Murphy's Top Twelve Laws of Win

8. To save your Windows configuration, hold down
Shift key and double-click on the Program Manager
Control box in the upper-left corner.

> *(More in Chapter 12 on keeping your Windows just so—see*
> *pages 135–146.)*

9. Run a virus scanner on all floppies you get from others.

> *(Chapter 21 tells why such paranoia is necessary—see*
> *page 256.)*

10. If File Manager gets confused about what's on your
floppy, press F5 to make File Manager look at the
floppy again.

> *(Chapter 13 will tell you a ridiculous amount about File*
> *Manager—see pages 147–172.)*

11. Keep your mouse ball spick-and-span.

> *(Chapter 3 tells you how—see page 36.)*

12. Keep a nerd on retainer.

> *(Chapter 22 has the rules—see page 276.)*

Smart Advice with a Smile
The Murphy's Laws Computer Book Series

Let's face it. Most computer books just don't feature the "can't put it down" excitement of an Ian Fleming spy novel or the heart-palpitating romance of Danielle Steel. But they don't have to put you to sleep, either. **The Murphy's Laws Computer Book Series** gives you the answers you need and keeps you entertained at the same time.

Written with wit and filled with useful information, **The Murphy's Laws Computer Book Series** *helps everyone*, even the most reluctant computer users, get the best of their computer and computing. In the series, there are books on word processing, spreadsheets, PCs, and operating systems—and even more books are planned. Every book in the series promises to give you the information you need on the software you use without boring you into oblivion.

Always smart, never stuffy. Every computer user will want to use **The Murphy's Laws Computer Book Series** whenever there are questions about the computer.

Look for **The Murphy's Laws Computer Book Series** at your favorite bookstore.

For a complete catalog of our publications:

SYBEX Inc.
2021 Challenger Drive, Alameda, CA 94501
Tel: (510) 523-8233/(800) 227-2346 Telex: 336311
SYBEX Fax: (510) 523-2373

This Book Is Only the Beginning.

Introducing the SYBEX Forum on CompuServe®.

Now, thanks to CompuServe, you can have online access to the authors and editors from SYBEX—publisher of the best computer books money can buy. From the privacy of your own home or office, you'll be able to establish a two-way dialog with SYBEX authors and editors.

Expert Advice at No Extra Charge.

It costs nothing to join the SYBEX Forum. All you have to do is access CompuServe and enter GO SYBEX. As a SYBEX Forum member, you'll have access to expert tips and hints about your computer and the most popular software programs.

What's more, you can download the source code from programs covered in SYBEX books, discover professional-quality shareware, share information with other SYBEX Forum users, and more—for no additional charge. All you pay for is your CompuServe membership and connect time charges.

Get a Free Serving of CompuServe.

If you're not already a CompuServe member, try it for free. Call, toll-free, 800•848•8199 and ask for representative #560. You'll get a personal ID number and password, one **FREE** month of basic service, a **FREE** subscription to *CompuServe Magazine,* and a $15 credit towards your CompuServe connect time charges. Once you're on CompuServe, simply enter GO SYBEX and start to explore the SYBEX Forum.

Tune In Today.

The SYBEX Forum can help make your computer an even more valuable tool. So turn on your computer, dial up CompuServe, and tune in to the SYBEX Forum. You'll be glad you did.

SYBEX. Help Yourself.

SYBEX

Murphy's Laws of

Windows™

Second Edition

Charlie Russel

Sharon Crawford

SYBEX®

San Francisco   Paris   Düsseldorf   Soest

Acquisitions Editor: Dianne King
Series Editor: Sharon Crawford
Developmental Editor: Kenyon Brown
Editor: Richard Mills
Editorial Supervisor: Kathleen Lattinville
Assistant Editor: Kristen Vanberg-Wolff
Technical Editor: Dean Denno
Book Designer: Claudia Smelser
Production Artist: Charlotte Carter
Technical Art and Screen Graphics: Cuong Le
Desktop Publishing Specialist: Dina F Quan
Proofreader/Production Assistant: Janet MacEachern
Indexer: Matthew Spence
Cover Illustration: Robert Kopecky
Cartoonist: Robert Kopecky
Special icon font created by Len Gilbert.
Screen reproductions produced with Collage Plus.

Collage Plus is a trademark of Inner Media Inc.

SYBEX is a registered trademark of SYBEX Inc.

Library of Congress Card Number: 93-85949
ISBN: 0-7821-1426-1

Manufactured in the United States of America
10 9 8 7

About the Authors

Charlie Russel and Sharon Crawford have the usual love-hate relationship with Windows. They've been sorting out and dealing with its bugs since version 2.

Charlie runs a DOS/UNIX network for a big manufacturer of cars and trucks. Sharon writes books and provides computer advice. Both feel that computers are ingenious tools to be enjoyed, if possible, and subdued, if necessary.

They are inveterate tinkerers and love computer spelunking, a hobby that has caused all sorts of expensive computer failures (and valuable lessons).

Together they have six cats, four computers, and a vegetable garden.

Acknowledgments

OUR HEARTFELT THANKS are extended to

Dianne King, who has been a source of encouragement and kindness to us as well as dozens of others;

Kenyon Brown, simply the best;

Richard Mills, an editor of great skill and gentlemanliness;

Dean Denno, who has been a great friend and offered many helpful suggestions;

and all the others who offered help, support, and amazing amounts of goodwill: typesetter Dina Quan, artist Charlotte Carter, proofreader/production assistant Janet MacEachern, technical artists Cuong Le and John Corrigan, and indexer Matthew Spence.

Many others at SYBEX and at New United Motors Manufacturing made contributions, the most basic of which was laughing at our jokes in the first place. It's *all* your fault!

Contents at a Glance

Table of Contents

Part 2

Getting to Know Windows

Part 3 A Gentle Guide to Windows Software

14 ☞ WORDS AND PICTURES (Write, Notepad, and Paintbrush)   173

15 ☞ THE REST OF THE FREEBIES   183

Part 4

DOS: It's Still Alive!!

Part 6   DECORATING WINDOWS

> **Murphy's Law:** Anything that can go wrong, will go wrong.

Murphy was absolutely right. And after everything has gone from bad to worse, the cycle will repeat itself. And in today's universe, the computer is the source of a lot of things that can go wrong. Everywhere the cry resounds: "How can I get this %&#@! thing to work?" or "I HATE computers!"

Murphy's Laws of Windows is the book that can make things go right for a change. This book shows you how to tame Windows and even have some fun along the way.

Here you will find all the answers about Windows that a real human would need. In English. Quickly. You can use your computer without having to have a degree in computer science or (worse) having to read a lot of pious platitudes about how The Computer Is Your Friend.

Who Are You?

All we assume about you is that you have a PC, a copy of Windows, and you want to use them both. You know pretty much what you want to do—you just need to get the computer to cooperate.

You have no interest in becoming a computer guru. Rest assured, it's not necessary. Just as you don't have to be an expert on the internal combustion engine in order to drive, you don't need a lot of technical knowledge to get results from a computer.

Inside This Book

This book is set up so that it can be used as an easy reference. You can jump in, find the answer to your question, and quickly escape. You will not be burdened with boring explanations you don't need to know because all that techie stuff is set aside in clearly marked boxes. If you're interested, you can read some (it *is* allowed), but you don't have to.

Part 1: The Bare Minimum (Skinny-Dipping into Windows)

Here's where you'll find all the basic stuff: what Windows can do for you, basic terms that everyone seems to expect you to know, as well as a review of the hardware and memory needs of Windows. The last chapter in this section tells you how to install Windows if you haven't done so already.

Part 2: Getting to Know Windows

Look here for the answers to your operating questions. Here are chapters on how to move around in Windows, what the basic parts do, and how to make them do what you want. This section includes the vital topic of making Windows look smashing.

Part 3: A Gentle Guide to Windows Software

In this section are the answers to all your questions about the programs that come with Windows, including Program Manager and File Manager. Here you'll find wonderful tips for making these free programs really valuable.

Part 4: DOS: It's Still Alive!!

This section covers just enough DOS to keep you afloat, plus how to use DOS programs in Windows. A chapter is included listing all the DOS commands you shouldn't use just in case the urge overcomes you.

Part 5: I'm Mad as %@$#! and I'm Not Gonna Take It Anymore!

Sooner or later your computer will commit some atrocity against your person and/or data. It may be strange behavior, mysterious messages, or outright failure to function. The chapters here cover what you can do to prevent such misfortune as well as steps to solve problems that inevitably happen.

Part 6: Decorating Windows

Here are some recommendations on how to part with some more of your hard-earned dough. The chapters in this section suggest hardware improvements and fun software that have practical implications as well as considerable potential for amusement.

What Those Things in the Margin Mean

 This guy is to alert you to really cool tips and shortcuts, particularly stuff you won't find in the Windows manuals.

 You'll see this guy when there's something that you should know about or you should remember.

 This is to let you know we're dealing with scary material. It means there's a possible risk to your files or your hardware or both. (The computer will not, however, blow up or catch on fire.)

 This icon is in a couple of places because it represents an opportunity to do something stunningly dumb. Read the warning and resist the temptation.

 This is to let you know that this is technical or background information that you certainly don't *have* to read. Mostly it's pretty interesting stuff, but if you skip it your life will go on without a hitch.

How to Use This Book

The intent is for this book to be used as a reference. Look for the topic you want in the table of contents or the index and you should be able to go right to the answer, because this book is equipped with the super-duper Mega-Index, the most useful on earth.

If you come across a term you don't know, it'll probably be explained in Chapter 2, "All the Stuff No One Ever Tells You," or in the glossary for normal people in the back of the book.

You should be able to find everything you need to know about Windows in this book. If you have an unwholesome interest in becoming an expert, there are a few recommendations scattered around for books you'll find helpful. The best, of course, are the other books in the *Murphy's* series—guaranteed not to be boring.

If you find an error or would like to make a suggestion (other than "drop dead"), write to us:

Charlie & Sharon
c/o SYBEX Computer Books
2021 Challenger Drive
Alameda, CA 94501

Or, if you have CompuServe, send a message to 76216,1463.

Praise is, of course, what we *really* want, but we'll deal with criticism as graciously as possible. And even try to fix what's wrong in the next printing.

So jump right in and have a good time.

PART 1

Look here for why Windows is so popular as well as what makes it a challenge. This part includes a chapter on hardware basics, a real-person's guide to memory, and a chapter explaining all the stuff people think you already know.

The Bare Minimum

(Skinny-Dipping into Windows)

Chapter 1

IF WINDOWS IS THE ANSWER, WHAT'S THE QUESTION?

Brown's Computer Law: The chief cause of problems is solutions.

MAYBE YOU ALREADY have Windows on your computer and don't know what to do with it, or some wiseguy nerd-type has told you that you absolutely, positively must get Windows. Like any sensible person, you're thinking: What *is* this new, exciting piece of technology and is there *any* way I can avoid it?

The short answer is *no*. Windows is everywhere and all the new programs of interest are being written for Windows.

But the long answer is that a Windows-based PC has so many advantages over a PC without Windows that you really don't want to avoid it. Here's what Windows can do for you:

☞ Make your computer a lot easier to use

☞ Let you do several things at once on the computer

☞ Let you take something (like a drawing) you make in one program and instantly put it somewhere else, even inside another program

How Windows Makes Life Easier

In Windows, programs all look a lot alike and actually work alike, too. The command to open a file is always on a menu called File on the left side of the screen, there's an Edit menu next to the File menu, and Help is always on the right side. The menus in between File and Help will vary, but many commands will be the same.

Windows also lets you copy and move files, format disks, and start programs without having to memorize commands. If you're using DOS, you have to type in what you want and tell DOS how to find it.

Windows replaces all that with simple menus and pictures. The result is that once you learn the *user interface* (geek-talk for the part of the

---

DOS—Windows' Ugly Brother

DOS (rhymes with "floss") is short for *disk operating system*. There are two "flavors" of DOS: MS-DOS (Microsoft's version) and IBM PC-DOS (IBM's version).

Up through version 5, they were virtually the same. But with version 6, they have gone off in opposite directions. Actually, the basic commands are identical, but the add-ons (the backup program, the text editor, and so forth) are very different.

In this book we assume the use of Microsoft DOS because if you're running it with Windows, it's still the safest and easiest option.

---

program you see on the screen) of one Windows program, you are well on your way to learning other Windows programs.

Windows uses a graphical user interface (GUI for short and pronounced "gooey"). This means that programs can be represented by small pictures called icons. Find the icon you want and click on it with your mouse and the program starts up without complaint.

☞ See "Menu Basics" on page 68 for all about menus.

☞ Chapter 7 has more than absolutely necessary about the GUI and how to use it.

Do Several Things at Once

With Windows you can have several programs open at once and switch between them (task switching), or you can have two or more programs actually doing stuff at the same time (multitasking).

For example, let's say you're writing a letter to your bookie, er, accountant and you want to do a few quick calculations. You can easily switch to a calculator program, do the figures, and switch back to the word processor. That's task switching.

Or you can print the letter and instead of having to wait for the printer to do its business before you can proceed, you can go on to something else. That's multitasking.

Cutting, Pasting, and
Stuff That Looks Like Magic

Another really cool thing that Windows lets you do is recycle your material. After you've typed something in, drawn a picture, or entered a whole lot of figures in a spreadsheet, you don't have to do it again, no matter how many ways you want to use the information.

Every Windows program has the ability to use an area of memory called the Clipboard. You copy your information from one program into the Clipboard. Then you can paste whatever's in the Clipboard into any other Windows program.

☞ Chapter 11 has all you'll ever need to know about using the Clipboard.

Windows also supports a kind of dynamic communication between programs. This means you can take, let's say, a chart made in your graphics program and put it into a letter in your word processor. Then, if you change the chart in your letter, the changes will also be made back in the original chart inside the graphics program. (Is that cool or what?)

This is called Object Linking and Embedding, and you'll find all you ever wanted to know about OLE (pronounced "O-lay") in Chapter 11.

Technical Drivel about
Operating Systems vs. Environments

Right on the box that your copy of Windows comes in, it says that Windows is an *operating system*. But it isn't, really. Windows is an *operating environment*. All this really means is that you can't have just Windows on your computer—you need to have DOS first, because DOS is the real operating system.

Typically, an operating system provides three basic services:

☞ It creates and manages a file system.

☞ It provides the tools for the user to interact with that file system.

☞ It provides a way to launch or run other programs.

Windows clearly provides the third, and to a more limited extent the second, function of an operating system. But it is left to DOS to handle the first function and much of the second.

Windows is an environment. It provides a layer of services to programs so that all Windows programs use the same set of video, sound, printer, and other hardware drivers. This makes it much easier for both hardware manufacturers and programmers who only need to create the driver once.

What about My DOS Programs?

The question arises: I have all these DOS programs I spent big bucks for, and I can't really afford to buy a whole bunch of new ones right away. Can I still use the old ones?

Sure. Virtually all your old DOS programs will run perfectly well in Windows, and you can update to new Windows versions as you have the money and the inclination.

In fact, you can run a DOS prompt from within Windows. If you have a 386 machine and enough memory, you can even run multiple DOS windows and applications at the same time. Though it's hard to imagine *why* you would want to.

☞ For information about 386 machines and all that stuff, see Chapter 3, "Hardware for Windows." More than you want to remember about memory is in Chapter 4.

☞ See Chapter 19, "DOS Programs and How to Run Them," for details on making your DOS programs run happily in Windows.

What Kinds of Windows Are There?

This book focuses on version 3.1 of Windows and version 6.0 of DOS (though DOS 5 will do). If you have an earlier version of Windows, stop right now and go get the upgrade. Please. Trundle off to your local software store and whip out the old VISA card. I'll wait right here.

Back already? Good. Now, go ahead and install it. (See Chapter 5 for help if you need it.)

You'll really like Windows 3.1, especially if you've ever used Windows 3.0. Not only does it have a screen saver and a new game, it is also a *lot* less likely to crash.

If you have a version of DOS before 5.0, you should definitely upgrade. If you have DOS 5, the decision to upgrade should be based on whether you already have your own versions of the add-ons that come with DOS 6, such as the backup, antivirus, and disk compression programs.

A Shameless Plug

If you really want to know all the cool things about DOS 6, look at *Murphy's Laws of DOS* (SYBEX, 1993) at your friendly neighborhood bookstore. We promise not to be offended if you even broke down and bought a copy.

The point here, though, is that DOS 5 and Windows 3.1 are the minimum versions you should be running. And they work well together, so you should go ahead and move up to at least that point.

To find out what version of DOS you're running, go to the DOS prompt (the thing that looks like C:\>) and type **VER**. *Your computer will "promptly" respond with the name and version of DOS.*

The version number for Windows appears on the first screen at start-up. You can also select About Program Manager from the Help menu in Program Manager. A window opens with the version number displayed near the top.

A Little Boring Background on Versions

Software is usually spoken of in terms of version numbers. You will see references to "Version X" or "Version X.xx" of various programs. What do the different numbers mean? Essentially the same rules apply to all programs:

☞ Whole numbers refer to major changes in the program. For example, if you have version 4.0 of a program, the release of version 5.0 is a major deal. With DOS, the change from DOS 4 to DOS 5 meant big changes. These are the sorts of changes that add real improvements. So, if you use the program a lot, you probably want to pay to get the new version.

☞ Changes of a tenth, such as from DOS 3.2 to DOS 3.3, usually provide an incremental improvement. Maybe only one significant feature is added. In the DOS 3.3 upgrade, support was added for high-density 3$\frac{1}{2}$-inch drives, as well as for large hard disks—actually, a pretty worthwhile update at the time. So whether or not to upgrade depends on how valuable the new feature is to you and how much they want you to pay. In the case of Windows, the change from 3.0 to 3.1 was *not* incremental, it was pretty dramatic. So there are exceptions.

☞ Changes of $\frac{1}{100}$th, such as from DOS 4.00 to DOS 4.01, generally provide no new features of significance—they just make the ones that *are* there work. Usually, this kind of version change is a bug fix. Maybe a minor improvement was made, but usually not enough that you would want to pay for it.

But the bug fixes can make a difference to you. If they are in areas you use, you should get the upgrade. And you shouldn't have to pay for it. If they tell you there is a charge, suggest that in your case this should be waived, since the only reason you are getting the new version is to fix bugs they made you pay for in the old version. If that doesn't work, ask for a supervisor. Persistence can save you some dough.

Colgan's Comment: Confusion is always the most honest response.

What You Need to Know Before You Decide to Do Windows

To run Windows, you need to understand that it's (and there's no nice way to say this) a hog.

It takes large amounts of memory and hard-disk space, and it puts more demands on your computer's hardware, especially the processor and video system, than plain-old DOS does.

How much memory and hard-disk space? That's a tough question to answer in a meaningful way. Don't try to get much use from Windows unless you have at least 20MB of free hard-disk space and 4MB of RAM. Many new Windows programs require 10–15MB of hard-disk space just to be installed and will not run well on a computer with less than 6–8MB of RAM installed. Fortunately, both hard disks and memory cost less now than they did a couple of years ago.

☞ See Chapter 4 for more on memory requirements.

Windows places high demands on your computer's main processor and video system. If you have anything less than an 80386 processor running at 25 MHz, you probably don't want to make the switch to Windows, and if you are buying a new computer, buy at least an 80486-based machine. The price differential is no longer that great, and you will be much happier.

Also, if you have an older, plain-vanilla VGA card, you will probably find you need to upgrade it. There are reasonably priced Super VGA cards that will provide a substantial improvement in your performance for reasonable sums of money, and there are special, high-end, coprocessor-based video cards that will provide truly remarkable improvements in performance for truly remarkable sums of money.

☞ For explanations of these ridiculous hardware terms, see Chapter 3, "Hardware for Windows."

☞ If you're confused about other terminology, you'll find fast, fast relief in Chapter 2, "All the Stuff No One Ever Tells You."

Chapter 2

ALL THE STUFF NO ONE EVER TELLS YOU

Alfie's Observation: Even paranoids have real enemies.

ONE OF THE reasons people get Windows is so they can get away from DOS-speak and other technobabble. Unfortunately, Windows has its own set of ridiculous terms. Worse, everybody acts as if you should already know what this stuff means. So rather than causing a moment of pained silence in the lunch room by asking a thoroughly embarrassing question, you can look in this chapter. Here, in alphabetical order, are some of the terms that Windows folk throw around with wild abandon.

Applications and Programs

An application is a collection of programs or a single program. For example, Harvard Graphics for Windows is an application. It's not just one program, it's a whole collection of programs and files of various kinds all grouped under a single name: Harvard Graphics.

You'll also hear of things like word processing applications and spreadsheet applications—these terms simply refer to the categories of applications that do word processing and spreadsheets.

For some reason, the free programs that come with Windows are called *applets.* No real person ever uses this word, largely because it sounds like a new brand of fruit snack.

Click, Double Click, Drag, and Drop

Windows is totally irrational without a mouse, so you'll need to know some of the mousy terminology. Before you start, make sure the mouse's "tail" (the cord that connects it to your computer) is on the side away from you.

Clicking

Clicking is what you do when you press and release the left mouse button. This is something you'll be doing *all* the time in Windows. You'll get an instruction to "click on" something or to use the mouse to "select" something. This means you move the mouse until the pointer is on the item in question, then you press and release the left mouse button. (If it's any other button on the mouse, it will be specified.)

☞ If you're left-handed and using a left-handed mouse, the button used to click is the one on the right. Lefty or righty, it's the button under your index finger.

Double clicking

Sometimes, you'll want to do more than just select something. If you double-click on an item, it means "take this item and do something with it." What the something is depends on, well, it depends. Trust me that double clicking is something you'll want to do. Just move the mouse pointer so that it's on the item in question, then press and release the left mouse button twice. You'll need to do it fairly quickly. If nothing happens it's because you didn't do it quickly enough.

☞ If you want to adjust the double-clicking speed, see "Disciplining Your Mouse" on page 104.

Dragging and dropping

Some things can be dragged around the screen by the simple expedient of putting the mouse pointer on them, holding down the mouse button, and moving the mouse to some other spot.

After you drag something, release the mouse button to drop whatever it was you were dragging.

The Command Line

The command line is the reason most people get Windows in the first place. It's not exactly a cozy spot. It's the location in DOS where you issue commands to the computer. If you type in a command that isn't *exactly* perfect, you'll get the grim message "File not found" or "Bad command or file name" or something equally helpful.

When you leave Windows, you will find yourself at a prompt that looks like

    C>

or

    C:\>

This is where you type in the command-line instructions.

With any luck at all (and Windows), you can avoid the command line almost all the time.

☞ However, if you must do something in DOS, see "A DOS Primer," Chapter 18, for the painless way to get around in DOS.

Nobody Tells
CH. 2

The Cursor

The cursor in DOS is pretty limited—just a flashing line or sometimes a rectangular block. In Windows, the cursor can have a number of forms. Most commonly, it's a blinking line that appears somewhere on the screen to signal that Windows is ready for *you* to do something.

The important thing to remember is that the cursor and the mouse pointer are not the same. The mouse pointer is the arrow or the non-blinking line (also called the I-beam) that moves when you move your mouse. The cursor is where any text you type will appear.

You can move the cursor by pressing the arrow keys (the ones with ↑, ↓, ←, → on them). Or you can move the mouse pointer to where you want the cursor to be. Click with the mouse and the cursor will move to the new location.

   ☞ See the table of "Mouse Disguises" on page 20, for all the ways your mouse pointer can look in Windows.

Defaults

Cathy's Verdict: If your life is getting you down, maybe you should change the default settings.

The default setting is what you get when you don't do anything. If you leave your hardware settings the way they came from the factory, that's the default. If you let your software install the way it wants to install, you have the default settings.

Lots of software, including Windows, lets you customize your settings. Whenever you make something look or act the way *you* want, you have moved away from the default.

The downside of default settings is that they can be so boring. The upside is that they (almost) always work.

Directories

A directory is a section of your hard drive. It is like a box you store things in. You can have big boxes or little boxes. And each box can contain things (files) or more boxes (directories), or a combination of the two. The name of the directory is the label on the outside of the box. It *should* tell you something about what is in the box, but if it doesn't, the only way to see what is inside is to open it up and take a look.

Your hard disk, then, is like a big box that has all the other boxes inside it. You create most directories yourself, so how many boxes and how many boxes inside boxes inside boxes you have is mostly a function of how compulsive you are about organizing.

☞ More on directories can be found in Chapter 13, "File Manager without Fear."

The DOS Prompt

The DOS prompt looks like this:

```
C:\>
```

If you find yourself looking at a screen that is blank except for this and a flashing cursor, you are at the DOS prompt. Some comfort, huh?

To get into Windows from here, just type

```
WIN
```

and press ↵.

If the computer responds with the message that you are already running Windows, just type

```
EXIT
```

and you'll be transported back into Windows.

Perfectly Useless Knowledge about "Shelling Out"

Because there are still a few things you can only do, or only do easily, in DOS and not in Windows, sometimes you will have to temporarily leave Windows and go to the DOS prompt. This is known as "shelling to DOS" or "shelling out." (And you thought you had done all your shelling out at the computer store.)

Shelling to DOS is done by double-clicking on the MS-DOS icon in the Main group window. It is important to remember, however, that shelling out to DOS is not the same as exiting Windows all the way to DOS. (For how to really and truly exit Windows—all the way to DOS—see "Quitting, Exiting, etc." on page 21). There are some DOS commands that you should only run when you have exited all the way to DOS. There's more on this in Chapter 20, "Don't Do Dis DOS."

Drivers

Drivers are little programs that allow your computer to communicate with equipment that's attached to it. Your printer has a driver, as do your monitor and even your mouse. Sometimes you have to install new ones because either your software or hardware has changed. Chapter 22, "Windows Problems and How to Solve Them," has the poop on how to do that.

Execute, Run, Load, and Start

All these terms mean the same thing in real life. Running and executing a program is the same as starting it. Loading means pretty much the same thing, though there is a formalistic way of interpreting it as meaning the process of a program retrieving a data file.

☞ You can start a program in Windows simply by double-clicking on its icon.

☞ Programs can also be urged into action by double-clicking on their names in the list of files in File Manager.

☞ If you really miss DOS, you can even start a program by using the command line in File Manager and Program Manager. If you have such impulses, you can get more info in Chapters 12 and 13.

Files

A file is a collection of information, representing a program or some sort of data, stored on a disk. Each file has a name, so you and the computer can identify it. A *program file* has a name with the extension .EXE, .COM, .PIF, or .BAT and actually causes something to happen. A *data file* can be text or numbers or a picture. It's something a program file acts on.

☞ File names in Windows have the same limitations as in DOS. Names can be up to eight characters long and can have an optional extension up to three characters.

☞ The rules for naming files are very specific. See page 155 in Chapter 13 for the baroque details.

GUI Basics

GUI stands for graphical user interface and is pronounced *gooey,* as in "Yuck!" Windows is GUI but so are other programs. Generally a GUI will have pretty pictures, buttons, boxes, and be cuter than a bagful of puppies.

If you've ever seen the plain-old DOS interface, you've seen the opposite of GUI. DOS has a command-line interface. You communicate there by typing in instructions at the command line.

Windows

Visually, the windows in Windows are the rectangular (usually) boxes that overrun your screen. An individual window can be very tiny or it can be *maximized* to cover the whole screen. If it can be moved but not resized, it's a dialog box and not a window.

Functionally, windows are the way programs are compartmentalized. Each program runs in its own window. Otherwise your WordPerfect would be fraternizing with your Lotus, a very unseemly situation. Windows provides a number of ways for programs to communicate and even exchange information, but they always maintain separate apartments, I mean, windows.

Desktop and wallpaper

In Windows, the desktop is the whole backdrop that isn't actively covered by a window. The default desktop is plain and boring. You can replace this tedium with wallpaper. Windows comes with some wallpaper, but within five minutes after Windows is installed in any office, the competition is on to see who can get the coolest wallpaper.

You can use as wallpaper any bitmapped file (a file with the extension .BMP, pronounced "bimp"), as well as files created in the Windows Paintbrush program (Chapter 14).

Icons

Icons are little pictures of things that you click on in Windows. Sometimes the icons are helpful—for example, a picture of a printer with the caption "Print Manager." That ought to be clear enough for anyone. Other times, some wiseguy has decided to use a heart as the symbol for WordPerfect or a happy face as the symbol for Excel.

Windows programs come with their own icons, but you can change any of them if you want. See page 144 for information on changing icons to whatever amuses you.

Hardware and Software

It's easy to define hardware; it's the stuff you can see and touch: the computer box, printer, monitor, mouse, floppy disks, and so forth.

Hardware doesn't do anything in the absence of software. Software is the information that the hardware processes in order to do something. Software comes on floppy disks (or, increasingly, on CDs).

Hardware is the medium; software is the message.

☞ You can find more on what Windows needs in terms of hardware in Chapter 3, "Hardware for Windows."

Kilobytes, Megabytes, and Other Astronomical Numbers

In computers the size of everything is in metric numbers. Don't look at *me,* it wasn't my idea!

Storage space as well as the things *in* the storage space (files) are measured in bytes. For all intents and purposes, a byte is a single character.

A thousand bytes is a kilobyte (abbreviated K or KB), a million bytes is a megabyte (abbreviated M, MB, or Meg), and a billion bytes is a gigabyte (abbreviated G, GB, or Gig). The numbers are somewhat approximate since computers count in multiples of two instead of multiples of ten. A nibble is 2^2, or 4, bits; a byte is 2^3, or 8, bits; and a word is 2^4, or 16, bits. Thus one kilobyte, which ought to be 1000 bytes, is actually 1024 (2^{10}) bytes, and one megabyte (one million bytes) is actually 1024 kilobytes, or 1,048,576 bytes, and one gigabyte is 1024 megabytes, or 1,048,576 kilobytes, or 1,073,741,824 bytes. And one terabyte is 1024 gigabytes, a number too big to even contemplate without getting a headache. For example, four tera-dollars would just about pay off the national debt.

Mouse Disguises

Depending on what your mouse is doing, the pointer assumes a variety of interesting disguises (Table 2.1). You should at least have a nodding acquaintance with these shapes so you can speculate about what's going on.

TABLE 2.1:
Mouse Disguises

What It Looks Like	What It Points At	What to Do with It
	Almost everything	Move it around until it's on top of whatever you want to click on.
	The side border of a window	Press the mouse button and hold it down while you move the mouse back and forth. When the window is the size you want it to be, release the mouse button.
	The top or bottom border of a window	To make the window taller or shorter, hold down the mouse button and move the mouse. Release the button when the window is right.
	The corner of a window	To pull or push a window to another size, press the mouse button and hold it down while you slide the mouse around. Let go of the button when the window is the right size.
	The divider between two parts of a window	Press the mouse button and hold it down while you move the mouse to the left or right. When the divider is where you want it, let go of the button.
	A place where text can be entered	This whatsis is called an "I-beam," and it means you are in a program or some other spot where text can be entered. If you click your mouse button, a cursor will appear very nearby.
	A window	This only appears when you've selected the Move or Size option from the Control menu. This is useful only for resizing the window using the cursor control keys. Click your mouse button anywhere on the screen and this thing will go away.
	A hot-linked word in the Windows help system	Click the mouse and you will get a definition or some additional information about the term.
	Anything you're not allowed to do	You get this symbol when you're trying to drag something to a location that's not allowed. Move the mouse and the symbol will change back when you're in a nonrestricted area.

TABLE 2.1: Mouse Disguises (Continued)	What It Looks Like	What It Points At	What to Do with It
	⏳	Nothing	Just hang in there; Windows is doing something and it can't be disturbed. You'll get this symbol while files are being saved or when you start a program and the files are being retrieved from the hard disk.

PIFs

PIFs are program information files that Windows needs to run DOS programs. Most programs now come with their own PIFs (files with the .PIF extension), and generally you don't have to mess with them. Even hardened Win-nerds are sometimes hesitant because of the reputation of the dread PIF Editor.

Honestly, it's not all that bad if you keep your wits about you and use the section on the PIF Editor in Chapter 19.

Quitting, Exiting, Leaving, Adios, etc.

Windows and all Windows applications have the happy faculty of closing in the same fashion. Hold down the Alt key and press the F4 key (in that block of function keys on the left side of your keyboard or strung out along the top of the keyboard). If you haven't saved your work, you'll be asked if that was an oversight.

☞ If you've had second thoughts, just click on the Cancel button and all will be as before.

☞ You can also exit a program by clicking on the box in the way-upper-left corner of the window. The box has a slotlike mark on it and is known as the Control box. One of the choices you'll get when you click on this box is "Close." Or you can double-click on the same box. Isn't it wonderful and annoying how there's never just one way to do something in Windows?

*Be sure to exit Windows in the prescribed manner. If you turn off the power with-
out having done the proper exit do-si-do, all sorts of rubble will be left on your
hard drive, plus things may not work so good the next time you start Windows.*

Reboot and Reset

Frequently, after a program gets done installing itself onto your computer, it will tell you to reboot or reset. This means telling your computer to start over from scratch, just as if it were waking up in the
morning.

There are three ways to reboot the computer—a warm boot, a cold
boot, and a power-off boot. The first is the quickest. Give your computer a "three-finger salute" by pressing and holding down the Ctrl,
Alt, and Delete keys all at the same time. This usually takes two hands,
just so you don't do it by accident. If you are running Windows, this
causes a special warning screen to come up that suggests that you
don't *really* want to do this. We agree. From within Windows, it is a bad
idea to reboot. Try to exit all the way out to DOS first.

A cold boot (sometimes called a reset) is even more emphatic than simply pressing Ctrl-Alt-Delete. First, not even Windows can stop you. If
you press the reset button (usually on the front of your computer box,
but sometimes hidden around back), your computer is going to reboot— regardless of what it was in the middle of doing. This is sort of
like hitting it over the head with a 2 × 4. It certainly gets the computer's
attention but may do some brain damage if the computer is in the middle of something.

Finally, there is the power-off reboot. Turn off the power, wait ten seconds, and turn it back on. This makes the computer forget anything it
ever knew about itself and go through the whole process of figuring it
all out again.

*Don't turn the power off and immediately back on. Because of the nature of com-
puter power supplies, this can cause additional electrical stress leading to prema-
ture component failure. In other words, you can fry a small and very expensive
little part whose primary job seems to be to protect that 50-cent fuse.*

*So be patient. Wait about ten seconds after you initially turn the power off before
turning it back on.*

Saving Your Work

No matter what you do on a computer, you'll have to save it if you ever want to see it again. Saving simply means telling the program you're using to create a file that contains the results of the work you've done. The file will be stored (usually on your hard disk) when you exit the program and turn off your computer.

Fortunately, in Windows, the Save command is the same in all programs. Just click on Save in the File menu (or press F while holding down the Alt key, then press S) and your work will be preserved.

The first time you save something, you'll have to give it a name and tell Windows where you want to store it. See page 155 for a whole section on good and bad ideas for file names.

All Windows programs also have a Save As feature. This just means that if you've opened a file, made some changes, and want to save the new version as well as the old version, you can. For example, if you have a letter called TOBILL and you've made a few changes and now want to save it as TOBOB, just select Save As from the File menu (or press Alt-F and then A). In the box that opens, you type in the new name, TOBOB.

☞ The first time you save a file, the Save and Save As commands work exactly the same.

☞ If you save a file a second time without changing its name, you erase the older version of it.

Task Switching vs. Multitasking

Boy, you'd think these were new Doritos flavors, the way computer nerds go on and on about them!

In fact, they're simple concepts. Task switching just means going from one task to another. If you're putting in your contact lenses and drop one down the drain, you have to switch from one task (putting in the lens) to another (cursing and swearing).

After you retrieve the lens and go back to putting it in your eye, if you continue swearing, you're multitasking—that is, doing two things at once. Multitasking is something that Windows does without much participation on your part.

Temp Files

When it comes to your hard disk, Windows is not the tidiest of tenants. It makes up a lot of temporary files while it's working and sometimes leaves them lying around.

If you exit from Windows correctly, this won't happen often.

Good Housekeeping: Getting Rid of .TMP Files

If you're pottering around in DOS, you can safely get rid of any files with the extension .TMP. Just type

```
DEL *.TMP
```

whenever you see some of the little devils. Just be sure that you're *not* in Windows when you do this or you'll be seriously sorry. If you think you *might* be in Windows, type

```
EXIT
```

at the prompt. If you're still running Windows, you'll be hurled back into its interior.

Chapter 3

HARDWARE FOR WINDOWS

Doubleday's Rule: When any mechanical contrivance fails, it will do so at the most inconvenient time possible.

YOU DON'T REALLY need to know anything about hardware to use Windows. In fact, once Windows is installed, you may never have any problems that have to do with hardware. But if you do, come back to this chapter and take a look.

If you read this chapter, you'll know enough to defend yourself from an aggressive salesperson or a nerd with an attitude.

The Computer

A computer is really the sum of all its parts. Most computers are built by hooking up a bunch of components, much like putting together a stereo. If you're a stereo nerd, you might want this amplifier, that receiver, those speakers, etc. If you're not a stereo nerd, you just go to the local Sounds 'R Us, point to one that looks good and sounds OK to you, and say "I'll take it."

The same goes for computers. If you know what you're doing, you can pick out a computer, piece by piece, or you can get one that is already put together.

For everything you need to know about how to buy a computer and not be bamboozled by "experts," go back to the bookstore and look at **Murphy's Laws of PCs** *by Gene Weisskopf (SYBEX, 1993). You could even be a real sport and buy* it.

Table 3.1 contains the basic hardware terms you will run across, the alternative names your favorite nerd may use for the same things, and real-world descriptions of what they are. For anything we've overlooked, see the glossary in the back of the book.

TABLE 3.1:
Computer Terms and Their English Translations

Main Name	Other Nerdy Names	Translation
Monitor	Video display, CRT, VDT, video display terminal	The thing that looks like a TV
Keyboard	Manual input device, 101-enhanced, 84-key	The part you type on
Computer box	System unit, tower case, desktop case	The main box that everything else plugs into
Mouse	Ergonomic graphical input device, rodent, pointing device	Mouse
Trackball	Ergonomic graphical input device, Trackman	Upside-down mouse

Hardware
CH. 3

TABLE 3.1:
Computer Terms and
Their English
Translations
(Continued)

Main Name	Other Nerdy Names	Translation
Floppy drive	5¼", 3½", removable storage drive, floppy	The slot in the front of the computer box you put a floppy disk into
Hard drive	Hard disk, Winchester, mass storage device, IDE, MFM, RLL, ESDI, SCSI	C: drive
Floppy disk	1.44, HD, DD, 1.2, 360, 720, 3½", 5¼"	What programs come on and where you back up to
Printer	Laser, dot matrix, ink jet, PostScript, PCL, hard-copy output device	Printer
Board	Card, PC board	Something you buy to increase the capabilities of your computer and that is installed inside the computer box
Motherboard	Motherboard	The main board inside the computer box that everything plugs into
Sound Blaster	Audio output card	A way to make everyone around listen to barfing noises
CD drive	CD-ROM, CD, compact disc	CD player

The Microprocessor

Two things determine how much basic horsepower your computer has: the type of microprocessor and the speed of the microprocessor.

The entire computer will sometimes be described in terms of the processor. For example, it may be described as a "386SX-20" or a "486-33." The first part refers to the processor itself and the second part to the speed of the processor. The processor, also known as the CPU (central processing unit) is the brains of the outfit. The entire range of PC processors can be summed up in the following numbers: 8088/8086, 80286, 80386, and 80486. (See "Boring Facts You Can Skip about the Processor Family Tree," below.)

The 8088 and 8086 are always referred to by their full numbers. But everyone re-fers to the last three processors as the 286, 386, and 486 (two-eighty-six, three-eighty-six, and four-eighty-six).

Generally speaking, the bigger the number, the more powerful the com-puter. And the more you'll have to pay for it. If you are buying a com-puter, don't buy anything less than an 80486-based computer. The prices have dropped like a stone over the past few years to the point where buying an underpowered machine makes no sense at all.

Most of the time it won't matter what chip is in your computer until you buy a piece of software that won't run on the processor you have. If you already have a computer, and you aren't sure what chip it has, ask a nerd.

Sometimes you can tell what kind of processor you have by watching the screen when you first turn on the computer. The processor number may be included in that gibberish that floats by during the boot-up.

What about all those letters after the numbers? The letters are less im-portant than the numbers, but they designate gradations within chips of the same basic category. The rules are:

☞ SX is less (powerful and expensive) than DX.

☞ DX2 is less (powerful and expensive) than DX at the same speed.

☞ SL is mostly for portable computers and uses less power than an equivalent DX.

Software that needs a 386 to run will run on *any* 386. It generally won't run as fast on a 386SX as on a 386DX, but it will run.

Software that runs on a 386 will run on any 486. (There are a few very weird exceptions to this, but none you're likely to encounter.)

The real break is between the 286 and the 386. Some software that runs on the 386 and 486 balks at having anything to do with the lowly 286.

Another topic directly related to the performance of your computer is memory, particularly in Windows. See Chapter 4, "Memory: How Does Windows Love It? (Let Us Count the Ways)," for the real scoop on memory.

Boring Facts You Can Skip about the Processor Family Tree

The first IBM Personal Computer (where "PC" got its start) in 1981 was based on the 8088 microprocessor, made by Intel. Since then, we've have had the 80286, the 80386, and the 80486. The first computers based on a chip called the Pentium are now appearing. The Pentium is really an 80586. Intel gave it a name so it could be trademarked.

Chip Speed: Adventures with Mind-Boggling Numbers

The internal speed of processors is measured in megahertz (MHz)—that's so many million pulses per second. So a chip described as a 386-25 allegedly performs 25 million somethings every single second! Don't think about this for too long or your brain will implode.

This seems like useful information. After all, a 386-33 should be able to do 8 million more somethings every second than a 386-25. But there are so many other factors involved, including whether your other hardware can take advantage of a faster chip, that the MHz figure alone can't tell you everything.

Within a given family of processors, the higher the speed number the faster the chip—and the more expensive. But the slowest of the next-highest family of chip is usually faster than the fastest of the previous family.

What???

Hardware CH. 3

Let's try again. Any 80386 chip will be faster than the fastest 80286, any 80486 will be faster than the fastest 80386, etc. There, that made a bit more sense. Sorry about that.

Math Coprocessors—What Are They and Do I Need One?

Computers are remarkably efficient at basic operations, such as adding two numbers. But conventional processors are very poor at doing complex calculations, such as those required to handle graphics and other math-intensive tasks. So, chip designers came up with chips specifically designed to handle these complex calculations. These chips are known as math coprocessors, and they work with the computer's main processor to handle the tasks that the main chip doesn't do too well. These chips follow the same designations as main processors, except that their numbers end in a "7" instead of a "6." Thus, an 80387 goes with an 80386.

With the introduction of the 80486, the math coprocessor was built right into the main chip. So don't let some enterprising salesperson try to sell you a math coprocessor for your new 80486DX or higher computer.

If you are still running on an 80386 or earlier processor, you *could* get a math coprocessor to speed up your computer. But it's probably a better investment to upgrade your whole computer.

Video 101

When you run Windows, your video system becomes lots more important than it was in DOS, since Windows puts so many more demands on the video system.

Your computer's video system is made up of the monitor and the video display adapter. The monitor is just the box that looks like a TV without the knobs. There'll be an on/off switch of some kind and controls for brightness and contrast, which you can fiddle with to make the screen look the way you want. There will probably be other controls either on the back or hidden behind a little door. Leave them alone.

By itself, the monitor doesn't do much. It's just a shell. The powers behind the throne are the main processor and the video display adapter. The video display adapter is the other half of the video system and is inside your computer box. It processes the information from your computer and then tells the monitor what to display and how to display it.

Usually the video display adapter is an actual circuit board (a "card" in nerd-talk) inside the computer box that can be removed and changed. In a growing number of new computers, the adapter is built into the main board of the computer.

The important thing to remember is that the monitor and the display adapter are a matched system. You can't just go out and buy a new version of one, without first considering how this will affect the other.

Picture Windows—Getting Good Video

Windows will run on a regular VGA or even on an EGA video system. But it may run reeeeaaaalllllly *slow*. The problem is that every time you change something, the screen has to be redrawn. This redrawing is handled by your computer's main processor, and it takes its own sweet time about it, too.

So, in the never-ending quest to part computer users from their dough, manufacturers have come up with goodies known as *video accelerators*. These guys have chips that take over some of the redrawing from the main processor.

If you are still using a fairly plain, somewhat older VGA card, upgrading to one of the newer, accelerated Super VGA or 8514/A cards can make a remarkable difference in how spiffy Windows looks on your computer.

Hardware
CH. 3

More Dweebish Terms You Will Wish You Could Forget

When talking about video, we run into all sorts of language never heard in polite society. Many of the terms below will be bandied about by computer-store salespeople and nerds, and will even be sprinkled through computer ads. No one will actually explain them, naturally. You are just supposed to *know.* This is, of course, very annoying, but here's a quick guide that will tell you everything you need to know short of turning into a dweeb yourself.

☞ **Pixel** The smallest unit of a graphics display. This is a single dot out of thousands or even millions. This isn't the only place you'll see *pixel* defined as a dot, but I cannot tell a lie: a dot it's not. A pixel is equal to a dot only at the highest resolution the monitor is capable of. At lower resolutions, a pixel can be made up of many dots.

☞ **Dot Pitch** The minimum size of each individual pixel on the screen. The smaller the number, the finer-grained picture you can get. Make sure you get a monitor with a dot pitch of 0.28 or smaller.

☞ **Interlaced** This means that only half the display is updated at a time. Interlaced displays tend to have a barely visible flicker that will eventually drive you insane or to the convenience store for beer, whichever comes first. What you definitely want is "noninterlaced."

☞ **Scan Rate/Refresh Rate** Refers to how often the display is updated. Look for a refresh rate no lower than 72 Hz. This means the screen is rewritten 72 times a second. Below that, you increase the strain on your eyes substantially. Higher is even better but is usually not cost-effective.

Hard Drives—What Windows Needs

Windows says right on the box it comes in that it requires 6MB of space on your hard disk and that 10MB is recommended.

Don't believe it!

While it *is* true that you can load Windows in that much space, you also need room for something called a "swap file," any additional fonts you may have, and any Windows programs you may add. So, if your current computer system hasn't got at least 20MB of free hard-disk space, don't even think about Windows.

If you haven't upgraded to DOS 6, do so and install its DoubleSpace program. Or get a copy of Stacker, a very good disk-compression program.

Or, if you already installed one of these programs and *still* don't have enough room, it's time to bite the bullet and get another hard disk. The good news is that this is a lot less painful than it used to be. New 120MB hard disks can be had for $200–$250, which is a good deal less than just a couple of years ago.

Disk Compression Programs— Something for (Almost) Nothing

Most files that are stored on your hard disk have a lot of "dead space" in them: either blank areas or repetitive areas. Disk compression programs, such as Stacker and DoubleSpace, take advantage of this to squeeze the files into less space.

When you install Stacker or DoubleSpace, it creates a new drive (more properly, a *volume*) on your computer, which looks like it is about twice as big as the original. Sort of like steroids for your hard disk. Your 80MB hard disk suddenly bulks up to 150MB or so. How much extra space you will gain depends on which programs you use and what kinds of files you keep on your hard disk. DoubleSpace generally gets about a 70 percent increase in space. Stacker seems to do a bit better—nearly 100 percent.

The only drawback is that it is tricky to go back once you have installed one of these programs. Both programs allow you to undo the change, but it's not the simplest process.

Not all files can be stored on the compressed disk. Some space has to be left for such things as a Windows swap file—what Windows resorts to when it gets short on memory.

So, beyond wanting a lot of hard-disk space, what else does Windows need? Well, Windows isn't really that all-fired fussy about what type of hard disk you have, just so long as you have a lot of it. These days, the best bargains are to be had in IDE drives. IDE is short for Integrated Device Electronics. They are the BIC pens of the hard-drive market. They're cheap and they work fine, but if one breaks you just throw it away, since it isn't worth trying to repair.

Clark's Second Rule: The goal of all inanimate objects is to resist man and to ultimately defeat him.

Floppy drives

Most computer boxes have two slots for floppy disks. These days you usually see one for $5\frac{1}{4}$-inch disks and one for $3\frac{1}{2}$-inch disks. Each one of these slots is a disk drive—one is drive A and the other is drive B. The one on the top is drive A unless some wiseacre has switched things around.

Windows requires a $5\frac{1}{4}$-inch high-density floppy drive or a $3\frac{1}{2}$-inch low- or high-density floppy drive.

Inserting a $5\frac{1}{4}$-inch disk

If there's a latch or door in the way, open it. Remove any disk already in the drive. Hold the disk by the label and slide it in the drive with the label side up. Close the latch or the door.

Removing a $5\frac{1}{4}$-inch disk

Open the latch or door and pull out the disk.

When the disk is not in the drive, it should be in its protective paper sleeve. You should never touch the shiny, exposed surface of the disk anyway, and if it's in the sleeve you *can't* touch it.

One of the best-kept secrets in computerland is how to tell high-density disks from low-density disks. Low-density (aka double-density) $5\frac{1}{4}$-inch disks (which hold about 360K of data) have a reinforcing hub ring around the hole in the middle of the disk. High-density disks (about 1.2MB capacity) do not have this ring.

Double-density $3\frac{1}{2}$-inch disks (about 720K capacity) have one hole in the plastic case (to the right of the label as you hold the disk facing you). High-density $3\frac{1}{2}$-inch disks (about 1.4MB capacity) have an additional hole to the left of the label.

Inserting a 3½-inch disk

Hold the disk by the label and slide it into the slot, label side up. When the disk is all the way in, you will hear a nice, satisfying click. The button under the slot will pop out (if it isn't out already).

Removing a 3½-inch disk

Push the button under the disk drive. The disk will pop out about an inch so you can pull it out.

Things That Will Make You Feel Stupid

☞ Don't put the disk in the little space between the two drives. Unless you have the computer box right in front of you *and* are very careful, eventually you will do this and feel unbelievably stupid. Especially since you will have to summon a nerd to dismantle your computer box and retrieve the disk. Save yourself this embarrassment and put a piece of tape over part of that space, so the disk won't go in by accident.

☞ In line with that, don't force the disk into the slot. If it doesn't go in easily, there is already a disk in the drive, or you are putting the disk in upside down or backward, or you have already embarrassed yourself as described above.

☞ 5¼-inch disks will slide in easily—even if they are upside down and backwards. They won't *work* that way (you'll get a "Drive not ready" error message), and it won't do your drive mechanism any good, either.

☞ Wait for the drive light to go off before removing the disk from the drive. The light means that something is happening and if you remove the disk, you will interrupt whatever's going on. Just like people, computers hate to be interrupted and will show their displeasure by fouling up whatever was being written to that disk. Don't risk it! Wait for the light to go off.

Hardware
CH. 3

Mice

The mouse is the gadget with the buttons that you slide around the desktop to move a pointer around the screen. A mouse is absolutely required to use Windows with any degree of comfort.

What kind of mouse you get depends on who's buying. If it's your dime, try out some at the local computer store. Make sure the mouse feels comfy in your hand.

Feel is more important than the number of buttons. Most Windows programs use only the left mouse button, though more and more are starting to use the right button for some things. Almost none of them use the third, middle button for anything.

☞ It is technically possible but painfully clunky to do Windows without a mouse. If your mouse has died and you're observing a decent interval of mourning, see page 73 for information on how to key your way around Windows.

What about trackballs?

A trackball is nothing more than an upside-down mouse. It behaves just like a mouse, uses the same drivers, and so forth, but instead of rolling it around on top of your desk or a mouse pad, you roll the little mouse ball around with your palm or thumb. Some people love trackballs, others can't stand them. Try one before you buy it, or make sure the store will take it back if you don't like it. And if you don't like the feel of one, you might like another, since they are not all alike. One advantage of a trackball is that it doesn't take up as much real estate on your desk as a mouse.

The care and feeding of your mouse

Your mouse needs more than Mouse Chow; a certain amount of care is required. Use a mouse pad because a nice, shiny desktop doesn't give your mouse the traction it needs.

If you are having problems with jerky mouse movement, you may be afflicted with a dirty mouse ball. Just take a damp cloth with a little bit of glass cleaner on it and wipe the outside of the mouse, then lay the cloth down and run the mouse around on it for ten seconds or so. Then do the same thing using a clean, dry cloth. This seems to do the trick.

Keyboards

Keyboards are still where you type in all the stuff and key in all the numbers. So how a keyboard feels to you has a lot to do with how happy you are at the computer.

Some keyboards make a nice, crisp click every time you press a key. However, *you* may hear this sound as clattery and chintzy sounding. If you are a touch typist, the placement of certain keys may drive you crazy, so be sure and try out a keyboard before you buy it.

Regardless of the type or manufacturer, all keyboards have four main parts.

Typewriter keys

The typewriter keys are the keys in the middle of the keyboard. The keys are arranged just like those on a typewriter (remember those?) and perform pretty much the same functions. Along the outside edge of these keys are the modifier keys. They are sometimes a darker gray and include Ctrl (Control), Alt (Alternate), Caps Lock, and Shift. Each of these keys modifies how the other keys on the keyboard behave.

Function keys

PC keyboards have ten or twelve function keys. These function keys, which are labeled F1, F2, and so forth, are arranged across the top of the keyboard or in a double row on the left side. Many programs attach special actions to each of these keys (though F11 and F12 are not called upon often). If you are a touch typist, get a keyboard with the function keys on the left.

Cursor control keys

The cursor control keys are ←, →, ↑, ↓, Home, End, Page Up, and Page Down, as well as Insert and Delete. These keys either form a special block of keys to the right of the typewriter keys or are combined with the numeric keypad on older computers.

These keys move the cursor around the screen without changing anything on the screen. The arrow keys work pretty much as you suspect. Depending on the program, the Home key will move the cursor to the beginning of the document, the beginning of the page, or the beginning of a line. The End key will move to the end of the document, the end of the page, or the end of the line.

Numeric keypad

Newer keyboards have a separate numeric keypad that doesn't share keys with the cursor control keys. This will help you to enter numbers while moving from cell to cell in your favorite spreadsheet program. Of course, if you use this block of keys primarily to move the cursor around, you may find the change more of a nuisance than an enhancement.

☞ *A computer really and truly cares about the difference between a 0 (zero) and a capital letter O. It can also get very huffy if you use a lower-case l (L) in place of the number one (1). If you mix them up you may get a rude error message (if you're lucky) or, worse, something won't work and you won't know why.*

☞ *The Tab key will move the cursor to the next tab stop. This will be the equivalent of five or eight spaces or whatever the program is set for. From the computer's point of view, this is a single character. When you backspace over a Tab, it disappears in one bite, not one space at a time.*

The toggle keys

The toggle keys are Caps Lock, Num Lock, and Scroll Lock. They change the state of certain other keys on the keyboard, and are either ON or OFF.

The Caps Lock key only affects the characters of the alphabet, converting "a" to "A", "b" to "B," and so forth, but has no effect on any other key, unlike the Shift key, which affects all the keys on your keyboard. If you use the Shift key while the Caps Lock key is ON, you get lowercase letters.

The Num Lock key converts the block of keys on the far right of the keyboard from cursor control keys to a numeric keypad and back. On enhanced keyboards, Num Lock is usually toggled to numeric keys by default, whereas the older, AT keyboards had this toggled to cursor control keys by default. In either case, however, tapping the Num Lock key switches this, and holding down the Shift key changes it for as long as you hold it down.

The Scroll Lock key toggles how some programs scroll the screen. Other programs completely ignore this key. But if you are working in a spreadsheet, for example, and suddenly your whole screen starts jumping around instead of just the cursor moving, try tapping the Scroll Lock key. That should fix it.

The Ctrl, Alt, and Shift keys

These are the modifier keys that affect every other key on the keyboard, and are frequently combined with other keys, and with each other, to perform special functions within programs.

These keys are never used by themselves. They are used to alter the meaning of a second key. For example, in Word for Windows you press the F7 function key to start the spelling checker, but if you hold down the Shift key while pressing F7, you start the thesaurus program. Some programs will also have three-way combos such as Alt-Shift-F12, which in Excel prints a spreadsheet. This means you hold down the Alt and Shift keys while pressing the F12 key.

Printers

Windows very nicely lets you install any number of printers to work with your system. You do it when you install Windows, or you can add a printer or two later. See Chapter 16 for everything about printers and printing.

Chapter 4

MEMORY: HOW DOES WINDOWS LOVE IT?

(Let Us Count the Ways)

Kofsky's Second Law: You'll never have enough time, money, or memory.

IF COMPUTER MEMORY had existed in Victorian times, it would have been the cause of people swooning and having attacks of the vapors.

It can be a confusing subject because there's more than one kind of memory and at least three different names for every kind. Even the most hardened techno-dweebs can find their brains softening in the middle of a discussion about memory.

If you don't think you have a problem with memory, skip this chapter. You can always come back to it.

Memory is where things happen in your computer. The processor does the work but can only hold so much information inside itself (not much).

The hard disk stores your programs and files but doesn't *do* anything. When you start up a program, the program and any files you need to work with are retrieved from the hard disk and loaded into memory. Once this stuff is in memory, the processor can do things with it.

Memory is also volatile (though it won't cause anything to blow up). Whatever you have in memory vanishes the instant your computer is turned off. This isn't a problem if you've saved your work to the hard disk, but if you haven't, you've lost your document or all the points you've built up in Space Blasters.

This is why all the books and all the computer yentas make such a fuss about saving your work in the programs you use. One blip in the power supply (or the baby pulls the plug out of the wall) and the work you've done since your last "save" is gone with the wind.

This memory is called random access memory, or RAM, and it rhymes with "Oh, damn!"

 It sometimes happens that folks confuse hard-disk storage space with RAM. This is because both are measured in megabytes and back in the bad old days, unfeeling computer geeks would refer to both *as memory. If you are perplexed, remember that the amount of RAM is always much smaller than even the smallest hard disk size. And don't call the hard disk "memory" and you won't be passing the error on to others.*

How Much Memory Is Enough?

See Kofsky's Law, above.

Windows loves memory. It needs a lot for itself, plus it encourages you to have so much happening that you need bunches of memory. Most programs will run better with lots of memory, and many programs require a substantial amount.

Fortunately, memory has gotten a good deal cheaper in recent years. Get as much as you can afford because the trend is not going to reverse any time soon.

When you buy software, the box will have on it somewhere the preposterous amount of memory needed to run the program. DOS programs state this in terms of the amount of conventional memory, expanded or extended memory, and hard-disk space needed. (Hold that thought—we'll explain in a minute.) Windows programs usually just give you a single, ridiculously large number for the amount of memory required, and an even more ridiculously large number for the amount of disk space required.

☞ If a program says it requires 2MB of memory but 4MB are "recommended," this means that it will sort of run with 2 but needs 4 to be functional. (And will be truly happy with 8MB or more.)

☞ Windows will sort of run with 2MB of RAM, but 4MB is much better.

☞ See the sections on conventional, expanded, and extended memory for information on those terms.

How Memory Is Measured

Memory is measured in bytes. A thousand bytes is a kilobyte (abbreviated K or KB), a million bytes is a megabyte (abbreviated M, MB, or Meg), and a billion bytes is a gigabyte (abbreviated G, GB, or Gig). Other kinds of storage, such as hard disks and floppy disks, also use these terms.

The numbers used to describe RAM are somewhat approximate since computers count in multiples of two instead of multiples of ten. A nibble is 2^2, or 4, bits; a byte is 2^3, or 8, bits; and a word is 2^4, or 16, bits. Thus one kilobyte, which ought to be 1000 bytes, is actually 1024 bytes; and one megabyte (one million bytes) is actually 1024 kilobytes, or 1,048,576 bytes; and one gigabyte is 1024 megabytes, or 1,048,576 kilobytes, or 1,073,741,824 bytes. And one terabyte is 1024 gigabytes, or a number too big to even contemplate without getting a headache.

Memory
CH. 4

Conventional Memory

Hall's Rule: Programs expand to fill the memory available.

Conventional memory is the first 640K of RAM in your computer. This is sometimes called DOS memory because DOS can run programs only in this part of memory. This is a limitation of DOS because your microprocessor could use any memory and in considerably larger quantities.

In theory, Windows gets around this limitation of DOS memory, but you will still run up against it sometimes, since certain programs and drivers need some of this memory to do their work in. Get too many going, and you will get an "Out of Memory" error message when you try to start up a new program. See Chapter 23, "Windows Error Messages You Love to Hate," for more on how to get around this.

To get the most out of conventional memory:

☞ *Upgrade to DOS 6. This will allow you to reduce the amount of memory that DOS uses in the first 640K, leaving more for your Windows programs.*

☞ *If you have a 386 processor or above (see Chapter 3, "Hardware for Windows," for details), use DOS 6's MemMaker program. If you don't have a 386, why are you trying to run Windows, anyway? If you do have a 386, see "Making the Most of Memory Using DOS 6" on page 228.*

Background Information of Dubious Value

When the original version of DOS was written in 1981, the typical personal computer had only 16 to 64 kilobytes of memory. So when the designers of DOS placed a limit of 640 kilobytes in DOS, they thought they had left *plenty* of room.

As a miscalculation this ranks right up there with New Coke and the PCjr.

Programmers have come up with some very ingenious tricks to get the most out of that 640K, and Windows is one of the most effective, but until Windows is a full operating system and we don't need DOS anymore, we will still bump up against this limitation.

How Much Memory Do I Have?

To see how much memory you have, from within Windows, pull down the Help menu of the Program Manager, and click on About Program Manager. At the bottom of the window, you will see how much free memory you still have (see Figure 4.1). No matter how much memory it says you have, when the system resources drop below about 40 percent free, Windows starts getting real droopy. Try closing some windows to ease the pressure.

FIGURE 4.1:

The About Program Manager window, which shows the amount of memory and percentage of system resources free

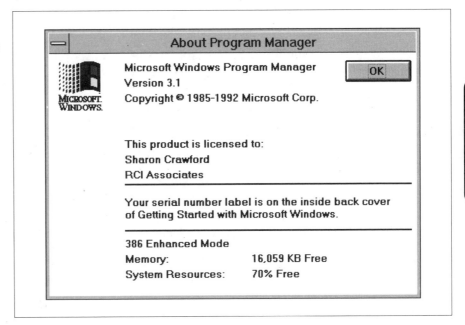

If you are running in standard mode, the number you see in the window is an accurate representation of how much memory you still have available. In 386 enhanced mode, this number is pretty meaningless. If *all* this seems pretty meaningless to you, see Chapter 6, "Starting Windows," for more on standard and 386 enhanced modes than you probably wanted to know.

For memory info while you're still in DOS, type **MEM** at the DOS prompt just before you start Windows. You'll see a summary that shows you all sorts of information about how much memory, and of what kind, you have.

Expanded Memory: Do I Still Need It?

When software designers starting figuring out that the 640K of conventional memory that DOS allows might not be enough, a group of them got together and came up with a standard way to get around this limit, called EMS (Expanded Memory Specification). This created a special kind of "paged" memory that is really smoke and mirrors, since this memory doesn't actually have an address. It's a lot like an old party phone line, where several houses share the same phone number, except here it is memory sharing the same address.

While this was great for DOS programs, and, in fact, was pretty much the only kind of memory most could use beyond the conventional 640K, it is pretty much useless for Windows. If you still have some older DOS programs that require this memory, and you aren't ready to abandon them for Windows versions, you will need to use a special program, called an Expanded Memory Manager, to simulate expanded memory out of your extended memory.

If you have DOS 5 or DOS 6, you already have an Expanded Memory Manager, called EMM386.EXE. You can read your DOS manual to find out how to install it. Or, if you're not into mortification of the flesh, get a copy of *Murphy's Laws of DOS* and do it the easy way.

Memory Terms You Can Probably Ignore

☞ **High DOS memory** The area between the end of DOS memory (conventional memory) and the start of extended memory. This is the area from 640K to 1024K (1MB). MemMaker (part of DOS 6) and other merry memory optimizers play neat tricks in here. The original DOS designers reserved this area of memory for device drivers of various types, so DOS can't normally touch it without the use of MemMaker or some other program.

☞ **UMBs** (upper memory blocks) Chunks of high DOS memory.

☞ **HMA** (High Memory Area) The area that DOS versions 5 and above can load themselves into. This is the first 64K of memory after 1MB.

☞ **XMS** (Extended Memory Specification) This is a standard way of allowing programs to share extended memory. It requires a driver, such as HIMEM.SYS, to do the controlling.

☞ **Address** The location of a given bit of memory. The numbers are expressed in the numbering system called hexadecimal, which is just as bad as it sounds.

☞ **Page frame** The area within DOS memory used by expanded memory to do its smoke-and-mirrors thing.

Extended Memory

Extended memory is memory whose address is higher than DOS memory or even high DOS memory—above 1MB. Windows loves this type of memory and won't even run if you don't have some of it. However, to keep programs from getting in each other's way and trying to use the same memory addresses, extended memory needs to be XMS extended memory (see "Memory Terms You Can Probably Ignore," above).

Memory Show and Tell

Figure 4.2 gives you an idea of the relationship among all the different types of memory. The memory does not *look* like this inside your

FIGURE 4.2:

What memory would
look like if it looked like
something

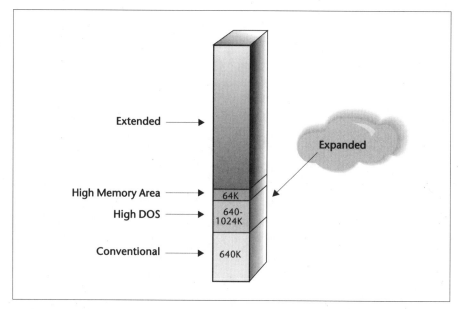

computer, but the addresses of memory locations are laid out like this
more or less in order.

Adding Memory

You actually *can* install memory yourself, but it means opening up the
computer box and deciding where to snap those little SIMMs in. It also
means figuring out how much memory you already have and in what
increments it's installed in order to figure out how to get where you
want to be.

Does this sound like something a sensible person would want to get involved in? Of course not.

Just put your little baby in the car and zip down to the shop. Tell the
techie there how much memory you think you'll need. Most stores
where you buy memory will install it for you at no extra cost. (Which
means they don't give you a discount if you install it yourself, so *let*
them do it.)

Other Reasons Not to Do It Yourself

Memory lives in your computer in one of three places:

☞ Your motherboard (the big circuit board inside your computer) may have some sockets on it about three inches long. Little cards called SIMMs or SIPs are plugged into these sockets. To add more memory, you have to know what kind of SIMMs or SIPs you have and what kind you need, because you may have to remove what you have and replace it.

☞ Or you may have a lot of little sockets on the motherboard into which memory chips go. To add more memory, you plug in more chips with extremely delicate little legs that you are likely to bend and therefore destroy.

☞ Or all your memory may live on an adapter card that plugs into one of the large sockets on the motherboard. To add memory, you have to plug in more of the very fragile chips as described above.

So unless you are very ambitious and very careful, it's not worth the grief to try to save a few bucks.

Wilkinson's Law: If it's worth doing, it's worth hiring someone who knows how to do it.

Memory
CH. 4

Chapter 5

TAKING THE PLUNGE: INSTALLING WINDOWS

Gates's Law: An ounce of image is worth a pound of performance.

MOST PROGRAMS THESE days have special installation programs, and Windows is no exception. But Windows goes one step farther. Microsoft built enough smarts into the installation program that all you need to do, besides feed disks to the computer when asked, is tell it what printer you have.

What to Do Before You Install

The first thing you need to do is turn on your computer. Good. Let's wait a few moments, till all that initial turning-on stuff settles down, and then we will be almost ready to start. If you find yourself at some sort of menu, exit all the way out to DOS. Windows needs to be able to take total control of your system.

Before you start to install Windows, or any program for that matter, you first need to make sure that you have everything you need to complete the installation, and that you protect yourself in case something goes wrong. After all, this is a book about Murphy. So, before you actually start, make a last check to see if you are ready.

Do you have the right DOS?

First, are you running MS-DOS or PC-DOS, version 3.1 or higher? According to Microsoft, this is the minimum version supported with Windows. But please don't waste your time with Windows if you don't have at least DOS 5.

Do you have enough hard-disk space?

Microsoft says that Windows requires a minimum of 6MB to 8MB of hard-disk space and that 10MB is suggested. Well, that's nice but ridiculous. You should figure on having at least 5MB beyond that so that Windows can create a permanent swap file. A swap file is where Windows sticks things it isn't using right now but might want later. A permanent one of these is nice, because it's faster.

Finally, if you don't have another 20MB beyond *that,* you're not going to be able to do much besides look at the Windows screen.

If you have DOS 6, you should run DEFRAG on your hard disk before you install Windows. DEFRAG will take all your programs and files and scrunch them all up on the front of your hard disk. This doesn't actually create any additional room on your hard disk, but it does make it easier for Windows to use what is left.

From the DOS prompt, type

```
DEFRAG C: /F
```

which will tell DOS to run its DEFRAG program on your C: drive and to fully optimize the drive. This will tidy up your hard drive by consolidating all the files and pieces of files that are lying around.

☞ See Chapter 9, "The Rest of the Control Panel," for more information about swap files and how to modify yours.

Is your mouse (and everything else) plugged in?

When you actually go to install Windows, you need to make sure that all the hardware you want it to know about is already in your computer. This means you need to make sure your mouse is plugged in, for example. Windows will question your computer closely to find out what is connected to or plugged into it, so you want to let it find everything possible the first time. Otherwise, you'll need to go back later and tell it about anything you have added.

Have you made an OOPS disk?

Don't forget this one. Any time you install a new program, you need to update your OOPS disk. The OOPS disk has on it all the stuff you need to bail yourself out of trouble. This protects you in case the program's installation process makes changes to your configuration files that turn out not to work. In a perfect world, of course, this never happens, but...

☞ For help on making your own OOPS disk, see page 246 in Chapter 21, "An Ounce of Prevention."

OK, So Let's DO IT Already!

First, rip open the box and paw through all the other stuff till you find the disks. They will be in one or more sealed plastic bags. Before you open these plastic bags, you are supposed to read and understand the legal mumbo jumbo in the Microsoft License Agreement, which is printed on the inside cover of the smaller of the two manuals you just discarded in your haste to find the disks. Go ahead, read it. Then take two aspirin for the headache and call us in the morning.

Installing CH. 5

So, at the DOS prompt, insert the first Windows disk in the A: drive, and type

    A:SETUP

If the disks you have will fit only in your B: drive, don't worry—just type **B:SETUP** instead of A:SETUP. Windows doesn't care, and we certainly don't, either.

One Windows Setup, Over Easy

After Windows Setup gets done checking out your system, it will offer you a chance to read a mostly useless help screen or proceed directly to the setup. Go ahead, read it.

See, we told you it was pretty useless. Now, press the Escape key to get out of that, and press Enter. Setup will offer you a choice between an Express setup and a Custom setup.

Stick to the Express setup and you can't go far wrong. Save the Custom setup for those with an incurable desire to tinker with stuff. That, after all, is why Microsoft put the option there in the first place.

If you are installing over a previous version, Windows will usually find it and ask you if you want to upgrade that installation or install to a new directory. Please, upgrade the old version. We can think of absolutely no reason to stick with an older version, and Windows will even save the Reversi game if it finds it there, so you have nothing to lose.

All you have to do now is feed disks to the Setup program as it asks for them. Everything else is handled automatically, until you get to the questions about printers. Along the way, Windows gets enough of itself loaded that it can switch over to a nice, cute Windows installation program. With any luck, this will be the last time you need to install anything from that ugly old DOS prompt.

Telling Windows about Your Printer

Finally, when Windows gets to the last disk of the installation, it will ask you to tell it about your printer. When Windows is ready to talk about printers, it will pop up a box on the screen, called the Printer Installation box.

You need to highlight a printer here. Use the cursor keys to go through the options until you find your printer, then press the Enter key.

☞ If your particular printer isn't listed, choose one it can emulate. Emulate is a fancy word that means a printer can pretend to be just like another printer. Your printer's manual will tell what other printers it can emulate.

☞ If you don't have a printer or don't want to install one now, just highlight the very first choice, which is "No Printers Attached." You can always handle this later. See Chapter 16, "Printing," for details on how to install a printer after you already have Windows up and running.

Want to move through the list of printers a bit quicker? Just type the first letter of your printer name. Zip, you move all the way down to the start of the printers whose names begin with that letter.

Consider installing at least one extra printer after you get everything going: a PostScript printer. This is a useful printer to use when you have a really cool presentation you created to justify the raise you are asking for. You can select this printer, print the job to a file on a floppy disk, and take the disk down to your local copy shop, where they can run it on one of their expensive PostScript printers to make everything look really professional.

Telling Windows about Your DOS Applications

Windows will search your entire hard disk, looking for the programs you already have. And it will do a remarkably good job of finding them all. Every once in a while it may have a hard time deciding which program you have. For example, when it encounters a program called Q.EXE, it has to ask you if this is Quicken or Quattro Pro. Just highlight the one that you have, and press Enter. If you have both, the program will tell you which directory it's asking about. Then it will keep going on about its business. Sometimes it will offer you choices, and none of them is correct. In that case, highlight None of the Above and then click on OK.

Installing CH. 5

☞ Even if Windows doesn't recognize one of your programs, you can add the program later. See Chapter 12 for how to do it.

No! Anything but Another Tutorial!

When Windows gets through installing itself, it will offer to let you take a tutorial that tells you all about Windows. If you have nothing better to do with your life for the next ten minutes or so, go ahead and start it. But frankly, don't be afraid to admit that it's a bore. Just press the Escape key any time in the middle of it to get out.

If you ever need a cure for insomnia and want to run the tutorial again, you can select it from the Help menu in Program Manager.

Return to DOS or Restart Windows

Finally, when the installation is complete, and you have escaped from the tutorial, Windows will ask you if you want to restart Windows, return to DOS, or (if Windows made changes to your configuration files) reboot your computer. Select the Reboot option, or if that choice isn't offered, select Return to DOS and then reboot your computer yourself.

☞ For more on rebooting your computer, see "Reboot and Reset" in Chapter 2.

Once you have rebooted your computer, just type

    WIN

from the DOS prompt and you will be back in Windows, hopefully to stay.

That's All, Folks—Exiting Windows

To leave Windows, double-click on the Control box (in the upper-left corner of the Program Manager window). If you've absentmindedly left a program running, Windows will be kind enough to notice and ask you if you want to save any changes.

After you've answered, you'll get a box with the message "This will end your Windows session." If this is OK with you, press Enter and after some clunking and beeping, Windows will disappear and you'll be back at the DOS prompt, where you started.

☞ If you decide you can't bear to leave Windows after all, click on the Cancel button.

To Turn It Off or Leave It On, That Is the Question

Probably the oldest debate in the world of PCs is whether you should turn your computer off when you're finished or leave the thing on all the time.

If you turn the computer off, you save a little bit of energy and maybe a bit of wear and tear on the hard-drive motor. This meant something years ago, but current hard drives are rated to run 100,000 hours or more without a failure.

Leaving it on reduces stress on the hard-drive motor caused by the initial surge of electricity when you flip the switch. And if you turn it on and off a lot, there's the problem of stress on the chips and connections caused by repeated heating up and cooling down.

So, we vote for leaving the computer on with the monitor turned off, but if it's too noisy for you or your dreams are haunted by Reddy Kilowatt, feel free to turn it off.

☞ If you want to leave the computer on all the time, turn the monitor off or better yet, use the Control Panel to turn on the Windows screen saver program. See Chapter 8, "Windows Treatments," for details on the screen saver.

☞ Don't like Windows' screen saver? There are lots of others out there. See Chapter 25 for some suggestions.

☞ Make sure the room where you keep the computer is kept reasonably cool. Computer innards generate a lot of heat, and if the room is too hot for you to work in, it's too hot for your computer to work in.

Installing
CH. 5

☞ Don't put a dust cover on any component that is turned on. The effect is that of a sauna and is not healthy for the machinery.

Never turn off your computer while Windows is running. Always exit by clicking on the little box in the upper-left corner of the Program Manager window and then selecting Close from the menu. Or you can press the Alt key plus the F4 key.

2

Here's where you'll get acquainted with Windows and its numerous charms. This part includes chapters on getting Windows started, setting up the Windows look, and getting Windows to work just the way you want.

Getting to Know Windows

Chapter 6

STARTING WINDOWS
(After All, This *Is* Why You Bought It)

Kollar's Rule: No task is impossible for the person who doesn't have to do it.

IN THIS CHAPTER we're actually going to make Windows do something besides look cute. In fact, here you'll see

☞ How to start up Windows, including a way even your favorite nerd may not know

☞ How to start a program in Windows

☞ How to open a file in the program

☞ How to save your work, and how to get out

We even include a primer on how to run Windows without a mouse. But trust us on this one. Do it *only* if you are desperate.

Firing It Up

So you think you are ready to blast off, do you? Fasten your seat belts then, and from the DOS prompt type

    WIN

and you are off to the wacky, wonderful world of Windows.

If everything works as it should, your screen will fill up with the Windows logo.

After this initial greeting, Windows continues on about its business and starts up. This can take anywhere from five or ten seconds to more than thirty.

☞ If, instead of the logo screen, DOS says "Bad command or filename," Windows isn't on your path. Time to call for some help from your favorite nerd.

☞ If all you get is the logo screen and nothing else happens, see Chapter 22, "Windows Problems and How to Solve Them," for help resolving the problem.

Getting Rid of the Start-up Screen

That initial logo screen is called a "splash" screen, and it is kind of cute. But after a while, you might get tired of it. To bypass the screen when you start Windows, type from the DOS prompt:

    WIN :

That's WIN to start Windows, a space, and then a colon. I guess the programmers who wrote Windows got tired of the splash screen, too, since they stuck that little trick in there.

Starting Windows and your favorite program at the same time

If you are starting Windows and just want to go straight to Quattro Pro for Windows to update your stock prices, just type

```
WIN QPW
```

That's WIN to start Windows, plus QPW to start Quattro Pro for Windows. If instead you want to run your word processor or some other program, just substitute the command for that program for QPW in the example.

More Than Anyone Wants to Know about Standard Mode and Enhanced Mode

Windows has two *modes* of operation, "standard" and "386 enhanced." Normally, you don't need to worry about the differences. Windows decides which you should be running depending on what kind of processor you have and how much memory is installed on your computer. And that will be the end of it.

However, if you have an incurable urge to know more (a sure sign of incipient nerddom), listen up.

Standard mode assumes that you have only a 286 processor and therefore can't take advantage of some of the neat memory tricks that were made possible with the advent of the 80386 processor. In this simpler mode, Windows *uses* your memory, but makes no effort to do any fancy tricks with it. This means that your DOS programs, for example, can only run full screen. You can't shrink them to windows in standard mode, though you can turn them into icons. While they are icons they don't run, however.

Running in 386 enhanced mode requires that you have an 80386 or higher processor, and at least 2MB of memory. (If you don't have at least this, you shouldn't be running Windows, anyway.) In this mode, Windows will let you run your old DOS applications in windows, and even run more than one of them in windows, if you want. Sounds good, right? So, what's the catch? Well, there really isn't one. Some Windows programs will run slightly slower in 386 mode as compared to standard mode, but the difference is pretty small and is frequently offset by Windows' faster disk performance in enhanced mode. So stick to 386 enhanced mode, unless you are specifically instructed to run in standard mode to test something.

About Program Manager

So, you have Windows up and running. Your screen looks something like Figure 6.1, with the Program Manager taking up most of your screen.

If it doesn't look like Figure 6.1, maybe it looks like Figure 6.2.

If you get the Figure 6.2 screen, double-click on the Program Manager icon and you'll get the full Windows.

Program Manager is itself a program. It consists of a window with a title bar and a menu bar. Inside the window are little squares representing other windows, called *group windows*. Behind the Program Manager window is a blank area called the *desktop*.

Double-click on any one of the group icons and it will pop open. Inside are icons—each one representing a program.

☞ Icons represent things in Windows. They are not the things themselves. So if you delete an icon, the program it represents is still on your computer somewhere.

FIGURE 6.1:
This is sort of how Windows will look when you start it up.

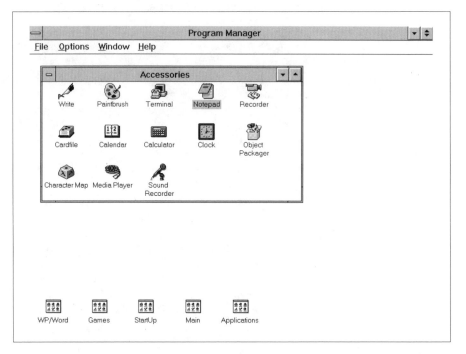

FIGURE 6.2:
This is the not-so-cute way Windows can look when you start.

☞ In Figure 6.1, there's a sort of shadow under the Notepad icon. That *highlighting* means that Notepad is ready to go and if you press Enter, it will start.

☞ Group icons can't be changed, but individual icons inside the group windows can be jazzed up considerably. See page 144 for how to get different icons.

Running a Program

Programs can be started lots of ways. The easiest is to find the icon representing the program and double-click on it.

Or click on the icon once and press the Enter key.

Maybe you don't know where the icon is. In that case, select Run from the File menu in Program Manager. Type in the full name of the program in the command-line text box and then click on OK. (If the program is not on your path in the AUTOEXEC.BAT file, you'll have to type the complete path in the text box.)

☞ Unclear on the double-click concept? Go back to page 12 for a quick brushup on clicking, double clicking, and so forth.

☞ Clear on the concept but still can't get the mouse to do what you want? See "Disciplining Your Mouse" on page 104 for information on how to bring that rodent into line.

Menu Basics

Windows uses what are called *pull-down menus.* This means that along the top of a program's window, just below the title bar, will be what is called the menu bar. This menu bar will have one or more words on it, such as File, Options, Help, and so forth. But each of these words is actually a gateway to a whole bunch of other possible commands.

If you click on the word "File," at the top of the Program Manager window, for example, a menu will drop down. On this menu will be a list of things that Program Manager can do related to files. For example, click on Run and type in **NOTEPAD.** Windows will open up its little text editor. On the menu bar for Notepad there are choices for File, Edit, Search, and Help.

Almost all Windows programs have a choice for file stuff on the far left of the menu bar and Help as the rightmost choice. In between these two, though, the choices will vary a good deal depending on what kind of program it is. Many programs will have a choice for Edit, as Notepad does, and when they do, it will be right next to the File choice. This is one of Windows' biggest strengths. Once you learn one Windows program, you are well on your way to learning the rest of them.

Opening a File

OK, since we have the Notepad program open, let's see how we use the File menu to open a file. Click on File, and then click on Open. The Open dialog box (Figure 6.3) will open.

FIGURE 6.3:
This is what you have to deal with whenever you open or save a file.

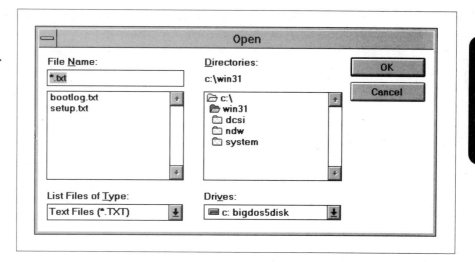

All the files in the Windows directory with the .TXT extension will be listed under File Name on the left. The Notepad program assumes that all files with that extension belong to it.

Even if your Windows program is brand new, you'll have a couple of Windows-generated files here, BOOTLOG.TXT and SETUP.TXT. Click on SETUP.TXT, and then click on OK. The dialog box goes away, and you are back at the main Notebook window, but now there's a lengthy file in the window. This file covers all the things that could have gone wrong, but didn't, during your initial installation of Windows. Interesting, but since we don't really need that right now, let's go back to the File menu, and this time, click on the choice for New.

Choosing New will close the current file, if there is one, and start a brand-new one.

☞ If the file you want has a different extension, click on the arrow next to the List Files of Type box. To see all the files in a directory, click on the All Files (*.*) option.

☞ If you don't see the file you want, it may be in a different directory. Double-click on the folders in the Directories list box. When you double-click on one, the contents of that directory will show up in the File Names box, and any subdirectories will show up in the Directories list box.

☞ Maybe the file you want is on a different drive altogether? In that case, click on the button next to the Drives list box. You'll get a list of drives to choose from.

☞ The good news is that once you know how to open a file in one program, you know how to open a file in all Windows programs.

Saving Your Work

It isn't a whole lot of fun to spend a couple of hours working on a memo to your boss about the raise you want, only to have the cat come along and pull the plug on your computer and lose all that work. In fact, it tends to make one want to throw things at the cat, which isn't really fair.

So, let's learn how to save our work. Click on File, then click on Save. Since we haven't given this important file a name yet, the Save As dialog box will open.

This box looks suspiciously like the Open dialog box you dealt with above.

Type in a name for the file, say SILLY.TXT. Then click on the OK button.

☞ You can save the file to a different directory or drive. Just select the drive from the Drives drop-down box. Click on a directory you like. Once you have everything just so, select the OK button.

☞ Once a file has been named and saved, you won't get the Save As box again with subsequent saves. Windows just assumes you want the file saved under the same name. However, if you want to save a copy of the file under a different name for reasons that are, of course, your business, just select Save As from the File menu and give the file a different name.

☞ Save your work often. That way, if something unexpected happens, you will only lose any work since the last time you saved.

Printing Out Your Work

Since this is a file-related action, we choose File from the menu. There are three printing-related options there: Print, Page Setup, and Print Setup. Let's leave the other two for later—just click on Print. A little information box opens up, telling you that Notepad is printing your file, and hopefully your printer starts making some printing-type noises.

For lots more about printing, see Chapter 16.

Two for the Price of One—
Running a Second Program

Windows' big selling point is the ability to run more than one program at the same time, right? This is a lot less difficult than you might think, since by opening Notepad, you already have two programs running: Notepad and Program Manager.

To switch between programs, just click on the one you want.

If you can't see the one you want, press Alt-Tab (hold down the Alt key and press the Tab key) and a small panel will open up in the middle of the screen. In it will be the name of a program that's open, as shown in Figure 6.4. If you already have several programs running, you can cycle through them this way to get to the one you want. Just hold down the Alt key and tap the Tab key as many times as it takes to get to the one you want, then let go. That program will now be on top!

☞ The order of programs as you cycle through them this way will change, depending on how recently you have used them. So, if you are switching back and forth between two programs, they will always be the first ones on the stack. Real handy if you have Solitaire open and your boss walks into your office! Just Alt-Tab and you are back in your spreadsheet.

☞ For more on moving windows and finding lost ones, see Chapter 10, "Windows Lost and Found."

FIGURE 6.4:
Alt-Tab gets you back quickly to where you were before.

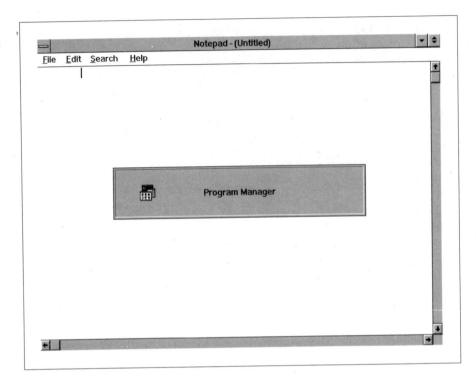

Keyboard Basics—ONLY for When Your Mouse Dies

It's very late and you've almost finished that presentation your boss wanted. One more quick tweak, and then print the flimsies out and you are done.

And your mouse chooses that moment to totally expire! Now what? There's no time to go get a new one, and none to spare in the department. Well, you *can* run Windows without it, though we recommend it only for emergencies this dire. Table 6.1 gives you the basic Windows keystrokes to get out of a jam.

TABLE 6.1:
Windows Keystrokes

Keystroke	What It Does
Alt-Tab	Switches to previous program.
Ctrl-Esc	Brings up Task List of open programs.
Alt-Enter	Switches DOS programs from full screen to windowed, and back. In Program Manager, brings up the Properties dialog box to change the properties of the item or group.
Alt-spacebar	Drops down the Control menu for the current window.
Alt	Activates the menu bar. Alt plus a letter drops down the menu that has that letter underlined.
Alt-F4	Exits the current program. If the current program is Program Manager, exits Windows.
Ctrl-F4	Closes the current window within a program.
Ctrl-Tab	Moves to the next icon or group window in Program Manager.
Alt-Esc	Iconizes a DOS window from full screen, or moves the focus to the next window or icon.
Enter	Executes, opens, activates, or generally *does* something; usually the same as double clicking.
Arrow keys	Moves the focus within a Program Manager group to a different icon. Within a dialog box, moves the highlight to different options in a list.
Tab	Within a dialog box, accepts the setting of the highlighted option and moves the focus to the next option.
Spacebar	Within a dialog box, toggles an option on or off.

All Good Things Must Come to an End—Leaving Windows

So you are done, and you want to stop Windows. Well, just close all your open programs and then select Exit from the File menu of Program Manager.

Actually, if all you have open are Windows programs, you don't need to close them first. Windows will let you know if there's any unsaved work and will prompt you to save it before closing.

But if you have any DOS programs open, you will need to shut them down individually first.

You will then get one last chance to change your mind about leaving Windows. Program Manager will always pop up the Exit Windows dialog box to make sure you really want to leave Windows. Click on OK to exit, or click on Cancel to return to Windows.

☞ The absolutely quickest way out of Windows is to press Alt-F4 while Program Manager is active, or double-click on the Program Manager Control box.

Always shut down Windows before you turn off the power to your computer or reset it. Failing to exit Windows properly can result in lost work if you haven't saved recently, or worse, damaged files if Windows is currently writing to a file.

Even if no work is damaged or lost, Windows will tend to leave around a bunch of temporary files that don't get deleted if you don't exit properly.

Getting Out of Program Jams

In a perfect world, with perfect people, none of us would ever do things we regret.

But let's get real here. If you try something in most Windows programs, and you decide that it was a horrible mistake, you can *undo* that mistake if you act immediately. Just click on the Edit menu, and then click on the Undo option in the drop-down menu. Or, press Alt-E, U to do the same thing.

In most programs with this lifesaving feature, you can get there even quicker by pressing Ctrl-Z (as in "Gad**Z**ooks but I didn't want to do that"). All right, maybe that isn't what Ctrl-Z is short for, but it works, so remember it to quickly undo what you didn't really mean to do in the first place.

You can even undo the undo you just did to get back to where you were before you undid it.

Getting Out of Jammed Windows

Sometimes you end up with a program that seems out to lunch and won't come back. If it is a Windows program, press Ctrl-Escape to bring up the Task List, make sure the program is highlighted, and then click on the End Task button. Of course, any work you hadn't saved before the program decided to take an extended lunch break is lost, but at least you managed to fire the program.

If it is a DOS program, it can be a bit trickier, since End Task won't get it done. If you are running in 386 enhanced mode, however, try this: Press Alt-Enter to switch the program to a window instead of full screen, and then either click on its Control box or press Alt-spacebar to open up the Control menu. Choose Settings, and then click on the Terminate button. Windows will throw up a final warning box like the one in Figure 6.5, and if you are sure this is what you want to do, click on the OK button.

FIGURE 6.5:

Using the Terminate button on a DOS application is a last resort, but sometimes the only one!

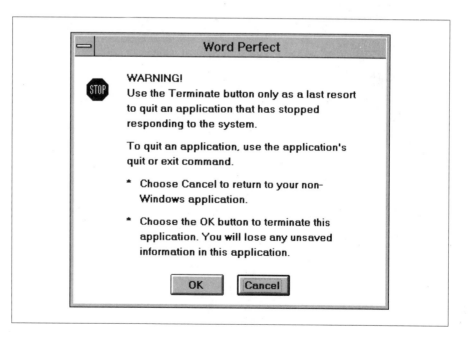

Finally, sometimes Windows itself seems to take an extended lunch. You're left looking at a screen where nothing is happening. Try the following steps:

1. Press the Escape key a few times. This probably won't work, but it'll make you feel better.

2. Press Ctrl, Alt, and Delete all at the same time. You'll get a screen telling you that you have an unresponsive application (as if you didn't know that!). Press Enter and Windows will close down the troublemaker.

3. If steps 1 and 2 don't work, press the reset button on the front of the computer box, or turn the power off. Wait ten seconds and then turn it back on. This will likely leave some temporary files scattered around your hard disk.

☞ See Chapter 22, "Windows Problems and How to Solve Them," for directions on finding these worthless temp files and deleting them.

Don't turn the power off and back on quickly. This is a good way to fry some expensive little part inside your computer.

Chapter 7

JUST LIKE A B MOVIE

(All about Buttons, Bars, Boxes, and Borders)

Wilson's Law: Internal consistency is valued more than efficiency.

WINDOWS IS LIKE most other computer stuff you come across. There are a million different little parts, and each part has a name that you can't remember five minutes after you've learned it.

Don't worry. It's not necessary to remember the names of anything. Once you've seen how to do most things in Windows, you'll remember how and the name won't matter. Use this chapter as a place to come back to, though, when you need a reminder about how one of these buttons or boxes or whatever works.

The Sum Is Greater Than the Parts

A window, as you no doubt suspect by now, is that rectangular box on your screen. The one with borders around it. Inside a window you can find a program or a bunch of icons representing programs.

Figure 7.1 shows a typical window.

FIGURE 7.1:
A window can have buttons, bars, boxes, and borders.

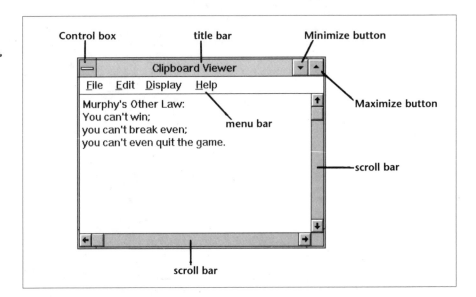

Staying within the Borders

Borders are the lines that go around the outside of a window. Really two lines very close together.

☞ You can use the border to change the size of a window. Position your mouse pointer over a border until the pointer develops two heads. Press and hold the left mouse button and move the mouse around. When you're done playing, release the mouse button.

☞ In Chapter 8, "Windows Treatments," you can read how to change the thickness of the borders. Strictly for those who border on the compulsive.

Step Up to the Bar

Every window in Windows has from one to three bars, which are the thick stripes along the edge.

Title bar

The title bar runs along the top of the window, with the program and file names in it.

Microsoft Word - Document1

If you're just starting to make a file and it doesn't have a name yet, it'll be shown as Untitled or Document1 or something like that. After you name the file, its name will be in the title bar.

☞ *The title bar is a handy place to grab onto a window and move it. Point the mouse at the title bar, hold down the mouse button, and move the mouse to some new spot. An outline of the window moves as you move the mouse. Let go of the mouse button and the window jumps to that spot.*

☞ *Double-click on the title bar to expand the window to full-screen size and cover up everything else on the screen. Double-click again on the title bar and the window shrinks back to normal size.*

☞ *The title bar of the window you're working in will be highlighted. That is, it'll be a different color from all the other open windows. The window with the highlighted title bar is also known as the active window.*

Menu bar

Every Windows program uses menu bars. Some have only a few choices, like Solitaire:

Game   Help

And some have a zillion choices, like Write:

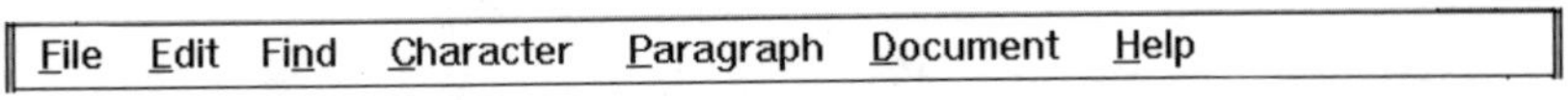

File   Edit   Find   Character   Paragraph   Document   Help

The menu bar is where most of a program's commands hang out when they're not busy. Click on one of the names in the menu bar and a whole list of options unfolds. As you can see in Figure 7.2, the choices on the Character menu all have to do with how individual characters will look. Once a menu is open, you move the mouse pointer to the option you want and click.

☞ You can also get to a menu easily by pressing the Alt key and then whatever letter is underlined in the menu name. Or press Alt and use the ← and → keys to get to the menu you want and then press Enter.

☞ If you accidentally select the wrong menu, just click on the right one and the old one will disappear just as the new one rolls down.

☞ To close all the menus, click anywhere else on the workspace or on the wallpaper.

☞ Sometimes commands appear on the menu bar. You can tell they're commands because they'll have an exclamation point next to them. Click on one of them and you won't get a menu, you'll get whatever the command does.

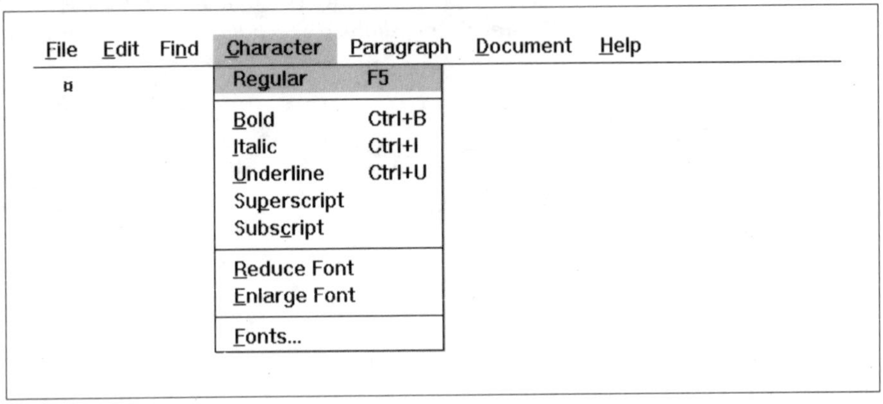

FIGURE 7.2:
On today's menu

File   Edit   Find   Character   Paragraph   Document   Help

Regular	F5
Bold	Ctrl+B
Italic	Ctrl+I
Underline	Ctrl+U
Superscript	
Subscript	
Reduce Font	
Enlarge Font	
Fonts...	

☞ Any menu choices that Windows just doesn't feel up to doing at the moment will be grayed out. For example, the Copy command will be grayed out if there's nothing in the window that could *be* copied.

Scroll bars let you get where you want to go

Scroll bars are at the right side and bottom of a window. Some windows will have both, some will have only one, a few will have none at all.

A scroll bar indicates there is some information beyond the border of the window. The vertical scroll bar represents the entire length of a document, and the horizontal scroll bar represents the width of the document.

Click on the little box inside the scroll bar. Hold down the mouse button, and drag the box up and down or back and forth in the bar.

☞ To move up a page, click on the scroll bar above the little sliding box. To move down a page, click on the scroll bar below the little sliding box. This is just like using the Page Up and Page Down keys.

☞ To move up a line in your document, click on the arrow at the top of the scroll bar. To move down a line, click on the arrow at the bottom of the scroll bar.

☞ Clicking on the little box inside the scroll bar doesn't do anything.

Windows Has Buttons for Everything

One of the coolest things about Windows is all the buttons, especially the ones you can click on and they actually appear to *move*. Wowser!

Command buttons

These are the buttons with words on them. They show up in dialog boxes in Windows and in the programs that run in Windows. Here are the common ones:

You click on the OK button to say you're through now and would like to move on, thank you. Pressing the Enter key does the same thing.

You've done something that you don't want to make permanent. Click on the Cancel button and whatever you've done in that box will disappear. Pressing the Esc key has the same effect.

Click this button and you'll get a help screen addressing the particular situation you're in.

Buttons like these, with arrows or dots, let you know that if you click on them, you'll get still another box to make selections from.

If you've clicked on the wrong command button and haven't lifted your finger from the mouse button, there's still a chance to save the situation. That's because the command doesn't take effect until you release the mouse button.

Keep pressing the mouse button and gingerly move the mouse pointer so that it's not on the command button. Release the mouse button and you're saved!

Robert's Rule of Order: We do the right thing accidentally far more often than on purpose.

Maximize and Minimize buttons

The Maximize and Minimize buttons are the up and down arrows at the upper-right corner of a window.

The up arrow is the *Maximize* button. When you click on it, the window fills the entire screen.

The down arrow is the *Minimize* button. Click on it and the window shrinks to the size of an icon.

When a window is maximized, the Maximize button changes into a double-sided arrow.

This is called the Restore button and when you click on it, the window shrinks back to the size it was before you maximized it.

☞ *When you shrink a program to an icon, the program is still open and waiting for you to do something. To bring it back to life, just double-click on the icon.*

☞ *If you're running a DOS program in a window, it can't be maximized to fill the whole screen. If you're not running a DOS program in a window, you can fill the whole screen. See Chapter 19 for ways to run your DOS programs so you can live with them.*

Radio buttons

Sometimes called option buttons, radio buttons are circles that are either empty or have a dot in the middle. The dot means that that option is selected.

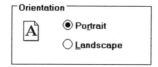

Radio buttons cut no slack at all. You have to choose one and only one of the options. When you select one, you are deselecting all the others.

Button bars, or what are all those little pictures?

Windows itself has not yet fallen prey to the button bar mania. But it seems like every program designed to run in Windows has to have not merely one button bar but a whole bunch of them. And you can turn them on or off, float them, make them vertical, horizontal, on top, on the bottom. And they all have these really useless little pictures on them. However, once you learn them, it can be very helpful to just click a button to

cut, copy or paste.

Having a Dialog with a Dialog Box

Whenever Windows want to solicit some information from you, it pops up something called a *dialog box*. A dialog box differs from a menu in that it wants you to type in some data (like a file name) or provide some other information it needs to go forward.

Inside dialog boxes are various *controls* (see Figure 7.3). Some of them are buttons, as covered earlier, but others are more boxes.

FIGURE 7.3:
A typical dialog box

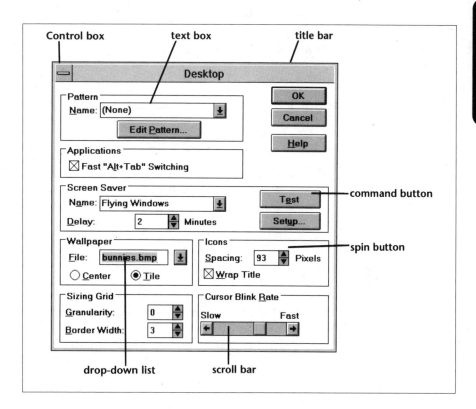

The Control box—why you don't need it

The Control box is in every dialog box and every window. If you click on it, you'll get a list of commands that are only useful if your mouse dies. Table 7.1 shows a list of the commands and how a person with a healthy rodent can avoid them.

TABLE 7.1:
What to Use instead of the Control Menu

Control Menu Option	What It Does	What to Really Do
Restore	Opens iconized program back into a window	Double-click on icon
Move, Size	Lets you use the cursor keys to move or resize a window	Grab the border or title bar with the mouse and drag
Minimize, Maximize	Makes the window smaller or bigger	Click on the Minimize or Maximize button
Close	Closes the window	Double-click on the Control box
Switch To	Opens the Task List	Double-click anywhere on the Windows background (the desktop)

☞ Not all the commands are in all the Control box menus.

☞ Closing a program is not the same as iconizing it. If you close it, the computer forgets all about it and to reopen, you have to load the thing into memory again. If the program is iconized, it is still open, just in a miniature form.

Text boxes

Text boxes are places in which you can (surprise!) type some text. Sometimes they start out with stuff in them, sometimes they're empty. If you position the mouse pointer in the text box, it turns into an "I-beam." Just click in the text box to start typing in it.

To replace all the text in the text box with something else, just double-click in the box and type in the new text.

Drop-down lists

To save space on the desktop (like with drop-down menus), Windows also does drop-down lists. Maybe it's a list of neat fonts, sometimes just a boring list of files. Depends on the context.

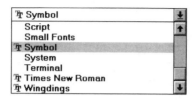

Sometimes you can click in the text box next to the button and the pointer will turn into a I-beam. This means you can type in your own choice. Other times, you'll find that Windows stubbornly refuses to recognize your existence. This means that you have to choose from the items in the list. Tough luck.

☞ To move around quickly in a drop-down list, press the first letter of the item you want. The first item beginning with that letter will be highlighted.

☞ If you don't *know* the first letter of the item, use the scroll bar next to the list. Click on the little slider box and drag it up and down until you find what you want.

☞ On some festive occasions you may need to select more than one item in a list. Hold down the Control key as you merrily click on the various items.

☞ For information on the I-beam and other mouse disguises, see Table 2.1 on page 20.

Spin buttons

You use these buttons to set days, times, numerical ranges, stuff like that.

Button, Bars, etc.
CH. 7

They tend to look a bit different from program to program. Just click on the up arrow to make the numbers go up and the down arrow to...oh, you can figure it out.

You can also click in the text box and enter a value directly, but why miss all the fun?

Son of scroll bars

Scroll bars can also appear inside dialog boxes, where they are used as a slider switch to adjust a value up or down. There's one in Figure 7.3 back on page 85. Grab hold of it by placing your mouse pointer on the little box and clicking on it. Holding down the mouse button, you can drag the box and adjust the cursor blinking speed from near-comatose to way-too-much-caffeine.

Check up on your options

Check boxes let you set or unset options. They are little square boxes that either have an X inside them or are blank. If they have an X, they're "on." If they're blank, they're "off."

You can click on the box to toggle the X on and off.

☞ Some programs, notably the Norton Desktop for Windows, have a variation on the normal check box scenario. You can have a check box that's checked (on), blank (off), or grayed (don't care). The grayed option means that you want the program to disregard a set of options altogether.

Chapter 8

WINDOWS TREATMENTS

Frank's Law: Nothing succeeds like the appearance of success.

BEAUTY MAY ONLY be skin deep, but it sure beats the alternative. And Windows can really look sensational given a chance. Left to its own devices, Windows shows up looking pretty drab. This chapter tells you how to turn it into a real beauty.

The gateway to changing all the things that make up your "desktop" is in the Control Panel. The Control Panel is in your Main group and has an icon that looks like this:

Control
Panel

Double-click on it to start up the Control Panel.

You will notice that there are lots of boring-looking things there, like Ports, Keyboard, Mouse, and Date/Time, as well as some stuff you know will be great, like Color and Fonts. This chapter will focus on the cool stuff, of which Desktop is the coolest, and the next chapter will focus on all the rest of the necessary but somewhat less exciting things in the Control Panel.

Have It Your Way—
Customizing Your Desktop

Desktop controls lots of stuff, both the neat and the mundane, but all have something to do with how your Windows desktop looks and behaves. So let's start by double-clicking on the Desktop icon, which looks like this:

Desktop

When you double-click on this, you get the Desktop dialog box, as shown in Figure 8.1. There you will see all sorts of buttons and boxes, and even a slide bar.

☞ If you have any doubts about how any of these buttons and so forth operate, jump back to Chapter 7, "Just Like a B Movie," for a quick refresher on them. Don't worry—we'll still be here when you get back.

FIGURE 8.1:

Here's where you can beautify your desktop.

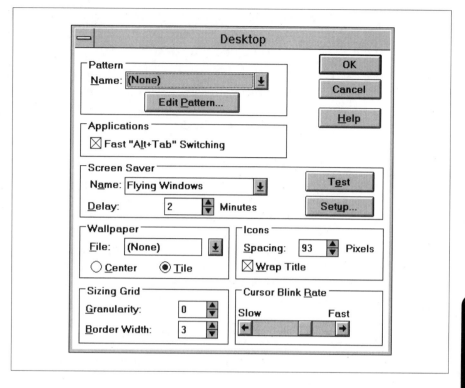

Choosing Your Pattern

The Pattern box lets you put a pattern over all the parts of your desktop that aren't covered with wallpaper. Windows ships with an assortment of 13 different patterns, ranging from a simple 50 percent gray screen to cute little Scottish terriers.

Click on the drop-down list arrow next to the Name box in the Pattern group. Pick a pattern and then click on OK. You can always return to the plain-old boring life you had before you started this by selecting None, which removes the pattern from your desktop.

☞ One problem with patterns is that they only show in areas where you don't have wallpaper. So if you have a wallpaper pattern covering your entire desktop, you won't see anything.

☞ You also won't see a change if you select a Windows color scheme that has a black desktop background. (See "Changing Your Windows Colors," on page 96.)

☞ If you find you have trouble reading the names under program icons on your screen, you might want to consider changing to a different pattern or abandoning patterns altogether. They can obscure the text and make it harder to read. (But you might decide this is a small price to pay for having cute little Scotties all over your screen.)

☞ If you are artistically inclined, or just love to fiddle with things, click on the Edit Pattern button. This will bring up the Desktop - Edit Pattern dialog box. Here you can mess around with any of the already existing patterns, or add a new one. Just remember that if you don't like what's happening and want to return to where you started, click on the Cancel button to leave the Edit Pattern dialog box without changing anything.

Using the Cool Switch

The absolutely best way to switch among your running applications is to use the Cool Switch. Hold down the Alt key and tap the Tab key. Each Tab tap brings up a banner in the middle of your screen with a program name and icon on it. When you get to the program you want, release both keys.

If Cool Switch is not on, using Alt-Tab is not nearly so gratifying. It just pops up the title bar of each open application wherever it happens to be on the screen.

When you install Windows, Cool Switch is automatically turned on. But if it's not working on your system, click on the Desktop icon in the Control Panel. In the Desktop dialog box, you'll see a check box marked Fast "Alt+Tab" Switching. Put a check in that box to enable Cool Switch, then click on the OK button.

Screen Savers

The purpose of a screen saver is to prevent a single pattern from "burning in" on your screen. With older monitors this was a problem. If you left an unchanged screen on your monitor while you went to lunch, say, you'd eventually find a ghost image of your spreadsheet permanently etched onto the surface of your monitor.

There's not the slightest bit of evidence that this is a significant problem with modern VGA screens, but without this "danger," there's no good excuse for having screen savers, so people still repeat the story.

Even when screen savers were actually needed, all that was necessary was something that would blank the screen when you weren't using it. How utterly boring. Since the alleged problem is the *same* thing being on your screen all the time, why not just provide something that is constantly changing? Thus was born the modern screen saver.

Click on the drop-down button in the Name list box and choose from five possibilities—from the totally tedious Blank Screen to the ingenious Mystify.

You can see how each of them looks by selecting the one you want and then clicking on the Test button. Most will also let you customize the screen saver to some extent by clicking on the Setup button.

Finally, click on the spin buttons next to the Delay box to set the idle time before your screen saver kicks in. Any keystroke or mouse movement resets this timer, so don't worry about making the time fairly short.

If you get bored with the Windows screen saver and want some more variety, wonderful screen savers are made by After Dark and Intermission. Both give you enough choices to totally boggle your mind and dazzle your coworkers.

Wallpaper

Probably the neatest thing you can do to your Windows desktop is have a really bizarre wallpaper that no one else has. Wallpaper envy is the only sign of life in many offices of our acquaintance.

Wallpaper is a graphical image, stored in a Windows bitmap file (these files have the extension .BMP). When you place a .BMP (pronounced "bimp") file in your Windows directory, it's automatically added to the list of available wallpapers.

To select a wallpaper, click on the drop-down arrow button next to the File text box, and then click on the wallpaper you want to use. Next, choose whether to center the image in the middle of your screen or to repeat versions of it over your entire screen. Then click on the OK button to close the Desktop dialog box, and the new wallpaper will be on your desktop.

☞ If your new wallpaper doesn't show, chances are it's a fairly small image and you selected "Center" instead of "Tile." Go back and change this setting and the new wallpaper will repeat over your entire screen.

☞ If you are using a video driver that only supports 16 colors, and your new wallpaper looks really weird and grainy, chances are it's designed for 256 colors. Very few 256-color .BMPs look anything *but* weird at 16 colors. To see how many colors your video driver supports, see Chapter 22.

☞ If you've somehow coerced someone into giving you a .BMP file on a floppy and you want to use it as wallpaper, see the section on copying files in Chapter 13 to learn how to get the file into the Windows directory.

More! I must have more wallpaper!

The best source of new wallpaper is a friend, especially one with nerdlike tendencies. If you walk by a computer and see a wallpaper you really like, go ahead and make that person's day! Ask them to give you a copy. Most will be happy to.

Another source is to make your own. You can use Paintbrush to draw something, and then when you save the drawing, choose Bitmap file as the file type and give the file a .BMP extension. (Chapter 14 has lots more on Paintbrush.)

☞ You can also, if you have access to a scanner, scan in a favorite picture. Or, if you know someone who has a scanner, ask them to do it for you. To get any sort of decent-looking wallpaper from a photograph will require that the image be 256 colors or more. The resulting Bitmap file can be copied into your Windows directory and used as wallpaper.

☞ Another good source is bulletin board systems (BBS's) or information services like CompuServe and GEnie. You need a modem to get to these services, so get some help setting up your computer to talk to CompuServe or a local BBS at least the first time. After that, you should be able to figure out how to do it. Most services and BBS's also have a novice area, where you can make mistakes and learn your way around, frequently at a reduced rate or even free.

☞ Most of the images on these services are stored in .GIF (rhymes with "if") format, which is short for Graphics Interchange Format. Get your favorite nerd to supply you with a conversion program to get files from .GIF to .BMP format.

If you are using a large, complicated, 256-color wallpaper, you are using a pretty fair amount of your computer's resources. This means that you could cause other programs not to have enough memory available to run. So, if you start getting "Not enough memory for that operation" error messages just after you switch wallpapers, try going back to a simpler wallpaper and see if the error message persists. If it goes away, chances are you will either have to have simpler tastes or get more memory.

The Rest of the Desktop Stuff

The last options in the Desktop dialog box are the least interesting. These are Sizing Grid, Icon Spacing, and Cursor Blink Rate.

The sizing grid has two settings. The first determines how big or small the invisible grid is that all the windows and icons on your desktop line up on. If you set this to zero, the grid is turned off. If you set this too high, it can be difficult to control the placement of windows on your desktop. The second setting determines how fat the borders on your windows are. The default setting of 3 should be fine for all except the most hardened twiddler.

The Icons box lets you change the number of pixels of space between each icon, and whether the title for the icon is allowed to "wrap" to a second line. If you find that your icon titles tend to overlap each other, you may want to crank this number up a bit.

Finally, the Cursor Blink Rate box has a slide bar from "Slow" to "Fast" to determine how fast the cursor blinks in your Windows applications. Again, if you are a confirmed twiddler, feel free. The rest of us will just leave it well enough alone.

Changing Your Windows Colors

Using the Desktop part of the Control Panel is nice, and you can change a lot about how your screen looks that way, but you are still left with the boring colors that Windows ships with as the default. So, fasten your seat belts and have at the Color dialog box. Here you can exercise your creativity to create a truly remarkable color scheme. Just double-click on the Color icon

Color

in the Control Panel group box and you will be whisked into the Color dialog box, shown in Figure 8.2.

This dialog box has a Color Schemes drop-down list box at the top, and a sample screen showing the current color settings in the middle, with some control buttons at the bottom. Let's start with the Color Schemes list box at the top.

Click on the drop-down button on the right-hand side of the box to see a list of predesigned color schemes that come with Windows. These range from the boring defaults to the positively hideous, such as Hot-dog Stand or Plasma Power Saver.

But hey, don't let me tell you what you like. Try them. Click on the one you want to try, and the sample screen in the middle shows you exactly what it will look like. Some color schemes are designed to look good on laptops, such as the LCD schemes and the Plasma Power Saver. These tend to look pretty weird in color, but some people actually like them. Don't be afraid to try, since it's easy to get back to where you started. When you are ready to spend some time with one, click on the OK button at the bottom of the window, and try it for a while.

FIGURE 8.2:
Double-click on the
Color icon to change
your screen colors.

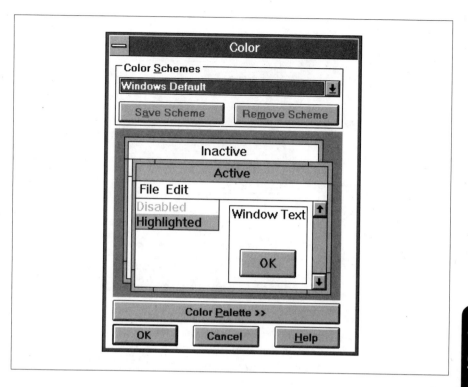

Once you have a feel for what you like, and what you don't, you can
create your very own color scheme. Just open up the Color dialog box
again, and click on the Color Palette button. This opens up the second
half of the Color dialog box, as shown in Figure 8.3.

This side shows a palette of Basic Colors, and a drop-down list box of locations, or "Screen Elements." In the sample box on the left side, click
with your mouse on the part of the screen you want to change. This
will put the name of that part in the Screen Element box, and then all
you need to do is click on the color you want it to be. The change
shows immediately in the sample box.

If none of the basic colors quite does what you want, click on the Define Custom Colors button. This brings up the Custom Color Selector
box, as shown in Figure 8.4. Use the mouse to move the open cross-hair
cursor around until you get the color you want, or do it manually by
using the spin buttons below the color map. When you have picked the

FIGURE 8.3:
You can design your
own color scheme for
Windows.

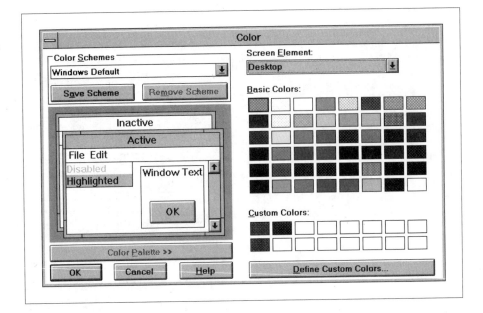

exact color you want, click on the Add Color button, and it will be
added to your color palette in the Custom Colors section.

Finally, when you have everything as you want it, click on the Save
Scheme button and the Save Scheme box will prompt you to give this
dynamite new color scheme a name. Type in a new name, or you will
overwrite one of the Windows default schemes. Click OK to accept the
name you typed in, and then click OK again at the bottom left of the
dialog box to change your Windows color scheme.

Fiddling with Fonts

Windows 3.1 introduced to the world a brand-new font technology
called "TrueType." This was a big break from the past, because it allowed users to create a document and have the fonts be an actual part
of the document. This way, if you shared a document with a friend, or
in a workgroup, all those special fonts you had didn't disappear just because your friend didn't have them installed on her computer.

In addition, TrueType fonts do a remarkably good job of showing on
screen exactly what you will see on the printed page. It isn't perfect,

FIGURE 8.4:

The Custom Color Selector box

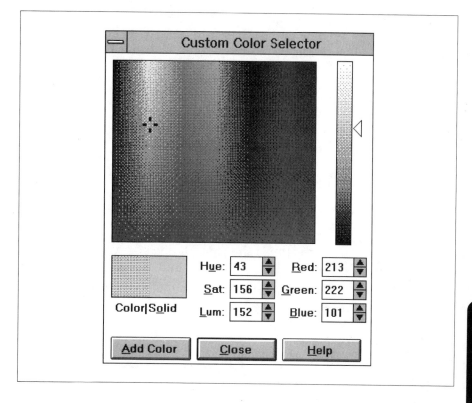

but it's a big improvement over what came with earlier versions of Windows. Plus, TrueType fonts are scalable, which means they take up less space on your hard disk.

A Horrible Note on Scalable Fonts

Scalable fonts are typefaces like balloons. No matter how big you blow them up to be, they retain their nice smooth outline. Other kinds of fonts are called bitmapped or raster fonts and they only look nice at certain sizes. When you blow them up, you really *would* like to blow them up.

And finally, the TrueType fonts in Windows are *device-independent*. This means that even if you are using a dot-matrix printer, you can use the same fonts as the person down the hall with the expensive PostScript laser printer. The laser printer's output will look better than yours, because of the differences in the way the printers work, but the font will clearly be the same.

Click on the Fonts icon

Fonts

and the Fonts dialog box shown in Figure 8.5 will open.

In the Fonts dialog box you can see which fonts are already installed, as well as add new ones or remove ones you never use.

At the top of the Fonts dialog box, you will see a list of installed fonts. As you select a different font, it is displayed below in the Sample box, along with some information about the size and type of font it is.

FIGURE 8.5:

Double-click on the Fonts icon to add or remove fonts.

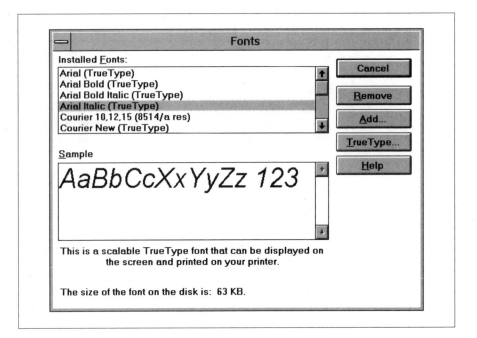

Adding a font

To add a font, click on the Add button. The Add Fonts dialog box will open, and you will see a list of fonts in your current directory, along with the usual Windows tools for changing drives and directories.

Once you have selected the fonts you want to add, click on the Copy Fonts to Windows Directory check box so that the fonts will be placed in your Windows system directory, and then click OK. The fonts will be copied from wherever they were before to your Windows system directory, and they will be available for all your Windows applications to use.

☞ In order to add fonts, you have to have them on your hard disk or on a floppy. Use the Directories and Drives boxes, to direct Windows' attention to the fonts you want to add.

Getting rid of a font

You can easily remove fonts you never use. Double-click on the Fonts icon in the Control Panel. Just highlight the font name in the Installed Fonts list box and then click on the Remove button. You will get a chance to confirm that you don't want to use the font anymore, and you can even delete it from your hard disk by checking the Delete Font File from Disk check box.

But why would you want to? After all, one of the ways to lord it over your friends is to have fonts they don't. However, if you have a space problem on your hard disk, you may want to cut back to the ones you actually use.

☞ To delete more than one font, press and hold down the Ctrl key while you use the mouse to highlight the fonts that you've decided to eliminate.

☞ If you don't check the Delete Font File from Disk box, the font will disappear from your list but it will still be taking up space on your hard disk.

Control Panel
CH. 8

☞ Be careful about deleting fonts that don't say TrueType next to them. Some of these are the system fonts Windows uses for dialog boxes, menus, etc.

☞ For more about fonts and the different font technologies, check out Chapter 16.

Chapter 9

THE REST OF THE CONTROL PANEL

Mary Ann's Law: You can always find what you're not looking for.

CHAPTER 8 DEALS with all the aesthetic stuff in the Control Panel and how to make your desktop into a scenic wonderland, etc., etc. But there's lots of other customizing you can do. In this chapter we deal with the other icons in the Control Panel—some of which are even useful.

Disciplining Your Mouse

You have to use a mouse all the time in Windows, and if it's not set up to suit you, you'll find it very annoying.

If you feel like your rodent could be better behaved, click on the Mouse icon in the Control Panel.

Mouse

Double-clicking your way

You can adjust the amount of time it takes for Windows to recognize a double click as just that and not two separate clicks. Double-click on the box marked TEST. This box will change color each time Windows recognizes your double click. Drag the slider box back and forth and experiment to get the double-click speed you want.

Mouse speed

Perhaps you'd rather your mouse didn't dart around the screen so readily. If so, you can adjust the mouse tracking speed by moving the slider box under Mouse Tracking Speed.

A slow speed means that you have to move the mouse quite a bit on the desktop to get a corresponding movement on screen. Faster mouse tracking means that you can barely move the mouse itself and the mouse pointer will take off like a shot.

☞ If you're left-handed, click on the Swap Left/Right Buttons check box. Then you can use the mouse in your left hand and still click with your index finger.

☞ If you click on the Mouse Trails check box, you'll get the weird effect of ghost arrows following your mouse around the screen. This feature was added to Windows for users of laptop computers. The screens on laptops often make the mouse pointer hard to see. This box may be grayed out if your system is using a video driver other than one of those that came with Windows.

What's a Port?

A port is a fortified wine served after dinner with Stilton cheese, of course!

But in computer-speak, a port is a connection point on your computer where things like printers and modems are hooked up. Unless you have a very good reason, stay away from the Ports icon

Ports

in the Control Panel. You can't do yourself any good there, and you can easily mess something up.

This Keyboard Is Too Weird

The Keyboard icon in the Control Panel

Keyboard

lets you set how fast a key will repeat when you hold it down.

The first slider box, Delay Before First Repeat, lets you control how long you have to hold down a key before it starts to repeat. The second slider box, Repeat Rate, sets how fast the key will repeat once it gets started. You can practice in the Test box until you get it right.

Setting the Date and Time

If you click on the Date/Time icon in the Control Panel, you can reset the date and the time.

Date/Time

Your computer puts a date and time on every new file you create. Having the right dates and times on your files can be very important when you're trying to track when some file was created or modified.

Highlight the number you want to change and then either type in the new number directly or use the spin buttons to set the date or time correctly. Click on the OK button when you're done.

386 Enhanced

If you are running Windows in 386 enhanced mode, you will see this icon in the Control Panel:

386 Enhanced

Double-click on this to bring up the 386 Enhanced dialog box. This box is really strictly the purview of nerds. You should not make changes here unless a program's documentation specifically tells you to.

☞ For more on modes, see "More Than Anyone Wants to Know About Standard Mode and Enhanced Mode" on page 65.

Permanent vs. Temporary Swap Files

The one thing you *might* want to change under 386 Enhanced is the setting for Virtual Memory. This setting controls how Windows uses your hard disk to make your computer think it has more memory.

If you have lots of hard-disk space, this should be what is called a permanent swap file. This means that Windows creates a special, hidden file on your hard disk that only it can use. In most cases, this makes Windows run faster than if you used a temporary swap file, since Windows has complete control of the area and doesn't have to ask for DOS to handle the file—it does it directly. The trade-off is that this space is *only* available for Windows and only for this specific purpose. So, don't create a permanent swap file unless you are sure you can afford to give up the space. A good rule of thumb is not to create a permanent swap file *smaller* than 5000K (5MB). And the optimum one should be no more than one to two times the size of your RAM memory.

If you do decide to create a permanent swap file, and you are running DOS 6, then first, before you do anything else, run DEFRAG from DOS *before* you start Windows.

After you start Windows, go to the Control Panel and click on the 386 Enhanced icon. In the 386 Enhanced dialog box, click on Virtual Memory. Then click on Change and make the necessary changes in the New Settings box.

- ☞ For more about DEFRAG, see Chapter 20, "Don't Do Dis DOS (Commands You Shouldn't Use in Windows)."

- ☞ If you see a box that says "Use 32-Bit Disk Access," leave it alone.

- ☞ You can't create a permanent swap file on a DoubleSpace or Stacker drive. You *can,* however, create one on the host drive if there is enough room.

- ☞ After you diddle around with this stuff for a while, you'll see that it mostly makes no difference what you do and that Windows was right in the first place.

More Control Panel CH. 9

Sound

If you have a sound adapter, you can use the dialog box behind this icon:

Sound

to set up all sorts of annoying sounds. Sounds can be assigned to various events in Windows. In the Sound dialog box, the events are listed on the left and the sound files on the right. Just click on the event and then the sound you want associated with it.

☞ *A sound adapter is a card that goes inside your computer and sends output to stereo speakers.*

☞ *See Chapter 25, "Ways to Spend Money and Have Fun," for more on sound cards and other cool stuff.*

☞ *Even without a sound card you can get a limited amount of sound by installing a program called SPEAK.EXE in your system. Bribe a nerd to get it for you off CompuServe. Since the speaker on your PC is about the size of a quarter, don't expect much in the way of sound quality.*

Changing Your Printer

Double-click on the Printers icon to bring up the Printers dialog box. There are all sorts of things you can do from here—like add or remove printers, set up the options on your printers, install font cartridges for them, and so on—but we will leave all that for Chapter 16, where we tell you more about printers and printing than you probably wanted to know. But *if* you have more than one printer installed on your system, you can use the Printers icon in the Control Panel

Printers

to change from one printer to another.

When you double-click on the Printers icon, you'll get the Printers dialog box, shown in Figure 9.1. Just highlight the printer you want to use in the Installed Printers box, and click on the Set As Default Printer button at the bottom. Then click on Close to get out.

FIGURE 9.1:
How to pick a printer

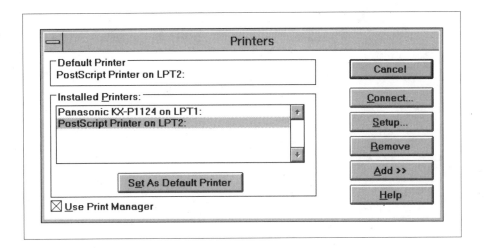

Stuff You Should Leave Alone

There are other icons you'll see in the Control Panel, but unless you have a very good reason, just leave them alone:

Drivers   Network   International

☞ Drivers Lets you add and change programs that control multimedia equipment, such as sound boards and audio CDs.

☞ Network You won't even see this unless you're on a network. And if you are, it's the network administrator's bailiwick.

☞ International This is where you change the date, language, and other settings to those of another country. You will probably have to play with this at least once. Just make sure you reset everything back to normal before you leave. If you're not quite sure what *is* normal, click on the Cancel button.

There may even be other icons, depending on how your system is set up. If you don't know what they are, you'd best leave them alone.

Holbrook's Other Law: Experience teaches you to recognize a mistake when you've made it again.

Chapter 10

WINDOWS LOST AND FOUND

Carter's Law: The window you need now will be the one buried the deepest.

WINDOWS MAKES IT possible to run several different programs at the same time. Which is great, except that it sometimes gets hard to find the one you want to switch to if it is buried under a bunch of other stuff. So, how to find the missing window? In this chapter we explore the different ways to arrange and rearrange your open windows, and how to find the one you want.

Putting the One You Want on Top

Windows lets you have your word processor, your spreadsheet, and Solitaire open all at the same time. But if you are playing Solitaire, its window will be the one on top. Which is fine, unless the boss walks in. So, to quickly put another window on top of the Solitaire window, just click on any exposed portion of another window. The other window comes to the top.

☞ The window you are working in, which is usually the one on top, is called the *active* window. We sometimes say that this window has the *focus*. All it means is that when you type, that is the window that is listening.

☞ Some small programs, like the Windows Clock and Windows for Workgroups Chat, have an option to always be on top. Just open the Control menu and you can click on the Always on Top option. This means the program in question will always be on top, whether active or not. Some folks find this helpful; others think it pushy.

Changing the Size of Your Windows

Windows lets you change the size and shape of your programs, making it easier to fit them to the task at hand. You can change the size of a window by moving the mouse pointer to the edge (any edge) of the window and the mouse pointer will change to a two-headed arrow, like the one on the left side of Figure 10.1.

When you see this two-headed arrow, just hold down the left mouse button and move the mouse in the direction you want the window to grow or shrink. You will see an outline of the new border of the window as you move the mouse. When you have it the size you want, let go of the left mouse button, and the window will be resized.

☞ If you resize from a corner instead of from one of the sides, you can change both the height and the width of the window at the same time.

☞ To do this with the keyboard, press Alt-spacebar, choose Size, and then use the arrow keys to change the size. Press Enter when the window is the size you want it to be.

FIGURE 10.1:

Grabbing the border of
a window

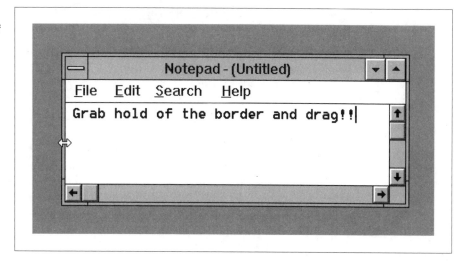

If the borders of your windows are too narrow, you may find it too hard to grab hold of them. Click on the Desktop icon in the Control Panel. At the bottom of the dialog box, you'll see a setting for Border Width. Increase the setting by a number or two.

Rearranging Your Windows

To move a window around on the screen, just place the mouse pointer anywhere on the title bar at the top of the window, and then hold down the left mouse button. As you move the pointer around the screen, an outline of the window follows. As soon as you release the mouse button, the window jumps to fill the outline.

☞ To do this with the keyboard, press Alt-spacebar, choose Move, and then use the arrow keys to move the window around. Press Enter when the window is where you want it to be.

Making a Window into an Icon

To make cute little pictures out of bigger windows (called "iconizing" the window), click on the down arrow button in the upper-right corner of the window. Iconized windows are still present and loaded into memory, just out of the way so you can do something else.

Lost & Found CH. 10

☞ To do this with the keyboard, press Alt-spacebar and choose Minimize.

☞ A window that has been iconized has lost none of its contents, nor has the program been closed. It's just sitting there waiting for you to pay attention to it again.

☞ Double-click on the icon to return the window to the size and place it was before you iconized it.

The program icon at the bottom of the screen and the program icon inside a window are not the same thing. The icon at the bottom of the screen represents an open program that is ready for quick recall. The icon in a program group stands for a program that is out on the hard disk someplace, which has not yet been loaded into memory.

It's possible, though usually highly undesirable, to load two or more versions of the same program into memory. It's undesirable because you can easily enter data into both versions and become hopelessly confused about where things are. Do you really need more confusion in your life?

Making an Icon into a Window

To get the icon back to a window, just double-click on it. Or if you have a thing for menus, click once on the icon to get a menu. You can click on Restore from that menu to pop the window back up.

Making a Big One out of a Little One (and Vice Versa)

All those windows arranged all over the desktop, in various sizes and shapes, are cute, but when you need to get some work done, you usually want to turn your active window into a big one that fills the entire screen. No problem. Just click on the upward-pointing arrow button in the top-right corner of the window. The window will grow to fill the screen (this is called "maximizing" the window), and the up arrow button will turn into a two-headed arrow button. Click on it to return the window to its former size and shape.

☞ Double-click on the title bar of a window and it will toggle between full-screen and windowed size.

☞ To make a DOS program that is in a window fill the screen, use Alt-Enter. This is a toggle, so you can take your full-screen DOS application and shrink it to a window with the same pair of keys.

☞ To maximize a window using the keyboard, press Alt-spacebar and select Maximize. To return it to its former size, press Alt-spacebar and select Restore.

The Task List—Better Than a Compass

In Chapter 6, you can see how to use Alt-Tab to move between programs, but there are a number of other ways to do this as well. One of the neatest ways to move between programs and rearrange them on your desktop is to use the Task List. This little gem has all sorts of goodies hidden in it.

To get the Task List, just double-click on a blank part of the desktop and it pops up with a handy list of every open program on your desktop. Double-click on the program you want to switch to and the program pops back on top, just like you left it. Or you can click once (highlight) the program you want using your mouse or the arrow keys and then press Enter or the Switch To button.

If you have a window covering the whole screen, you can't click on the desktop because it isn't visible. So you'll need to call the Task List using the keyboard. Press the Ctrl and Esc keys and the Task List will pop to the front.

Cascading Down Windows

When you get a desktop with windows all over the place and looking like the real desk of a slightly scatterbrained software engineer or computer book writer, you can use the Task List to do a quick cleanup. Pop up the Task List by double-clicking on any open spot on the desktop, and then click on the Cascade button. Faster than a speeding bullet, Windows cleans up all that mess and clutter, leaving you with neatly laid-out windows just like Figure 10.2. Any programs that were icons

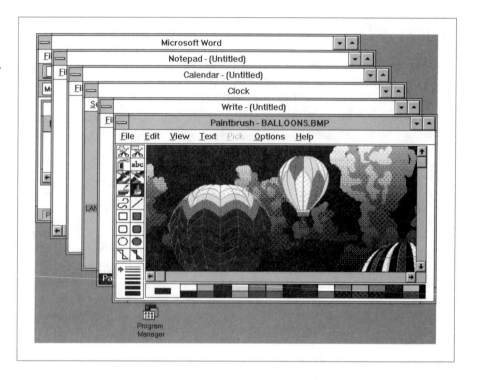

before will remain icons, but all your open windows will be neatly rearranged.

☞ To cascade your open windows using the keyboard, press Ctrl-Escape to bring up the Task List, then Alt-C for Cascade.

☞ With your windows cascaded, it is easy to move between them by clicking on the title bar of the one you want. Or double-click on the title bar, and the window pops up to full screen. Then double-click on it again, to return it to its cascaded size.

Tiling Your Windows

Don't like the look of cascaded windows? How about taking all your open windows and squeezing them so that they all fit on the screen at once? This is called tiling and is another trick of the Task List. Just double-click on an open part of the desktop to bring up the Task List, then choose Tile. You will get something that looks like Figure 10.3.

FIGURE 10.3:

The Tile option from the Task List is interesting but not much help.

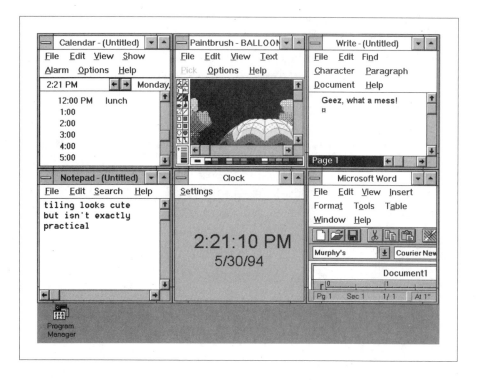

We didn't say it would be actually *useful,* just that you could do it. With only a couple of windows open, this can sometimes be informative, but with much more than that the windows are just too small.

☞ To tile your open windows using the keyboard, press Ctrl-Escape to bring up the Task List, then Alt-T for Tile.

If you want to compare the contents of two windows, tiling can help. But if you're comparing text, you'll want to tile them horizontally. *Press the Shift key while you click on the Tile button and Windows will arrange the two windows so that you can actually compare sentences.*

Finding a Lost Window

Another use for the Task List is to find a lost window. If you get totally carried away with moving your windows around, sometimes you can end up with the window so far from any sort of "normal" position that you can't see it. Call up the Task List, either by double-clicking on an open area of the desktop or by pressing Ctrl-Escape. Highlight the missing program and press Enter. If the window pops up, it was just a lost icon. But if you still can't find it anywhere, call up the Task List one more time and choose Cascade. That'll get the little sucker! Your lost window is now part of the Windows Waterfall.

Chapter 11

TWO FOR THE PRICE OF ONE: SHARING WITHIN AND BETWEEN APPLICATIONS

Andrew's Law: If you can't produce results, show furious activity.

YOUR MOTHER ALWAYS told you it was nice to share, didn't she? Perhaps you remember the circumstances under which she told you that.

Didn't it always mean you had to give up your favorite toy to your odious cousin Ralphie?

But Windows gives you a pleasant way to share. In the Windows environment, stuff can be moved around and shared without any program getting that deprived feeling.

In this chapter you'll see how to

☞ Highlight and select what you need

☞ Cut, copy, and paste using the Clipboard

☞ Copy something from one Windows program to another

☞ Copy stuff from Windows applications to DOS applications and vice versa

☞ Make changes to stuff after you've copied it to another program

☞ Get the drift of OLE, DDE, and other scary acronyms

Getting What You Need—Selecting Data

If you want to move something from one window to another, you first have to select it. The best way to do that is to highlight it using your mouse.

Move the mouse arrow to the beginning of the information you want. Hold down the left mouse button, move the mouse to the end of the information, and release the button. The information will now have a differently colored background. An example is shown in Figure 11.1.

If you're using the keyboard, use the arrow keys to get to the beginning of the stuff you want. Hold down the Shift key and use the arrow keys to highlight what you want.

FIGURE 11.1:

Highlighted text shows up in another color.

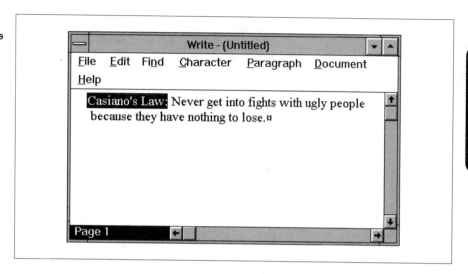

Sharing CH. 11

The Clipboard—Myth or What?

The Clipboard is a reserved piece of memory used as a temporary way station for stuff you're moving around in Windows. It's easy to confuse it with a real program since there's an icon big as life in your Main group, called Clipboard Viewer, that looks like this:

Clipboard
Viewer

But don't be fooled. The viewer is just that—it only lets you look at what's in that piece of memory.

To see what's currently in the Clipboard, double-click on the Clipboard Viewer icon.

☞ Almost all Windows programs have the commands Cut, Copy, and Paste. When some bit of information is cut or copied from a program, it is deposited in the Clipboard area of memory. You can then use the Paste command to copy what's in the Clipboard into another spot—either in the same Windows program or into another place altogether.

☞ The Clipboard can hold only one "thing" at a time, whether it's a single word, a graphic, or a whole chapter of your book on alien abductions. When you cut or copy something else, the content of the Clipboard is replaced.

☞ On the other hand, anything placed in the Clipboard stays there until you cut or copy something else. So you can paste whatever's in the Clipboard over and over without using it up.

☞ To save what's in the Clipboard, click on the Clipboard Viewer icon. Select Save As from the File menu. Type in a file name and click on OK.

When you copy some big piece of something to the Clipboard, it just sits there taking up memory. So after you're done cutting and pasting, clear the Clipboard so that memory can be put to good use. Click on the Clipboard Viewer icon and then press the Delete key. You'll be asked if you want to clear the Clipboard. Be brave and click on Yes. Then close the Clipboard Viewer too.

You don't need the Clipboard Viewer to move things between documents. The Clipboard functions automatically and invisibly.

Deleting and Cutting— Sounds like the Same Thing

Deleting and cutting sound like the same thing, but in Windows they are most assuredly different.

If you hit the Delete key or Backspace key after highlighting some information, it's deleted. Gone. Finis. History. If you act immediately, you can usually get it back by holding down the Ctrl key and pressing the letter Z. But if you've done anything else in between—even hit the spacebar, for example—it's gone for good.

Cutting the highlighted data wipes it off the screen, too. But at the same instant the data is cut, a copy of the same data is deposited in the Clipboard.

To cut your highlighted material, just hold down the Ctrl key and press the letter X (or select Cut from the Edit menu). The info vanishes from your screen and leaps to the Clipboard.

This seems so unlikely a scenario that you'll want to try it a few times to make sure it works.

Copying Stuff

To copy from one Windows program to another, first highlight the text you want to copy. Select Copy from the Edit menu (or press Ctrl-C).

☞ Since copying is so undramatic, you may wonder if anything in fact happened when you used the Ctrl-C key combo. To reassure yourself, you can keep the Clipboard Viewer open at the bottom of the screen so you can see what's happening. It's not necessary, but it does calm the nerves.

☞ To put a copy of your whole Windows desktop into the Clipboard, press the Print Screen key (sometimes called PrtScr or some such). To get just a copy of your *active* window, hold down the Alt key while you press Print Screen.

Getting Pasted

After you've cut or copied something, you can paste it to another part of the same window, to another window in the same program, or to another program entirely.

Click the mouse in the spot where you want the stuff to appear and then hold down the Ctrl key and press V. Whatever's in the Clipboard will appear in the spot you selected.

☞ The Paste operation copies the contents of the Clipboard to the spot you pick. The original information is still in the Clipboard so you can paste it into various locations as long as it amuses you. It will still be on the Clipboard until you use the Cut or Copy command to put something else there.

☞ You can also select Paste from the Edit menu. Just make sure you don't select Paste Special—that's for Object Linking and Embedding (also known as OLE), which is covered later in this chapter.

Background Information for the Nonconformist

You can also use another set of Cut, Copy, and Paste keystrokes:

Cut   Shift-Del

Copy   Ctrl-Ins

Paste   Shift-Ins

These were the keystrokes in Windows 3.0, and they still work in Windows 3.1. They were dropped because it was decided that it was easier to remember Ctrl-X and Ctrl-C as being shortened for Cut and Copy. This in no way explains Ctrl-V for Paste, but there you are.

From Windows to DOS

You can move text from Windows programs to DOS programs, but graphics have to stay in Windows, where they are properly looked after. The process is not complicated, just different, based on whether you're running the DOS program in a window or full screen.

The DOS program is in a window

1. In the Windows program, highlight the stuff you want. Select Cut or Copy from the Edit menu.

2. Switch to the DOS program either by clicking somewhere in its window or by pressing Alt-Tab. Make sure the cursor is where you want the new text to appear.

3. Click on the Control box in the upper-left corner of the window.

4. Choose Edit from the Control menu that opens. From the next menu, select Paste.

All the stuff you selected is typed into the DOS window instantly.

The DOS program is full screen

If the DOS program is running full screen, hold down the Alt key and press Tab as many times as it takes to get to Program Manager. The

DOS program will be minimized to an icon at the bottom of your screen.

1. In the Windows program, highlight the stuff you want. Select Cut or Copy from the Edit menu.

2. Click once on the DOS program's icon and its Control menu will open.

3. Once again, select Edit and then, from the next menu that opens, select Paste.

The word "Paste" appears in the title of the iconized program. Here's how it looks when you paste into WordPerfect for DOS:

Wait until the Paste word goes away before trying to do anything else.

☞ *To toggle a DOS program from full screen to its own window and back again, the magic key combination is Alt-Enter.*

☞ *You can't paste anything **into** a DOS program when it's running full screen.*

From DOS to Windows

You can copy stuff from DOS programs to Windows, but it can get complicated. If you have to do a lot of copying between programs, get rid of your DOS programs and become all-Windows. It will save you much grief in the long run.

An occasional paste between friends is OK, as long as you understand the rules:

☞ You have to run the DOS program under Windows but not necessarily *in* a window.

☞ You can't *cut* text or anything else from a DOS program in Windows. You can only copy.

☞ You need to decide if you want to copy actual words (text) from the DOS program or take a picture of the DOS window.

Copying text from DOS to Windows

To copy some text from a DOS program to a Windows program, first run the DOS program in a window, then follow these steps:

1. Click on the DOS program's Control box to unroll the Control menu as shown in Figure 11.2.

2. Select Edit from the Control menu and then Mark from the next menu.

3. Use the mouse to highlight the text you want. Then all you have to do is press the Enter key and the text is copied to the Clipboard.

4. Switch to the Windows program, and use the Paste command to put the text where you want it.

If you want to copy a whole screenful of text, run the DOS program full screen. Press the Print Screen button and all the text showing will be copied to the Clipboard.

FIGURE 11.2:

The Control menu of a DOS program when it's running in Windows

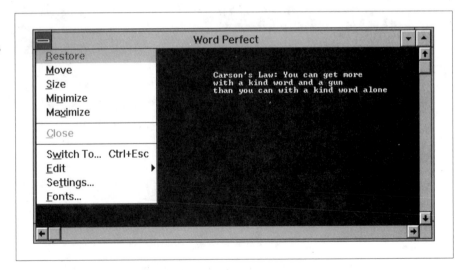

Taking a picture of a DOS window

You can take a snapshot of a DOS window and then copy it into Windows.

Run the DOS program in its own window, then hold down the Alt key while pressing the Print Screen key. This will copy a graphic image of the window to the Clipboard. From there you can copy it to Paintbrush and fuss with it if you want before copying it somewhere else.

☞ Remember, this is just a snapshot, not actual text. You can "draw" on it with Paintbrush, but you can't rearrange the sentences or copy it into a word processor.

What's This OLE Stuff?

The Clipboard works fine for most things, but Object Linking and Embedding (known by its cheerful nickname, OLE, pronounced "O-lay") offers a truly cool way to put information (like pictures or sounds) created in one program into another program. Like most things created by nerds, OLE is considerably easier than it sounds at first.

We'll deal with embedding and linking shortly. They're easy. The brain twister here is, what's an object? Actually, the answer isn't so hard. An object is anything in a Windows program that you can select and copy to the Clipboard. It can be a word, a sentence, or a chapter; a drawing, a chart, or part of a spreadsheet.

When you use the Clipboard to paste a picture into your word processing document, that's all you get—a picture. But when you use OLE, you get a picture that remembers where it came from.

Embedding

When you embed an object, it looks like it was pasted in the usual way. The difference is, if you double-click on it, the originating program opens and you can edit the object.

Let's say you write a letter to your mom and you embed in it a graph showing the kids' growth over the past year. You put off mailing the letter for a couple of months, during which time little Murgatroyd sprouts another two inches. All you need to do is open the letter in your word processor and double-click on the chart. The spreadsheet that created the chart will start with the chart already loaded so you can make the change. When you're done, just close the spreadsheet and the updated chart is sitting in your letter.

With an embedded object, you don't need to remember the file name or even the program that created it. The embedded object is self-contained. If you open the spreadsheet program and change the chart there, the chart in your letter stays blissfully unchanged and unaware. All the chart in your letter knows is what program made it, not what might be happening to its original version back at the old homestead.

Linking

A linked object looks like a pasted or embedded one but has a different relationship to the source program.

For example, let's say that when you wrote that letter to Mom, you also wrote to your Aunt Opal and to your Aunt Jewel and put the same chart in their letters too. Only this time you *linked* the chart rather than embedded it. Later, after Murgatroyd's unexpected expansion, you only needed to change the original of the chart for all the letters to be updated.

That's because with a linked object, there's only one version of the file. When you change one, you change 'em all.

Paste stuff when you're pretty sure you're not going to want to change it later. Embed objects that you want to be able to edit later. Use linking if you want to be able to put the same version of an object in several different programs.

OLE Facts

☞ Not all programs support linking and embedding. If you don't see Links or Paste Special or some such in the program's Edit menu, the program doesn't support OLE.

☞ In Windows 3.1, only Write, Paintbrush, Sound Recorder, Cardfile, and Object Packager support OLE.

☞ If you link stuff in a document and then send it to someone as a file, they won't get the linked stuff because it's still in your computer.

☞ If you want to send Mom the letter and make it possible for her to edit the chart, you should embed the chart and not link it. Then you can send her the word processor file, and assuming she also has the spreadsheet whence came the chart, she can work on it just as you could.

DDE—for Nerds Only

DDE (Dynamic Data Exchange) is the old version of OLE. It works similarly, except the link is more one-way than reciprocal. With DDE, when you link something into a document (like Murgatroyd's growth chart), you can update it in the spreadsheet program and the change will be reflected in Mom's letter the next time you open it. But if you're in the word processor and double-click on the chart, you get a great big nothing.

Programs are still around that support DDE but not OLE, so check your programs' manuals.

What's This Weird-Looking Object Packager?

The Object Packager is in the Accessories window and unlike many Windows programs, you can poke and prod it and never figure out what it's for.

But Object Packager fits right in with this OLE stuff because it lets you make a package (an OLE object containing other objects). You can then insert this package into still another document, where it's represented by an icon. The lucky recipient can then double-click on the icon and up pops the contents of the package.

Using Object Packager

To give you an idea of how Object Packager works, here's a simple example. We'll take CHIMES.WAV, a sound that comes with Windows 3.1, package it in a microphone icon, and embed it in a Write document.

1. Double-click on the Object Packager icon:

Object
Packager

2. Select Import from the File menu.

3. In the Import dialog box, select the file CHIMES.WAV in the Windows directory and then click on OK.

4. Now you'll see a microphone icon on the left side of the Object Packager window and "Copy of CHIMES.WAV" on the right side. Select Copy Package from the Edit menu and your new package is copied to the Clipboard.

5. Start the Write program and type in your message—like "Hi, Mom, click on this picture to hear a song." Then select Paste from the Edit menu and the microphone icon will plop right into your letter to Mom.

You can do all this stuff but you still won't get any sounds unless you have a working sound card in your computer (see Chapter 25, "Ways to Spend Money and Have Fun") or you have a speaker driver.

A speaker driver does not come with Windows, but a program called SPEAKER.DRV can be obtained from Microsoft or downloaded from CompuServe. Get a favorite nerd to download this program for you and install it as a driver in Windows. The sound quality will be limited by your quarter-sized PC speakers, but you can get some amusing and annoying effects.

This part covers all the programs—large and
small—that come with Windows. There's
also a chapter on unlocking the secrets of
successful printing and a chapter on the
additional features that come with Windows
for Workgroups.

A Gentle Guide

to Windows Software

Chapter 12

PROGRAM MANAGER IS EVERYWHERE

Keith's Law: Just because the water is calm doesn't mean there are no crocodiles.

IN THE BAD old days, B.W. (Before Windows), you had to type in long strings of text to get the computer to do *anything*. The original idea behind Windows was to introduce push-button ease to computing. And you can almost do that. Except that what you do is click on an icon, which looks like a little picture.

In this chapter you will see what makes the Program Manager tick, how to start programs from it, and how to add groups, programs, and icons to it.

What Program Manager Is and Why

The Program Manager is the *shell* for Windows. This means that it is the part of Windows that you do the most interacting with. Everything you do in Windows begins from the Program Manager and is ultimately controlled by the Program Manager.

When you start Windows, Program Manager is the first window you see. And when you close Program Manager, you're shutting down Windows.

One view of Program Manager is in Figure 12.1. This setup is designed to put a lot of programs in easy reach, but your Program Manager may look a lot different because of how your system has been put together.

FIGURE 12.1:
One way of setting up Program Manager. Each icon represents a program or a program group.

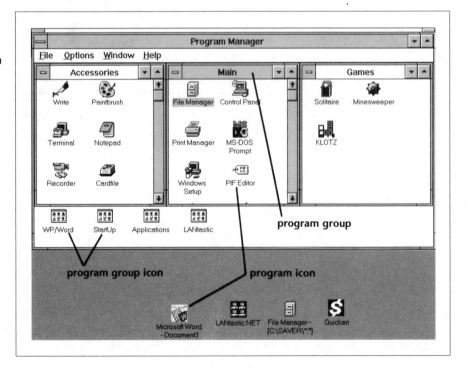

☞ Like any other window, the Program Manager can be minimized into an icon, which looks like this:

To bring it back up to full size, double-click on the icon.

☞ The program icons in Program Manager represent programs but are not the same thing as the programs. If you delete an icon, the program itself remains on your hard disk as before.

☞ If a window has a scroll bar, it means there are so many icons in it that they're not all visible. Use the scroll bar to take a peek. For a brushup on scroll bars, see Chapter 7, "Just Like a B Movie (All about Buttons, Bars, Boxes, and Borders)."

Want to Sound Cool? Read This

The Program Manager is the official name for the main Windows program, but among nerds and those who aspire to nerddom, you will mostly hear it called "ProgMan." This is pronounced "prAHg-man," which rhymes with "frAHg-man," which is what a Bostonian might call an underwater diver. But don't pronounce it "prAWg-man" to rhyme with "frog-man." This will make you sound merely dorky instead of nerdy.

Windows, Icons, and Groups

So, you have the Program Manager sitting there, taking up most or even all of your screen. Inside the Program Manager window, you have a bunch of other windows and icons. Maybe you have windows called "Main" and "Games" and "Accessories" open, plus group icons and program icons, on the screen. Something like Figure 12.1.

Main, Games, and Accessories are *groups*. But then, so are the little icons down at the bottom of the Program Manager window, such as StartUp and Applications. A group is like a box in which you store your programs. It can be like Main or Accessories—each of which is a group created by Windows during the installation program—or it can be one you created yourself.

☞ The icons at the very bottom of the screen are program icons and represent programs that are loaded in memory, but just sitting around waiting for you to give them orders.

Say you have a monthly dog-and-pony show that you do at work. It starts out life as a spreadsheet, then you plug the numbers into a graphics program, and finally you pull the graphics into your word processor for final spiffing up. You could just leave the individual programs in a big group called "Applications," but you could also create a group called "Monthly" and put your Quattro Pro for Windows, Harvard Graphics, and Ami Pro programs in it. See "Making a Group," on page 140, to see how to make your own groups.

Starting Programs from Program Manager

The Program Manager is one of the Windows programs that lets you start programs. The other is the File Manager (Chapter 13 gives you the lowdown on *that*), but most of the time, you will use the Program Manager to fire off new programs. And like everything else in Windows, there are about a zillion ways to start programs from the Program Manager. We'll use just the two most common ones:

☞ The simplest way to start a program from Program Manager is to double-click on the program's icon. Double-click on the group that the program you want is in. Then double-click on the program's icon, and you are off and running.

☞ The second way to start a program from Program Manager is to select Run from the File menu and type the program's name in the Run dialog box. Well, actually the name of the executable file for the program. So, for example, for Microsoft Word for Windows, you would type

WINWORD

You may have to include the path for the file so Windows can find it. If you don't know what a path is, see Chapter 13.

☞ *Keep your programs in logical groups like "Spreadsheets" or "Monthly Report" to make them easier to find.*

☞ *If you don't know the exact name of the file you want, click the Browse button and look around.*

☞ *If you're not sure what a file is or exactly what to type in the Command Line box, see Chapter 13 for everything about files.*

☞ *When you use the Run command to start your program, you can include the name of a file to open and any other command options to your program as well.*

What's a Group?

Groups are individual windows inside Program Manager, each with a descriptive title and containing program icons. When you install Windows, it creates several groups all on its own. These are Main (where all the boring but necessary stuff is), Accessories (where all the freebies are hidden), Games (the reason you bought Windows in the first place), and StartUp (which is initially empty). In addition, Windows will create one or more groups called "Applications 1," "Applications 2," and so on, depending on how many programs you have stashed on your hard disk.

That's nice, but not real helpful for getting your life with Windows in order. We find Windows much easier to use if you create some groups of your own that put your programs together in ways that make sense. They don't have to make sense to us, just to you.

Some people like to group their programs together by task, so they might have a group for their Monthly Report called, say, Monthly. Others like to group all their programs that do similar things together, so they might have a group called Graphics, in which they have Harvard Graphics for Windows, CorelDRAW, and AutoCAD, for example. How you do this is really up to you, but the result you want is to make *your* computer easier for *you* to use.

Tidying Up Your Program Groups

Perhaps you like to set up your groups just so, and you want to make sure they stay that way. To make Windows open up on Tuesday morning just the way you closed it on Monday night, select Save Settings on Exit from the Options menu in Program Manager.

On the other hand, maybe you like Windows always to open up in a particular way, but after you've flailed around in Windows for a while, you have icons strewn all about the landscape, program groups in disarray, etc. To make Windows open up on Tuesday morning just the way it did on Monday morning, set up things just the way you want them. Then while holding down the Shift key, double-click on the Program Manager Control box (in the upper-left corner).

Then no matter how you mess about, Program Manager will always open up looking just the way it did when you double-clicked. (For this to work, make sure the Save Settings on Exit option is *not* selected.)

Making a Group

To make a group, click on the File menu on the menu bar of Program Manager, and then select New from the drop-down menu. A dialog box will open like this:

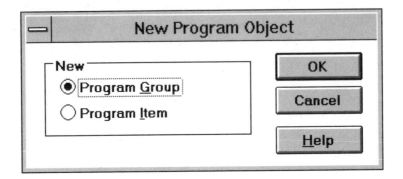

Click on Program Group, and then click on the OK button. Now you have the Program Group Properties dialog box. First, type in a description of the group. This description becomes the title underneath its icon.

Next type in the file name for the group. Only eight characters are allowed here, since Windows will add its own .GRP extension to it. (If you don't supply a file name, Windows will use the first eight letters of your description.) Click on OK one more time, and you have a new group. Stay tuned, and in the next section we will show you how to add items to this new and still empty group.

☞ Wonder why the group name can't be more than eight characters long? It's because Windows is still a captive to that ole debbil DOS, and DOS says file names can't have more than eight characters. DOS also imposes rules on just what characters you can use, so see the sections on legal and illegal names for files on page 155 for the rules.

Deleting a Group

If you're tired of a group and want to zap it or you've created too many groups and you just want to tidy up, it's easy to delete a group. Just minimize it to an icon, make sure it is highlighted, and press the Del key.

☞ The programs represented by icons in a deleted group are not deleted themselves; they're still on your hard disk. You can add them to another group whenever you want. Just follow the steps in "Adding a New Program to a Group" on page 142.

☞ If you accidentally delete one of Windows' own groups—Main, Accessories, StartUp, Games, or Applications—you can make Windows rebuild it. Select Run from the File menu in Program Manager. In the Command Line box, type

    SETUP / P

and click on OK. You may end up with a few extra icons this time, but you can always delete them. You can consider them as the price of being too hasty with the Del key.

King's Rule: Even if you're on the right track, you'll get run over if you just sit there.

Adding a New Program to a Group

OK, so you created this new group for your monthly dog-and-pony show to upper management. Now you want to put the programs in this group that you use to create this ticket to success. No sweat.

First, let's add your word processor, Ami Pro, to this group. Let's say that for some reason Ami Pro isn't in any of your other groups, either, so we will add it the hard way. To add a program that's on your hard disk, but which isn't in any other group:

1. Open up the group you want to add the program to by double-clicking on its icon. If it's already open, click once on the title bar to make it active.

2. Click on File on the menu bar, then select New. Up will pop the same dialog box you get when making a group. Only this time you click on the Program Item button and then click OK.

3. Next will pop up a box called the Program Item Properties box. Fill in the Description, Command Line, and Working Directory text boxes.

4. Click on OK when you're done.

☞ Description means the name you want to appear under the program's icon. This can be up to forty characters long, but keep it short or you'll end up with a mess.

☞ If you don't know or can't remember what the command-line entry is for this program, use the Browse box to hunt around till you find your wonderful new program. Click on the file name, then on OK, and your command-line entry will be filled in automatically.

☞ If you don't know about command lines, read Chapter 18 and come back.

☞ Working Directory is for those programs that are too brain dead to know where their files are. This is not generally a problem, but if you make a new program item and when you click on it, it seems confused, have a friendly nerd determine the correct working directory and type it in on this line.

☞ If you already have an icon in a group and just want to move or copy it to another group, see the next two sections.

Moving Icons from Group to Group

Windows programs have this habit of creating their own little program groups to put themselves into, which is fine, if you happen to want your programs to all be in their own little group. But if you want to organize things your own way, here's how to move those icons around.

First, open up both the group you want to move the icon into and the group it will be coming from. Now, place the mouse pointer on top of the icon you will be moving and hold down the left mouse button. Good. Now, with the button still down, drag the icon over to where you want it to be.

That's all there is to it. In fact, you can even short-circuit it further. Don't bother to open up the group you are putting the icon into. Just open up the one you are coming from and drag the program icon over to where the icon of the group you are going to is and drop it on top.

Copying Icons from Group to Group

Sometimes, for convenience' sake, you'll want to have a program in more than one group. For example, say it turns out that you use Quattro Pro for Windows for more than just your monthly dog-and-pony show—you also keep track of your investment portfolio with it. So you really need it in two places, your Monthly group and your Stocks group. No problem.

To add it to a second group, just follow the exact same steps you did to move it, except this time do it while holding down the Ctrl key. This time you are copying the icon instead of moving it.

☞ You can also use the Copy option on the File menu to do this. The advantage of this method is that you can choose from a list of all your groups. And it might save you from accidentally moving the icon instead of copying it.

Changing Icons

Most Windows programs come with their own icons, and some of them are downright cute. But if you add a DOS program to a group, Windows will give it a really ugly icon that looks just like this:

The worst part of that is that they are all exactly the same. Yuck. Who wants that?

To change an icon, click on it once to select it. You'll know it's selected because the name under the icon will be highlighted. Then choose Properties from the File menu.

This brings up the Program Item Properties dialog box, with the name of the program already filled in:

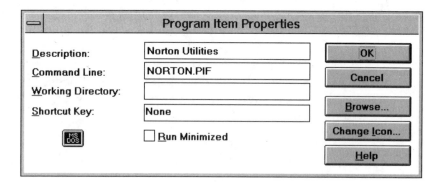

Click on the Change Icon button. You will either get a choice of icons that came with the program or you can choose from a whole mess of icons that come with PROGMAN.EXE.

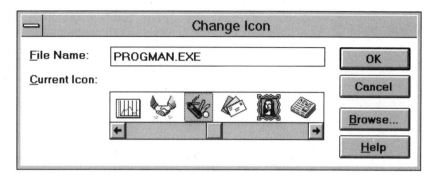

Use the scroll bar to stroll through the icons. When you find one you like, double-click on it. Click on OK one more time and the new icon will replace the old one.

☞ Icons are stored in files that end with the .ICO extension, as well as in some files with .DLL and .EXE extensions. So if you don't like the ones in PROGMAN.EXE, hit the Browse key and look for others. You'll find a file called MORICONS.DLL in the Windows directory. Double-click on that for even more icons.

Starting Programs Automatically (the StartUp Group)

There are two ways to start up programs automatically when you start Windows. The first is a relic from the older versions of Windows. You can take Notepad or some other text editor and add a line to your WIN.INI file that says

```
LOAD=program.exe
```

but what a pain. If you wanted to be editing start-up files and all that stuff, you would still be running DOS.

The *much* simpler way is to use the StartUp group. This is an empty group that Windows 3.1 creates when it's installed. Add a new icon to your StartUp group or copy an icon there and every time you start Windows, you will automatically start the program.

☞ See "Adding a New Program to a Group" or the sections on moving and copying icons earlier in this chapter for help in getting a program icon into the StartUp group.

☞ If you want the program to run as an icon when it first starts, highlight the icon in the StartUp group, press Alt-Enter, and click on the Run Minimized check box to check it, and then click OK. The next time you start Windows, the program will start up and turn itself into a little icon on the bottom of your screen.

There HAS to Be a Better Way—Other Shells

Once you have gotten familiar with the Program Manager and have learned how to do the things it does, you may find some of its limitations driving you nuts. For one, you can't create a group within a group.

Not to worry, there are bunches of substitutes for Program Manager out there. Some are fairly simple, like Dashboard from Hewlett-Packard, while others, like PC Tools from Central Point Software, are extremely sophisticated and complex.

The best known of these, and our personal favorite, is the Norton Desktop for Windows. For more on the Norton Desktop, take a look at Chapter 24, "Ways to Make Your Pocketbook Thinner and Windows Happier."

Chapter 13

FILE MANAGER WITHOUT FEAR

Dr. Hart's Conclusion: Education is what you have left over after you've forgotten everything you've learned.

FILE MANAGER IS the other half of the "core" of Windows. While Program Manager lets you arrange, copy, move, delete, and launch programs and their icons, the File Manager lets you do the same kinds of things with files. The File Manager icon, found in the Main group, looks like this:

File Manager

 A word of warning is in order. At times we are going to have to get almost nerdy here, and we will even talk about some of those icky DOS things, like directories, paths, and whatnot. Stay away from the stuff in boxes, especially if it has that guy with the propeller beanie next to it, and you will avoid all the really nasty stuff. And if you do feel adventurous sometime, you can always come back to those boxes.

File Manager—A Smooth Operator

File Manager gives you an easy-to-use picture of the files and directories on your computer. Without having to deal directly with DOS, you can do most of the stuff that DOS does. You can do file and directory stuff, like copying, renaming, moving, and deleting, and you can also format and copy disks. You can do network tasks, like using the File Manager to connect and disconnect from network drives. You can even use the File Manager to launch programs.

In fact, about the only DOSish things you *can't* do from the File Manager are those sorts of low-level, nasty things that we tell you, in Chapter 20, to *never* use in Windows anyway.

Another Shameless Plug

As long as Windows still requires DOS, we will, however much we may regret it, live in a DOS world. If you find yourself having to cope with DOS and want more help than this wonderful book on Windows gives you—run, don't walk, back to your nearest bookstore and buy *Murphy's Laws of DOS* (SYBEX, 1993).

Suspenders AND a Belt

Before you do anything to your precious files with the File Manager, take one precaution first. Turn on all the not inconsiderable protection that File Manager has.

Select Confirmation from the Options menu. Make sure that all the boxes have checks in them. If some of them are not checked, click on them to check them. Click on OK when you're done.

With these options on, File Manager will give you one last chance to change your mind before you do something that'll affect a file.

> **Aylesworth's Observation:** If someone is determined to be stupid, no force on earth can stop him.

Opening Up a Drive Window

Inside the File Manager (Figure 13.1) there are one or more open *drive windows.* Normally, each drive window is divided into two *panes.* The left pane is called the *tree pane,* and the right pane is called the *file pane.* To open an additional drive window, click on New in the Window menu.

To change which drive a window is looking at, click on the icon for the drive you want to look at on the drive button bar just below the title bar of the drive window. To open another drive window, double-click on the icon for the drive you want to look at.

FIGURE 13.1:
Pieces of the File
Manager

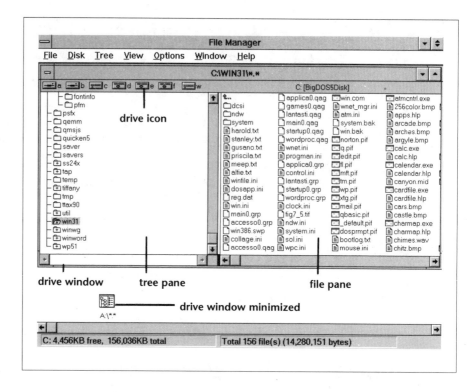

Closing Down a Drive Window

To close a drive window without closing File Manager, click on the little Control box to the left of the menu bar

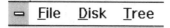

and select Close from the menu that rolls down.

This only applies if the drive window is at its maximum size. If it looks like this

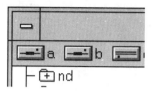

then click on the Control box on the drive's title bar.

☞ No matter what you do, File Manager always insists on having at least one drive window open.

Switching among Open Drive Windows

If you click on the Window menu in File Manager, you'll see a list of the drives you have open. Just use your mouse to highlight the one you want, and it'll pop to the front.

Back to DOS—Directories, Subdirectories

On the left-hand side of the File Manager drive window is the *tree pane*. This gives us a visual image of how the directories on the drive are arranged. But what *is* a directory, you ask?

Think of a directory as a box to put things in. You can have big boxes or little boxes. And each box can contain things (files) or more boxes (directories), or a combination of the two. The name of the directory is like the label on the outside of the box. It *should* tell you something about what is in the box, but if it doesn't, the only way to see what is inside is to open it up and take a look.

The other thing you need to keep in mind is that a directory and a subdirectory are really the same thing. The only directory that isn't a subdirectory is the *root* directory, which is the main box that all the other boxes and files fit into for each drive. So all the rest of the directories are subdirectories of the root directory.

About Paths—Horribly Nerdy Stuff That You Should Read Anyway

A path name is a like a road map telling Windows and DOS how to find a particular location on your hard disk. A full path name starts with the drive and proceeds through every layer of directory to get to a specific spot.

For example, if you have a file called TREES.WP5 in your POEMS directory under your WPWIN directory on your C: drive, the full path name for this treasure would be

```
C:\WPWIN\POEMS\TREES.WP5
```

This would be enough information for the File Manager, or any other Windows program, to locate the file. That's

C:	Drive name
\	Root directory
WPWIN	Directory in the root directory
POEMS	Subdirectory inside the WPWIN directory
TREES.WPS	File inside the POEMS subdirectory

Making a Directory

To make a directory, select Create Directory from the File menu. Type in the name you want. If you don't want the directory to be in the current directory (shown at the top of the dialog box), type in the full path.

☞ Directory names should be kept as short as possible while remaining descriptive.

☞ Directories are subject to the same naming rules as files. They can have up to eight characters, plus up to three characters for an extension. It's not a good idea to use extensions when naming directories because they end up looking like files.

☞ Legal and illegal file names are covered later in this chapter.

What Are All Those Little Pictures?

In the File Manager, there are a whole bunch of little icons in the drive windows. Each one has a slightly different meaning. Table 13.1 shows you all that we could find, complete with descriptions of what they actually mean.

TABLE 13.1:
Drive Windows Have
Lots of Icons

What It Looks Like	What It Means
	A subdirectory. The folder is open, so this is the one you are currently looking at in the file pane.
	A subdirectory. The folder is open, so this is the one you are currently looking at in the file pane. And it has a + in the middle of the folder, so there are other directories not shown inside this one. Double-click on this icon to see the subdirectories under it.
	A subdirectory. The folder is closed, so you can't see which files are in it without clicking on it.
	A program file. If you double-click on this icon, the program will execute.
	A data file. File Manager knows what program owns this file, and if you double-click on it, File Manager will open both the file and the program that owns it.
	A file. File Manager doesn't know much about this file except that it is a file. If you double-click on this, all you get for your trouble is a message box telling you that File Manager doesn't have an association for that file.
	A hidden or system file. File Manager is politely trying to warn you to leave it well enough alone. Take its advice.
	The mouse pointer when you are copying a file.

TABLE 13.1:
Drive Windows Have
Lots of Icons
(Continued)

What It Looks Like	What It Means
	The mouse pointer when you are moving a file.
	Double-click on this, and you are looking at the next higher directory.

Expanding and Collapsing Your Subdirectories

The File Manager can show you all of your subdirectories, and all of the subdirectories and all of the subdirectories of the subdirectories, *ad nauseam*.

This is called an expanded view. To see this view, press Ctrl-* (that's the asterisk on your numeric keypad, *not* the one above the number 8). This view gives you a lot of information, but it can be a bit cluttered.

To get rid of some of the clutter, just double-click on the little folder icon for one of the subdirectories that has more subdirectories under it you don't want to see. This will collapse the view so that you don't see any of the subdirectories under this directory. And it puts a little plus sign inside the folder icon so you know there are more folders hidden beneath this one.

If you don't see little tiny plus and minus signs in the middle of some of the icons in the tree pane of your drive window, you may have goofed and accidentally turned off this little gem of a feature. Just click on Tree on the menu bar and click on Indicate Expandable Branches to put a check mark next to it.

Legal Names for Files

DOS sets the rules for file names, unfortunately. And they are rather strict. The first eight characters of a file name can be any letters or numbers. The following names would be OK with the DOS Police:

WHATSUP
401
UNCLE

File names can also include the following characters from the keyboard:

_ ' ~ ! @ # $ % ^ & ( ){ } –

If you want to add your own extension, you can. You must specify the period and then add up to three more characters:

WHATSUP.DOC
401.K
UNCLE.SAM

☞ Some programs add their own extensions. You just provide the first part of the file name and the program provides the extension.

☞ File names are not case sensitive. You can enter names in either upper- or lowercase.

☞ The extension is normally used to identify file types. For example, the .DOC extension indicates a Word file, and the .XLS extension indicates an Excel file. It really is more efficient to use the main file name to define the contents of the file and the extension to define the file type.

Illegal Names for Files

If you try to use any of the following characters in a file name, you will be treated rudely:

* + = \ ¦ [ ] ; : " , < > ? /

In addition to these, you can't use a period, except to divide the main name from the extension, and you can't use a space. All these characters have special meaning to DOS (and therefore to Windows) and are not for the likes of you.

☞ Your file cannot be named any of the following: CLOCK$, CON, AUX, PRN, NUL, LPT1, LPT2, LPT3, COM1, COM2, COM3, or COM4. These are DOS device names and as you know, it's not nice to confuse DOS.

Seeing More Than You Wanted to about Files

When you first install Windows, the file pane of File Manager shows you all of your files, sorted by the name of the file. But that's all you get, except for the little icon.

If you want to be able to see lots more information about each file, just click on View on the menu bar and then select All File Details. The file pane changes to look like Figure 13.2. Now it still shows you the name of each file, but in addition you have the size of the file, the date it was last modified, the time it was last modified, and the file attributes.

To get a little more control of what you see, select Partial Details from the same View menu. This pops up the Partial Details dialog box, and you can check the boxes to tell File Manager how much detail to show in the file pane. A good compromise is to check the Size and Date options, since these are the two things you are most likely to want to know about the file.

Hopelessly Boring Information

Files have up to four attributes. These attributes help to determine how a file behaves and how it can be treated. The four attributes are A, R, H, and S.

☞ A is for *archive*. When this attribute is "on," or set, the file has not been backed up since it was last changed. This attribute is used by backup programs, such as Microsoft Windows Backup, which is included in DOS 6, to determine if the file should be backed up. See Chapter 21, "An Ounce of Prevention."

☞ R is for *read-only*. This is the "Look but don't touch" attribute. You can copy, print, and view the file, but you can't change it in any way.

☞ H is for *hidden*. With this attribute on, the file is hidden from normal view. This is only limited protection, though, since there are lots of ways to see what files have been hidden.

☞ S is for *system*. This attribute means the file is a special file used by DOS. Like hidden files, system files are not normally visible in the File Manager.

To see hidden or system files in the File Manager, click on the View option of the menu bar and then on the By File Type choice all the way at the bottom. You will see the By File Type dialog box. Check the Show Hidden/System Files box and now you will be able to see those hidden files. But you probably should leave this box off most of the time. It makes it *much* less likely that you'll do something stupid to one of these special files.

Don't fool around with the attributes of files, especially those marked system or hidden. It is easy to do something you really didn't mean to do.

FIGURE 13.2:

By selecting All File Details, you can have File Manager tell you far more than anybody needs to know.

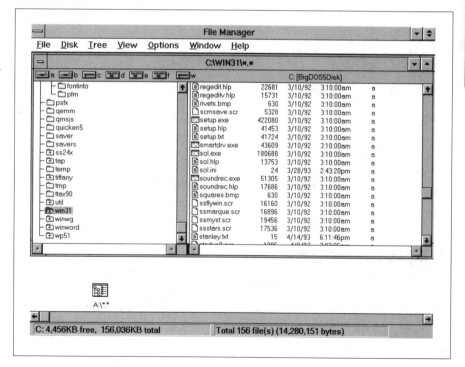

File Manager

CH. 13

Selecting Files

Before you can move or copy or do anything else to a file, you need to *select* it. And you can just as easily copy or move or whatever a bunch of files as a single file, but first you need to select the files you want to act on.

To select a single file, click on it with the mouse. Now you can do whatever it is you planned to do with the file.

To select several files, all in a row in File Manager, select the first one by clicking on it with the mouse, then press the Shift key and click on the last one. Zip! Windows just highlighted all of them. This is called a "Shift-click," by the way.

Great, but what if you want one file here, and another one several files down in the list, and another one even farther down the list? No sweat. Click on the first one, then press the Ctrl key and while holding it down, click on each of the others. This is called a "Control-click." Each of the files stays selected. If you accidentally clicked on one you didn't want, just Control-click on the one you want to remove.

Selecting Files by Name or Type

Maybe you want to select *all* the files in a pane or all the files with a particular extension. Click on the File menu and then on Select Files. A dialog box opens in which you can specify the files you want to select. Use *.* to select everything. Use *.BAK to select all the files with the extension .BAK.

☞ See "What's a Wildcard?" on page 163 if you have no idea what *.* might mean.

Copying Files

File Manager makes it easy to make a copy of a file for safe-keeping. To copy a file to a floppy in your A: drive, put the floppy in drive A:, and then highlight the file in the file pane and drag it to the A: icon at the top of the drive window.

If you want to copy multiple files, select them first, then drag from any selected file to the destination drive icon—you'll get the whole bunch.

It is just as easy to copy a file to another directory on your current drive, with one difference. Instead of simply dragging the file, you must first press the Ctrl key and hold it down during the operation. Otherwise, Windows will move the file instead of copying it.

☞ If you want to have a dialog box to type in the destination, highlight the files you want to copy, and then press the F8 key. The Copy dialog box will open, and you can type in the destination.

Moving Files

To move a file from your hard disk to a floppy disk, just highlight the file, and then press and hold the Alt key while you drag it to the floppy drive's button at the top of the drive window.

To move a file from a floppy back to your hard disk, though, requires a bit more work. The best way is to open drive windows for both the floppy and your hard disk. Then, highlight the file (or files) in the window for your floppy drive, and press the Alt key while you drag the files to the window for your hard disk. When the little file icon is over the top of the directory you want the file to go to on your hard disk, drop it by releasing the mouse button.

To move files around on your hard disk, simply highlight the files you want to move and then drag them to the directory where you want them to go and drop them. Couldn't be simpler.

☞ If you want to have a dialog box to type in the destination, highlight the files you want to move, and then press the F7 key. The Move dialog box will open, and you can type in the destination.

Deleting Files

To delete files using File Manager, simply select the files you want to delete, and press the Delete key. You will be asked to confirm that you want to delete the files, and when you click on OK they will be history.

However, if you followed our advice under "Suspenders AND a Belt" above, and turned on confirmation, you will have a second chance, as shown in Figure 13.3, to say "NO! I didn't mean *that* file!" before it's gone. The nice part about this second confirmation is that you can have File Manager prompt you for each individual file, or just say Yes to All and be done with it.

FIGURE 13.3:

A last chance to save your file before it is foully murdered

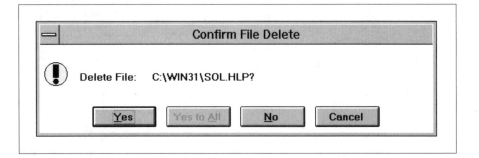

Confirm File Delete

Delete File: C:\WIN31\SOL.HLP?

[Yes]   [Yes to All]   [No]   [Cancel]

☞ If, in spite of all the chances to change your mind, you still manage to delete a file you didn't want to, do nothing till you check out Chapter 21, "An Ounce of Prevention," for instructions on running the DOS 6 undelete.

File Manager lets you delete a subdirectory just as easily as a file. But getting a deleted subdirectory back is always a bit iffier, if not downright impossible. So be especially sure you're fully awake before doing this.

Changing the Names to Protect the Innocent (Renaming a File or Directory)

To change the name of a file or subdirectory, simply select it and then choose Rename from the File menu. This will open up the Rename dialog box, and you can type in the new name.

You can easily change the extension of a bunch of files, using the Rename function of File Manager. Suppose you want to change a bunch of .BAK files to have .SAV extensions. First, select the files you want to change, then choose Rename from the File menu. When the Rename dialog box opens, type ***.SAV** in the To: box and click on OK.

☞ For help on selecting multiple files, see "Selecting Files" on page 158.

☞ See "What's a Wildcard?" on page 163 for instructions on using the * wildcard.

Windows is very fussy about where it thinks program files are located. Think twice or even three times before you start renaming subdirectories that Windows or your programs created. The File Manager makes it extremely easy, but it is generally not a good idea.

Ah, Refreshing

Sometimes when you are working with files in Windows, especially if you run a program from a DOS window, the drive window in File Manager gets out of date and loses track of where everything is. It is a good idea to periodically *refresh* the window, especially if you have been running a DOS program. To refresh the window, just press the F5 key while the window is active.

☞ You can tell which drive window is the active one if you have more than one open, because its title bar is a different color.

☞ Whenever you change floppy disks and you have a drive window open for that drive, it is a good idea to refresh it.

☞ When you connect to a network drive outside of File Manager, you will want to refresh to add the new drive's button to your drive button bar.

Rohmer's Law: If you don't know where you're going, any road will get you there.

Finding Lost Files

File Manager makes it pretty simple to find a lost file, assuming you know what its name is, or at least part of what the name is. Say you wrote a letter to your Uncle George, and now you can't find it. You remember the name of the file was UNCLEGEO.LET, and you are sure it is somewhere on your C: drive.

1. Click on File and then click on Search.

2. In the Search dialog box, type **UNCLEGEO.LET** in the Search For: box, and press the Tab key.

3. Type **C:** in the Start From: box.

4. Make sure the Search All Subdirectories box is checked, and then press the Enter key or click on OK.

File Manager will now search your entire hard disk and find the file UNCLEGEO.LET. When it finds it, it will throw up a Search Results window, much like Figure 13.4.

If you can't exactly remember the name you gave the file, but you remember it started with UNCLE, you follow the exact same steps as above, but in the Search For: box you type in **UNCLE*.*** to tell the File Manager you want to find *all* the files that start with UNCLE. This might find some files for your Uncle Bob, too, but you should have no problems figuring out which ones those are.

☞ See "What's a Wildcard?" below for help on using the * wildcard.

FIGURE 13.4:
Uncle George is found at last.

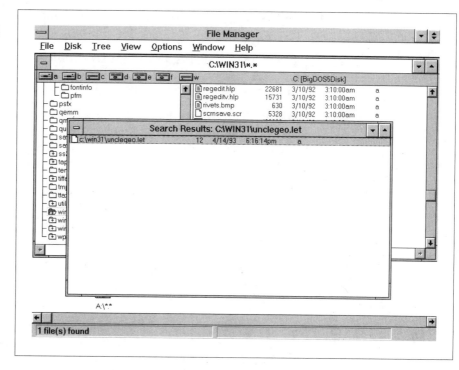

What's a Wildcard?

Windows recognizes two wildcards—characters that stand in for other characters. One is the * (usually referred to as the star, even though we both know it's really an asterisk), and the other is the ? (referred to as the question mark, even though we both know it's really a query).

The * stands for any group of characters, and the ? stands for any single character. But the ? wildcard is strictly for those who do things just to prove they can. Stick with * and save ? for the pocket-protector crowd.

Using the * Wildcard

You can use the * wildcard to stand in for one or more characters in a file name. The best way to understand the use of the * is to see some examples.

☞ The wildcard file name *.* matches *all* files.

☞ The wildcard file name *.WK1 matches all files with the extension .WK1.

☞ The wildcard file name SHERMAN.* matches all files that start with SHERMAN regardless of extension, including SHERMAN.DOC, SHERMAN, and SHERMAN.BAK.

☞ The wildcard file name SHER*.* matches all files that start with SHER regardless of how they finish up. This would include all the SHERMAN files above, plus the files SHERWOOD.DOC and SHERYL.RES.

One truly weird limitation of the star wildcard is that you can't use it in the middle of a name. For example, if you type in **C*L.DOC** in an attempt to find all your files that start with C, end with L, and have the extension .DOC, you instead get a listing of all the files that start with C and end with the extension .DOC. This is because once DOS sees the *, it ignores all the characters to the right.

Click on a Program and Open It

Most of the time you'll be starting your programs by double-clicking on their icons in Program Manager. But you can, if it amuses you, run programs directly from File Manager. You just double-click on a program file in the file list.

You can tell which files are program files, because File Manager kindly draws you a picture. Program files all have a little program icon next to them, like this:

▢cardfile.exe
▢charmap.exe
▢clipbrd.exe
▢clock.exe

Any file name with this picture next to it is a program and will run when you double-click on it.

☞ Most of the programs you'll use have the extension .EXE, which is short for **EXE**cutable because another name for a program is an *executable file*. Other extensions you might see on program files are .COM (for command) and .BAT (for batch).

☞ .PIF files are files that help Windows run DOS programs. PIF stands for *program information file*. A whole lot of tedious information about PIFs can be found in Chapter 19, "DOS Programs and How to Run Them."

It's not a good idea to go around randomly double-clicking on strange programs. Some DOS programs, like APPEND.EXE and VSAFE.COM, should definitely not be run in Windows. Some programs, like RECOVER.COM, should never be run at all! So approach strange programs with caution. If you don't know what they're for, you'd best ask before exercising that itchy mouse finger.

Click on a File and Open It

Perhaps you'd like to start a program with a file all ready to go. All you need to do is double-click on a file in File Manager. Windows checks to see if the file has an *association* with a program. If the association exists, Windows will cheerfully start the program and load the file you clicked on. Is that cool or what?

For example, double-clicking on a file with the .TXT extension will start the Windows Notepad program and plop the file down in it. You can then edit or print or just admire it.

This works because Windows automatically knows that certain extensions go with certain programs. Table 13.2 shows some of the extensions Windows knows about—if you double-click on a file with one of these extensions, you will launch the associated program.

☞ If you click on a file and get the Cannot Run Program box, you can instruct Windows to associate the file extension with a program. See "Associating with the Right Crowd," on page 167.

File Manager CH. 13

TABLE 13.2:
Common File
Extensions That
Windows Recognizes

File Extension	Associated Program
BMP	Paintbrush
CRD	Cardfile
DOC	Word for Windows
HLP	Windows Help
TRM	Terminal
TXT	Notepad
WB1	Quattro Pro for Windows
WK3	1-2-3 for Windows
WRI	Windows Write
XLS	Excel

Drag and Drop a File to Open It

Another way to get at stuff quickly is to click on a file name and while holding down the mouse button, drag the file to someplace useful and drop it. For example, you can

Drop into an open program window	The file automatically loads into the program.
Drop on a minimized program icon	The file loads into the program. If you drop onto a minimized Print Manager, for example, the file will print.
Drop into a program group	A quick way of making up a new group window.

☞ For more on making and filling up group windows, see Chapter 12, "Program Manager Is Everywhere."

☞ Not all programs support drag-and-drop. So you may drop a file and it'll just sit there looking goofy. It doesn't do any harm to try, however.

Associating with the Right Crowd

If you want to make Windows recognize the files from your favorite program, you can easily introduce them by making an association. That way, when you double-click on a file in File Manager, Windows will snap to attention and open your program with that clicked-on file already loaded.

1. Open File Manager and highlight a file with the extension you want to teach Windows about.

2. Select Associate from the File menu. You'll get a standard-issue dialog box. The extension of the highlighted file will already be in the box at the top. You can look through the list in the box under Associate With and see if your program is there. If it is, highlight it, and go to step 4. But it won't be, so just go to the next step.

3. Click on the Browse button. Find the program name you're looking for. Double-click on it so you can get back to the Associate dialog box.

4. When you have the right extension in the Files With Extension box and the right program in the Associate With box, you can click on OK and the deed is done.

You can have more than one extension associated with a program. For example, .RIF and .RAF can both be associated with WP.EXE (that's WordPerfect's program file). But you can't associate an extension with more than one program. So neither .RIF nor .RAF can also be associated with WINWORD.EXE (Word for Windows' program file), at least not at the same time.

Disassociating Yourself

If you have a program associated with an extension, there may come a time when you want to use that extension elsewhere. Since an extension can associate with only one program at a time, you may want to make a change.

To remove an association, just open the File Manager and highlight a file with the extension you want Windows to forget about. Select Associate from the File menu. In the Associate With list, highlight (None) and click on OK.

Now you can associate that extension with another program if you want.

A Brief Treatise on Floppy Disks

Floppy disks are made of thin sheets of plastic and are called floppies to set them apart from "hard" disks, which are inside your computer. Floppies are also called diskettes, flexible disks, and sometimes just disks. They come in two physical sizes:

☞ The $5\frac{1}{4}$-inch size is (surprise!) $5\frac{1}{4}$ inches in diameter and looks like an old 45-rpm record inside a paper or plastic sleeve.

☞ The $3\frac{1}{2}$-inch size is also made of mylar, but it's inside a rigid, more-or-less square plastic case.

The $5\frac{1}{4}$-inch disk comes in two capacities:

☞ 360K—called double-density, or low-density, this size will hold up to 360,000 bytes worth of files.

☞ 1.2MB—called high-density, this size will hold up to 1,200,000 bytes worth of files.

The $3\frac{1}{2}$-inch disk also comes in two capacities:

☞ 720K—called double-density, or low-density, this size will hold up to 720,000 bytes of information.

☞ 1.4MB—called high-density, this size will hold up to 1,440,000 bytes of information.

TECHNONOTE

Only Aspiring Technoids Should Read This

The numbers used above are somewhat approximate since computers count in multiples of two instead of multiples of ten. A nibble is 2^2, or 4, bits, a byte is 2^3, or 8, bits, etc. Thus one kilobyte, which ought to be 1000 bytes, is actually 1024 bytes, and one megabyte (one million bytes) is actually 1024 kilobytes, or 1,048,576 bytes. But for most purposes, stick to the simple numbers. A kilobyte is 1000 bytes, and a megabyte is 1,000,000 bytes. Discussions of this issue have been known to cause brain damage.

Formatting a Floppy Disk

To format a disk, put it in the drive, label side up. If you have only one floppy drive, it's drive A:. If you have two, the top one is A: and the bottom one is B: (unless some nerd-from-hell has switched them around).

Select Format Disk from the Disk menu. In the dialog box

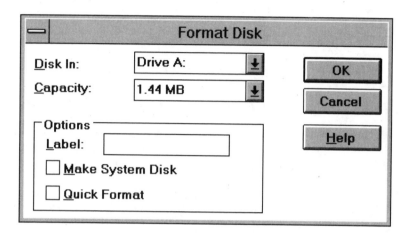

fool around with the arrows until the correct drive and capacity are highlighted. Click on OK to start formatting.

Copying One Disk onto Another—Same Size and Type

To copy a whole disk, you use File Manager's Copy Disk command on the Disk menu. You'll get a dialog box that is awesome in its simplicity. All you need to do is specify the drives and click on OK.

☞ The two disks must be of the same size and capacity. Put the original in drive A: and the blank disk in drive B:.

☞ If you have only one disk drive, select it as both the source and destination. Follow the instructions. You may have to swap the two disks in and out of the drive a few times.

☞ To copy a disk in drive B:, just select B as both the source and destination.

☞ With the Copy Disk command, you get an exact copy of the original disk. Not only are files copied but so are any disk labels and hidden files.

The Copy Disk command does not check to see if there's anything you might want on the destination disk. It just wipes out any files you have there. So be sure the disk is blank or doesn't have anything important on it.

Copying One Disk onto Another—Different Size and Type

With floppy disks of different sizes and types, you can't make an exact copy. But you can take all the files on one disk and copy them to another disk as long as the destination has enough room for all the files.

1. Put the source and destination disks in their respective drives. Click on the drive icon for the source disk.

2. Click on Select Files in the File menu. In the Select Files dialog box, type ***.*** and click on the Select button.

3. All the files will be highlighted in the file pane. Just position your mouse pointer anywhere over that highlighted area, and drag the whole lot to the icon of the destination floppy disk.

For more on selecting files, see the section cleverly called "Selecting Files" on page 158.

Your Very Own Floppy Decoder Ring

Disks usually have manufacturer's labels to tell you what capacity they are. But if you're reusing disks, those original labels may be pasted over. So here's an easy way to tell *without* a label.

Double-density 5¼-inch disks have a reinforcing hub ring around the hole in the middle of the disk. High-density disks do not have this ring.

Double-density 3½-inch disks have one hole in the plastic case (to the right of the label as you hold the disk facing you). High-density 3½-inch disks have an additional hole to the left of the label.

What's Write Protect?

When copying files or formatting, you can get a callous message like that in Figure 13.5.

A disk that is write-protected is made read-only. That means you can read whatever's on the disk and you can copy files from it, but you can't change or delete anything on the disk.

FIGURE 13.5:

This rudeness can pop up when you are formatting or copying.

File Manager CH. 13

Write-protecting a 5¼-inch floppy

Take one of the little black sticky tabs that came with the disk, and place it over the notch on the side of the floppy (see the left half of Figure 13.6). When the notch is covered, the disk is write-protected and you can't alter the contents in any way.

To remove the write protection, peel off the sticky tab. Be careful not to damage the disk with overenthusiastic peeling.

FIGURE 13.6:
Here's where the write-protect stuff is.

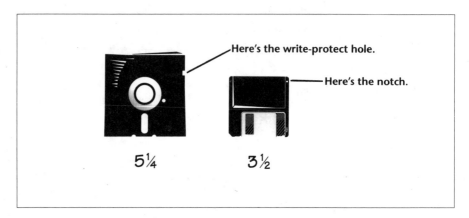

Here's the write-protect hole.

Here's the notch.

5¼   3½

Write-protecting a 3½-inch floppy

Look for the hole on the right side of the label (see the right half of Figure 13.6). This little hole has a sort of window shade in the back that lets you open and close the hole. Slide the cover so the window is open and the disk is write-protected. Slide the cover back so you can't see through the hole, and you can write to the disk, delete files, reformat it, or whatever.

Chapter 14

WORDS AND PICTURES
(Write, Notepad, and Paintbrush)

Kienan's Law: It's better to know some of the questions than all of the answers.

THE PROGRAMS THAT come with Windows range from the sublime to the ridiculous. In this chapter, we lean ever so slightly toward the sublime end of the spectrum. Here's where you'll find the lowdown on Write, a thoroughly respectable word processor; Notepad, Write's baby brother; and Paintbrush, a very cool paint program that will enable you to waste many pleasurable hours.

Doing the Write Thing

First the bad news. Write doesn't have a spell checker or elaborate formatting, or a grammar checker like the big-time word processors.

Now the good news. Write doesn't cost $300 like those big-time packages—you got it free when you bought Windows. And it can do plenty of fancy stuff. The icon for Write is in the Accessories group and looks like this:

Write

Double-click on the icon. If the Write window is less than full screen, click on the Maximize button in the upper-right corner. Your screen will look like Figure 14.1.

FIGURE 14.1:
The Write window and its various parts

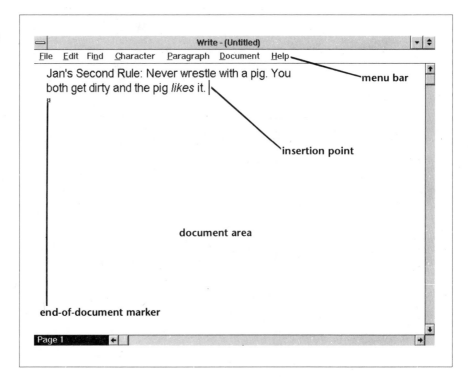

☞ The flashing vertical bar is called the *insertion point* (sometimes called the *cursor,* too). That's where anything you type will appear.

☞ The four-pointed thing is the "end of document" symbol. Your document ends there, not necessarily where the last bit of text is.

Entering text

Just start typing away. You don't need to press Enter when you reach the end of a line. Write has word wrap, which automatically moves the cursor to the next line.

Press the Delete key to delete characters to the right of the insertion point. Press the Backspace key to remove text to the left of the insertion point.

Use the arrow keys to move the insertion point around. Or move your mouse pointer to the spot and click once. The insertion point will leap to the new location.

The page number display at the bottom of the Write window can be confusing because it seems to remain at Page 1 all the time. To use any of the page-oriented features in Write, you have to repaginate. To do that, select Repaginate from the File menu.

Prettying things up

Write has some advanced features that will let you dress up your document so you can show it to company.

☞ To make text bold or italic, select it with the mouse. Click on the Character menu and select **Bold** or *Italic.* You can also use this menu to make something <u>underlined</u> or ^{superscript} or $_{subscript}$.

☞ From the Character menu, choose Enlarge Font or Reduce Font to jump the point size up or down two points. Or just click on Fonts to get the Font dialog box, shown in Figure 14.2. There you can play around with all the fonts on your system and even get a sample.

FIGURE 14.2:
Font play time!

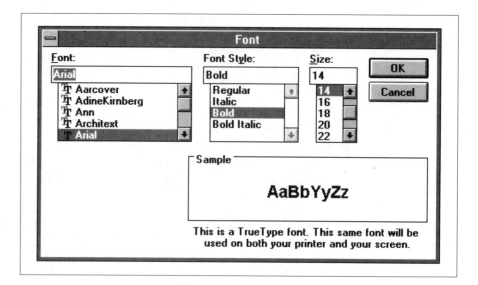

☞ Documents are saved in Write as they are in other Windows programs. Select Save from the File menu and type in the name
you want to use. For more on making directories for your files,
schedule a brief consultation with Chapter 13, "File Manager
without Fear."

Write into ASCII?

When Write does its thing, it puts lots of mysterious codes in the file along
with your deathless prose. So when you try to open a Write file in another
word processor, the prose is intact but there's also a lot of other stuff in there
with it.

If you want to give your file to someone using another word processor, you
can save your Write file in ASCII (pronounced ASK-ee). Select Save As from
the File menu. Click on the arrow next to the Save File as Type box and
choose Text Files (*.TXT).

ASCII just means plain text without italics, boldface, or other formatting
stuff.

Leaving Write now

When you're done with Write, select Exit from the File menu. The program will zip up and you'll be back in Program Manager.

Notepad, Write's Baby Brother

Notepad is in many ways Write's speedier (but dumber) baby brother. It loads much faster than Write but it can't do nearly as many smart things. The icon for Notepad, which is in the Accessories group, looks like this:

Notepad

☞ Notepad is strictly a text editor, which means it doesn't give you a lot of choices about how things look. To write a letter or a report, use Write. Notepad is just for quickish notes to yourself.

☞ Notepad does not automatically wrap the text to the next line. You have to select Word Wrap from the Edit menu. And you have to select it all over again the next time you open Notepad!

☞ To get anything to print out of Notepad and not look completely goofy, you need to set things up using the Page Setup option on the File menu. The document will print out according to the margin settings there—not according to how it looks on the screen.

☞ Notepad also has the quirk of printing the file's name at the top center of the page. To get rid of that, select Page Setup from the File menu. The Page Setup dialog box opens with a code highlighted in the Header box. Press Del to clear the box. You can also clear the Footer box if you want to get rid of the automatic page numbering. Click on OK when you're finished.

Notepad does have the cool facility of letting you keep a log with the date and time stamped on it. Just type in .LOG (exactly like this—include the period and use capital letters) in the very top-left corner of the window. Save the file and then whenever you open it, it's stamped with the current time and date right ahead of where you'll be typing in your text.

Christine's Commentary on Software: There is no direct relationship between the quality of a program and its cost.

Paintbrush

Paintbrush lets you spend many hours dabbling in computer art when you should be doing something useful. It's really just a tidier version of the messy finger-painting you did in kindergarten. The icon for Paintbrush, which is in the Accessories group, looks like this:

Paintbrush

And when you double-click on the icon, you get a window like that in Figure 14.3.

Selecting your tools

Paintbrush comes with a whole selection of tools, represented by icons down the left side of the window. Some are pretty self-explanatory but not all, so look in Table 14.1 for what each of them does.

At the bottom of the screen is the color palette, which shows you the colors you can choose from. The color in the box to the left is the currently selected color. No matter what tool you're using, that's the color it will be drawing or painting with. The color behind that box is the current background color.

FIGURE 14.3:

The Paintbrush window before it's been messed up

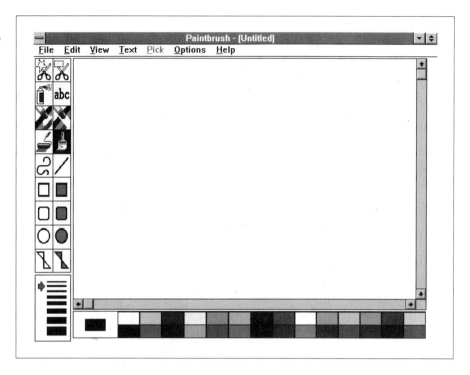

TABLE 14.1:

Paintbrush Tools

What It Looks Like	What It Is	What It Does
Scissors	Scissors	Outlines a piece of a drawing. You can then cut and paste, copy, or use the mouse to drag the outlined piece to another part of the drawing.
Pick	Pick	Takes a rectangular bite of your picture. You can cut and paste it elsewhere. Or you can just drag it to another part of your drawing.
Air brush	Air brush	Gives the effect of spray paint.
abc	Text	Use this tool to add text to the drawing.

TABLE 14.1:
Paintbrush Tools
(Continued)

What It Looks Like	What It Is	What It Does
	Color eraser	Wipes out the currently selected color only.
	Eraser	Wipes out everything in its path.
	Paint roller	Fills up a closed area with the selected color.
	Brush	Draws stuff. Difficult to use even with a steady hand.
	Curve	Draws a straight line. Use the mouse to pull at the line to curve it.
	Line	Draws a straight line. Hold down the Shift key to make it snap to 45-degree angles.
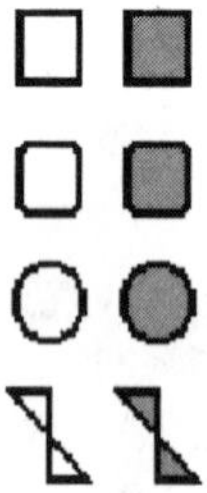	Various boxes and shapes	Creates the shape depicted. The shaded ones are filled in with whatever foreground color is selected.
	Line sizes	Changes the width of the line drawn by the selected tool.

To select a foreground color, click on it in the palette using the left mouse button. To select the background color, click on the color you want in the palette using the right mouse button.

Using the tools

Just click on the icon for the tool you want to use. The mouse pointer will change to some weird representation of the tool. Point your mouse and press the left button. As long as you hold down the left mouse button, you're in business with that tool. Let go of the mouse button when you're done drawing or whatever.

☞ To draw a perfectly straight line with the Brush tool, hold down the Shift key while you draw.

☞ Double-click on the Brush tool to get a window where you can select different Brush tips.

☞ When you're typing in text, use the right mouse button to select a color other than white. Then select Shadow or Outline from the Text menu to get an effect like this:

Hi There!

Click with the right mouse button on white to return to normal.

☞ You can change the color of objects you've already drawn quite easily. For example, to change your blue stuff to red, click on blue in the palette with the left mouse button, then click on red with the right mouse button. Then click on the Color Eraser tool. Put the pointer over the blue thing you want to change and rub the eraser around on it (making sure to hold down the left mouse button).

☞ To clear the whole window at once, double-click on the Eraser tool. Then answer No when you're asked if you want to save your work.

Making new wallpaper with Paintbrush

When you save a file in Paintbrush, the default format is .BMP, which just so happens to be the format Windows uses as wallpaper. After you've saved your work, as say, PICASSO.BMP, go to the Control Panel and select Desktop. In the Wallpaper drop-down list box, select PICASSO.BMP and then click on OK.

☞ For more on wallpaper and its meaning in the great scheme of life, see Chapter 8, "Windows Treatments."

Chapter 15

THE REST OF THE FREEBIES

Smelser's Law of Windows: The more windows you have open, the more likely you are to fall out of one of them.

IF YOU'VE WONDERED about all the other icons you see in Windows, this is the chapter for you. Some you've probably been able to figure out, like the Clock is a clock and the Calculator is a calculator. Not much of a challenge there.

But there are other, more mysterious ones like Character Map and Terminal that may have you baffled. Here, in alphabetical order, is enough information to satisfy the curious. You might even find one or more of these little programs useful.

Calculator

The Calculator works pretty much like any other simple calculator you've seen. Just double-click on this icon in the Accessories group:

Calculator

If you want to turn it into a scientific calculator, just select Scientific from the View menu.

☞ Use the mouse to click on the on-screen number pad. If that's too slow, use the numeric key on your keyboard. (Be sure the Num Lock light is on.)

☞ Press Ctrl-C to copy your answer to the Clipboard. Then click in the window where you want the answer to appear and press Ctrl-V.

☞ If you enter a number with a lot of zeroes in the decimal part, like 530.0000001, you won't see the zeroes until you enter the nonzero value. So when you enter 530.0000001, it will show as 530.0 until you enter the 1.

Calendar

If you have a very elaborate and complicated appointment schedule, Calendar is not for you. But if you have just a few things to keep track of, like the occasional dentist's appointment or budget meeting, it can do just fine. The icon for Calendar is in the Accessories group and looks like this:

Calendar

Double-click on it and a one-day-at-a-time view pops up, like in Figure 15.1.

FIGURE 15.1:
This is how the Calendar starts no matter what you do.

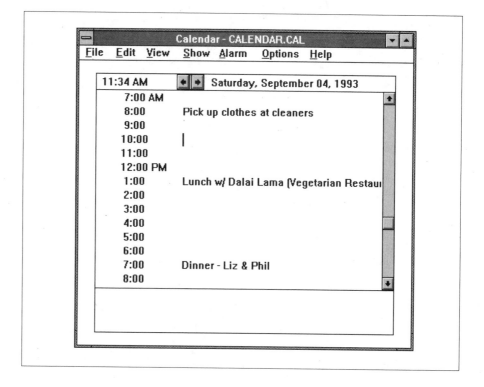

To get a whole month's view, press the F9 key. Press F8 to get back to the day view. In the month view, the calendar looks like Figure 15.2. Much more useful, we think.

☞ To mark a special day, select Mark from the Options menu.

☞ To jump to a specific date, press F4.

☞ To set an appointment for a very specific time, press F7. This only works in the day view.

☞ To remind yourself of appointments, select Controls from the Alarm menu. Set a time up to 10 minutes in the Early Ring box, and make sure the Sound box is checked. Then select Set from the Alarm menu. A little bell-shaped icon appears next to your appointment, and a box with a beep will pop up to remind you at the time set. You can only set an appointment in the day view, but the box will pop up if you're in the month view or even if Calendar is minimized to an icon.

Freebies
CH. 15

FIGURE 15.2:
This way you can mark paydays and holidays and stuff like that.

If you are using the alarm in Calendar and the screen saver is active, your alarm won't be displayed until you press a key or move the mouse. This means you may miss that important meeting, get fired, and end up not being able to make an honest living and have to go to law school. So don't rely on the alarm!

Cardfile

Cardfile is a sort of electronic box of Rolodex cards. The icon even looks like that:

Cardfile

Cardfile is in the Accessories group. It's supposed to help you keep track of phone numbers, addresses, stuff like that. It is, however, difficult to master. Though if you need it, it might be worth the effort.

Making a cardfile

To make a new card:

1. Select Index from the Edit menu (or press F6). In the Index dialog box, type in the characters you want. The cards will be sorted alphabetically by the first word on the index line. Include the phone number on the index line if you want to be able to use Autodial. Click on OK or press Enter.

2. Type in any text you want to appear on the card.

3. Go to the next card by selecting Add from the Card menu.

4. When you have a bunch, select Save from the File menu. Give your file a name, and click on OK. Next time you want to look at your cards, select Open from the File menu and click on the name.

☞ To look at a card, click on the index line and the card will pop to the top of the pile.

☞ You can look at your cards as a list of index lines. Just select List from the View menu.

☞ To search for a name, select Go To from the Search menu. Type in the name you want and click on OK.

☞ To search through the text on the cards for the guy whose nickname is "Weasel," select Find from the Search menu. Type in **Weasel** and click on Find Next.

Making Cardfile dial your phone

If you have a modem and it's hooked up and in working order, you can use Cardfile to call any of the folks in your cardfile. Click on any card you want. Press F5 and then click on OK. Cardfile will dial the first string of numbers it finds on the card.

☞ Put the phone number on the index line. If any other numbers, like the address, are ahead of the phone number, Cardfile will be very confused.

☞ If you want to dial something other than the first string of numbers on the card, highlight the number you want dialed and then press F5.

Freebies
CH. 15

☞ If you have to dial a 9 or some other prefix to get an outside line, check the Use Prefix box inside the Autodial dialog box, and make sure the prefix shown is the right one. Put a comma after the prefix and you'll cause a two-second pause between the dialing of the prefix and the dialing of the rest of the number.

Character Map

To get foreign characters like µ or special characters like ñ into your document, you can use Character Map. Double-click on the icon in the Accessories group that looks like this:

Character Map

After you start Character Map, check in the Font box that you have the font you want. Then follow these steps:

1. Double-click on the character you want.

2. Click on Copy. Then select Close.

3. Go to the document where you want the character to appear, and click on the exact spot.

4. Press Ctrl-V and the character appears.

☞ *Put your mouse pointer over a character and hold down the mouse button. You'll get an enlarged version of the teeny-tiny character so you can actually see it.*

☞ *You can get more than one character at a time. Just keep double-clicking until they're all in the Copy box.*

Clock

The Clock is not very mysterious. It looks just like a clock. It is in the Accessories group.

Clock

☞ Drag the Clock icon to the StartUp group and you'll have the Clock on your desktop whenever you start Windows. Shrink it to an icon and it's out of the way, but still useful.

☞ You can change the Clock from analog to digital using the Settings menu. Once it's set to be digital, you can also choose the font. Don't get too fancy with fonts or the Clock won't be readable when you shrink it back to an icon.

☞ Also in the Settings menu is the option No Title. Click on that and the title bar disappears. To get it back, double-click on the clock face.

☞ In the Clock's Control menu, you can select Always On Top. That way, when the clock is iconized, it's always peeping through any other documents to remind you how near it is to lunchtime.

Play It Again, Sam (Macro Recorder)

No Windows program, including Windows, would be complete without a macro recorder. In Windows it is called the Recorder and the icon looks like this (it's in the Accessories group):

Recorder

A macro is a way of automating repetitive tasks. You record the keystrokes and then the computer plays them back a zillion times without getting tired.

The problem is that the macro recorder in Windows is not very good. You can play around with it if you want, but if you have some task you'd like to automate, you'd be better off investigating the macro facility in a word processor or spreadsheet or some such program.

Media Player

Media Player is for people who have invested tons of dough in compact discs, MIDI keyboards, and other high-tech wonders. The icon for it is in the Accessories group and looks like this:

Media Player

You can also use Media Player to play sound files, including some that come with Windows, but only if you have a sound card installed in your computer. Sorry.

☞ For more on sound cards, see Chapter 25, "Ways to Spend Money *and* Have Fun (As If You Needed Help)."

Minesweeper

People either love Minesweeper or fail to see the point. To try it out, double-click on the Minesweeper icon (in the Games group):

Minesweeper

The window is supposed to be a mine field. The object is to click on one square at a time until you clear all the mines. Start by clicking on any old square. If it has a bomb underneath, you lose on the very first click.

☞ If there's a number in the square, there are that many bombs surrounding the square.

☞ If you think there's a mine under the square, click on it using the right mouse button. That puts a flag in the square.

☞ Keep clicking squares until you either clear all the squares that don't have a bomb or get blown up.

☞ If you clear all the squares, you win. If you get blown up, press F2 to get a new game or select Exit from the Game menu.

☞ If you get good and addicted to this game, the Game menu gives you a chance to change the difficulty level as well as record your best times.

Solitaire

Solitaire is just like the card game except the opportunities to cheat are very limited. To play Solitaire, double-click on this icon in the Games group:

Solitaire

☞ Click on the deck (in the upper-left corner) to deal three cards. You can then drag a card to the stacks. To put a card in one of the stacks along the top of the window, just double-click on the card.

☞ When all the cards have been dealt, click on the big green O to turn the deck back over.

☞ When the boss walks by, click on the Minimize button in the upper-right corner. Better yet, keep your spreadsheet program open and use Alt-Tab to switch to it instantly.

Cheating at Solitaire? You Ought to Be Ashamed

If you're doing the three-card-at-a-time deal in Solitaire (see Options on the Game menu), there's a chance the card you want won't get dealt. To force Solitaire to deal the next card in the deck, hold down Ctrl-Alt-Shift while you click on the deck. You'll feel a bit guilty, but it won't last.

Freebies CH. 15

Sound Recorder

The Sound Recorder lets you play, record, or edit sounds on your computer. To start it, double-click on this icon in the Accessories group:

Sound
Recorder

☞ Sound Recorder is useless to you unless you already have a sound card in your computer. For more on sound cards, see Chapter 25, "Ways to Spend Money *and* Have Fun (As If You Needed Help)."

☞ You'll also have to install programs called drivers so that Windows knows how to talk to your sound card. You can find more on drivers in Chapter 22.

☞ Don't get carried away with recording sounds because sound files are really large and will fill up your hard disk in no time.

Terminal

If you have a modem hooked up to your computer, you can use Terminal to transmit stuff across phone lines. The Terminal icon, found in the Accessories group, looks like this:

Terminal

Once Terminal is set up, it's pretty easy to use. But getting it set up is not for the faint of heart. Con a nerdy friend into doing it for you. Offer her or him some nice, high-calorie, low-nutrition treat and you can probably get it done for no more than the cost of the treat and having to listen to the nerd explain far more than you wanted to know about how to do it.

☞ If you're going to want to use your modem a lot, invest in a useful communications program, such as PROCOMM for Windows. Much nicer than Terminal.

Chapter 16

PRINTING

Turner's Law: No matter how many pages you have to print, the printer will run out of paper before you finish.

Croley's Commentary on Turner's Law: The last person to print never refills the paper.

PUNDITS HAVE BEEN proclaiming the dawn of the paperless office for years now, but it hasn't happened yet, and doesn't show much sign of happening any time soon. So, no matter what you are using your computer and Windows for, almost inevitably you will want to print out the results.

Windows makes it both easier and harder to print than plain-old DOS. Harder, because there are more layers in between your document and the actual printer, so that troubleshooting involves more steps, but easier, because all printers are the same to your application. Windows handles the differences.

Printer Basics

There are three basic kinds of printers on the market today—laser printers, ink-jet printers, and dot-matrix printers. In each class of printer, there is a wide variation in price and performance. And if you run DOS applications, even inside Windows, your application must know a great deal about each printer that it supports in order for it to work well with it.

Windows programs, however, simply need to know how to print to Windows, and the rest is handled for them. This means that each program automatically supports thousands of printers and produces remarkably similar output on each of them.

Laser printers

Laser printers are what we all wish we had. They are relatively fast, quiet, and produce excellent output. There are two principal types of laser printers, those that use the PostScript language and those that are based on Hewlett-Packard's Printer Control Language (PCL). Both provide excellent output, and both work equally well from Windows.

The choice between the two depends on what your primary printing is. If most of your printing involves complex graphics, the PostScript-based lasers will generally do a better job.

Ink-jet printers

Ink-jet printers work by squirting a bunch of tiny little drops of ink onto the paper. They are very quiet, moderately inexpensive, and produce output that rivals that of laser printers. However, they are fairly expensive to use, since the ink cartridges are not cheap and don't last that long, and they are a good deal slower than laser printers. They make a good compromise for home or home office use, but are not really appropriate for business use.

Dot-matrix printers

The lowly dot-matrix printer has been around for years. It is noisy, and its output varies from the respectable to the horrible. But it is cheap, and it is the only way you can print multiple-page forms, so it is unlikely to disappear any time soon.

When used in their fastest mode, usually called draft mode, the fastest of these printers are pretty speedy, but produce output that could best be described as barely readable. But when used at their highest resolution, these printers can produce quite acceptable output, if slowly.

A Note about Color Printers

All three kinds of printers are also available in color. Each produces color output roughly as good as their black-and-white output.

So, should you buy color? Well, unless you have a lot of money to burn, probably not. At least not yet.

Color certainly makes fliers and presentations look special, but the trade-offs are substantial. Except at the dot-matrix level, the extra cost for a color printer is not trivial, and they are definitely more expensive to use. But more to the point, color is a *lot* slower and not really appropriate for day-to-day use.

When the price comes down, you may want to consider it, but for the moment I would hold off, unless your primary output is graphics-based presentations. In the meantime, there are lots of commercial places with color PostScript printers that will take a disk from you and produce truly outstanding output.

Sending Stuff to the Printer

Windows programs all use the same basic printing interface. This is one of the things that really makes Windows a pleasure.

The File menu contains the options to send output to your printer. Just select Print from the File menu, and you are off and running. Some programs, like Write, will give you a chance to make additional choices at this point and will throw up a Print dialog box like Figure 16.1 to let you have a little say in exactly *how* your printing will be done. Others, like Notepad, will simply start printing the current document without any additional input from you.

FIGURE 16.1:

The Print dialog box in Write lets you choose how to print your document.

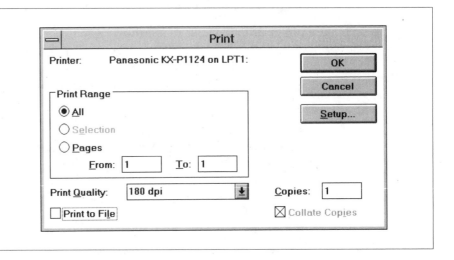

Printing When You Don't Have a Printer

If you want to print to a file so you can later print the file on a printer, select Print from the File menu. In the Printer dialog box, click on the Print to File box. You'll be asked to provide an output file name. Just type in a name for your file and click on OK.

Later, you can copy the file to a floppy. Take it to another computer and put the floppy in the A: drive. At the DOS prompt, type

```
COPY A:filename PRN /b
```

where *filename* is the exact name of the file.

Why, you ask, would you even want to print to a file?

☞ The computer you actually print from doesn't have the same programs you do. For example, you have a Word document and you want to print it from a computer that doesn't have Word installed.

☞ You're creating the file on a computer that doesn't have a printer at all—a laptop, for instance.

The Print Manager Program

When you print something from Write, or Notepad, or, in fact, any Windows program, that program sends the output to Windows, not directly to the printer itself. Windows then uses its Print Manager program to print your precious document unless you have specifically turned off the Print Manager. We'll talk about that possibility later, but for the moment let's assume you left well enough alone and it's still turned on.

Print Manager is a program that comes with Windows and *spools* your printed output to your hard disk and then sends it to the printer while you go on about your business doing other things. It works in the background without your really even having to be aware of it, so you don't have to wait to update your resume while your 120-page thesis is printing.

When you tell a Windows program to print something, Windows handles the starting of Print Manager automatically. It even closes the Print Manager when the printing finishes.

☞ If you are on a network and don't have a printer connected to your computer, you probably don't use or need Print Manager. The network handles all the messy details.

☞ If your network is Windows for Workgroups, you must be running Print Manager to share your printer with others in your workgroup. (Workgroup stuff can be found in the next chapter.)

If Print Manager Doesn't Start Automatically When You Print

Normally, Print Manager will start when you go to print—unless you are using a network printer—but if someone has screwed around with the Control Panel, it may not work right. To turn the Print Manager back on, open the Control Panel and double-click on the Printers icon. The Printers dialog box (Figure 16.2) will open.

In the bottom-left corner is the Use Print Manager check box. Make sure this is checked, and then click on Close. Now, when you go to print, Print Manager should work like it is supposed to.

FIGURE 16.2:

The Printers dialog box

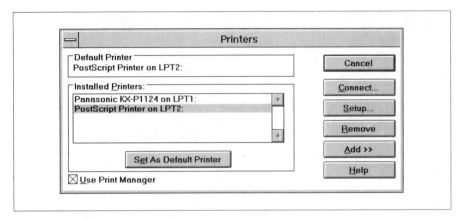

☞ If you are using one of the many third-party print spoolers, such as PrintCache from Laser Tools, it may disable the Print Manager when it is installed. Leave well enough alone, in that case.

☞ If you are printing on a network, and the printer is not attached to your computer, you probably won't see the Print Manager regardless of what the Use Print Manager setting is. Don't worry about it; the network software will handle things in this case.

☞ If you are printing from DOS or a DOS program, Print Manager doesn't get involved. You will just have to wait patiently for the printing to finish. See "Windows vs. DOS Printing" for more details.

Windows vs. DOS Printing

When you print from a Windows program, you will see a little information window open up to tell you that printing has begun and what page is currently printing. When this is finished, your Windows application will come back, and you can go on about your business. Meanwhile, Print Manager will handle the actual printing in the background. What you are seeing while your application is ticking off the pages is not what page is actually being printed by the printer but what page is currently being sent to the Print Manager.

What about printing from your older, DOS applications? Each one has a different set of commands, and it may look different while it's printing, but the result is the same. Print Manager doesn't work with DOS programs, so you'll have to wait patiently for a DOS program to do its printing if you want to continue to work, *in that program,* while the process goes on.

You can, however, let your DOS program go on about its printing business while you fire up another program to get some work done. For details on how to set your DOS program to run in the background, see "Getting That DOS Program to Print in the Background" on page 234.

Faster, Faster!

Printing from Windows is not always as fast as you might want, especially if all you need is a quick printout of a simple text file. Here are some ways to get a little extra speed out of Windows:

☞ Install the Generic/Text Only printer in Windows and use that for simple text files. For details, see the section below on adding a printer.

☞ Lower the resolution of the printer you are using. If you are printing to a laser printer at 300 dots per inch, switch to 150 dots per inch. For details, see the section below on modifying your printer setup.

☞ Open the Print Manager by double-clicking on its icon in the Main group. Click on Options in the menu bar, and select High Priority. This will tend to make your other Windows applications run slower, but will give more time to the printer. On a fast computer, you will probably never notice the difference in your other applications, but you will definitely see a difference in how fast the printing goes.

☞ Get one of the third-party Windows printing enhancers. Good ones that we know about are PrintCache 3.1 from LaserTools, PowerPak from PC-Kwik, the WinJet and WinPrinter series from Laser-Master, and SuperPrint from Zenographics. Some of these are Windows-only solutions, and some work with DOS applications as well. Probably the best general-purpose solution regardless of printer, for both DOS and Windows applications, is PrintCache from LaserTools.

Drag-and-Drop Printing

To quickly print some kinds of files, such as a Windows Write file or a text file, you can use the File Manager's drag-and-drop capabilities. If the Print Manager isn't open, open it and shrink it to an icon at the bottom of the screen. Then, open the File Manager and find the file or files you want to print, and drag the file to the Print Manager icon at the bottom of the screen and drop it. If it is a file for an application that Print Manager knows how to handle, it will open up the application and print out the file, closing the application when the file is printed. Pretty slick, huh?

Adding a Printer

When you first installed Windows, you probably installed at least one printer, but sooner or later you may need to change this. You get attached to a network that has a better printer, you buy a new one, whatever. You could just call up your favorite nerd, offer her or him a suitable bribe, and handle it that way, but you really don't need to. Save your credit with the nerd for when you really need help, and do this one yourself.

First, dig out your original Windows disks. You will probably need these unless your new printer is a close relative of one of the ones you already have installed. Next, open up the Control Panel and double-click on the Printers icon. This will open the Printers dialog box, where you should click on the Add button. OK, it should look something like Figure 16.3 now. All that is left to do is to pick your printer and do the actual installation.

To pick your new printer, use the scroll bar to move through the list of printers available. When you find yours, highlight it with the mouse and click on the Install button. If you don't find your printer, you will need to consult the printer's documentation to find out what printers it can pretend to be (the nerdish scientific term is *emulate*), and select one of those. If Windows doesn't find a driver it can use for your printer on its hard disk, it will ask you to insert one of the original Windows disks, usually disk 6, in the A: drive. Humor it, and put the disk in.

FIGURE 16.3:

Adding a printer to
your collection

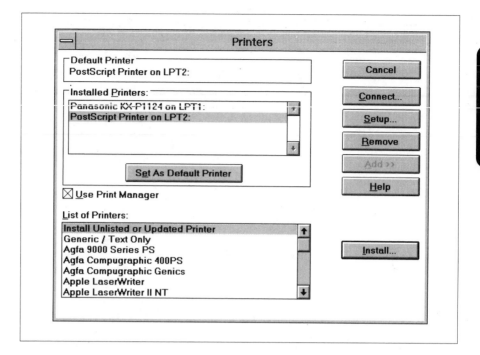

Windows will copy the necessary file from the floppy drive, and your
new printer will now show up in the Installed Printers box. Great. Now
all you need to do is check to make sure it is set for the correct printer
port, and you are done.

The new listing will say something like "HP LaserJet IIIP on LPT1." The
key words here are "on LPT1." This says the printer is attached to your
primary printer port. If it is connected to something else, like LPT2, you
need to click on the Connect button and tell Windows where the
printer is actually attached.

☞ If you have no idea what port your printer is attached to or even
   what a port *is,* try LPT1 first. Then print something. If it doesn't
   work, try LPT2. You can't do any harm, and you might stumble
   on the right answer (how 90 percent of all troubleshooting is
   done).

☞ If this is a network printer, you should get your network administrator to give you exact instructions about how to connect to the
   printer.

Changing Your Printer Setup

Windows generally thinks that you always want to print to your printer at the highest-possible resolution and that you will be using regular, letter-size paper. Well, that is nice, but sometimes you need something a bit different. Most Windows applications let you change your printer setup from within the application. Just select Printer Setup from the File menu. If your application is one of these, great. Just poke your way through the dialog boxes and change what you need to change. Just remember that what you change in one Windows application will generally change it for *all* Windows applications.

☞ Most spreadsheet programs, though, can be set to print in a landscape orientation without changing the orientation for other Windows programs.

If your application doesn't offer you a Printer Setup choice, you need to go to the Control Panel again. Double-click on the Printers icon, and highlight the printer you want to change. Now click on Setup and change whatever it is you want to change. There are settings for which way to print on the paper (Orientation), the paper size and source, the resolution, and all sorts of other options, depending on the particular printer. Just set everything the way you want it, and click on OK enough times to get back to the main Printers dialog box. There you want to click on the Set As Default Printer button to make the printer you have changed the current printer, and then click on Close to exit. Now when you start your application, it will use the new settings for your printer.

Printer Drivers and Where to Get Them

New printers are being made all the time, and Windows knows nothing about them at all if they were released after Windows. So, you may well need to install a new driver to go with your new printer. Your new printer should come with drivers and instructions for how to install them. (Help with drivers can also be found in Chapter 22.)

Follow the instructions from your printer manufacturer, and if you get stuck, don't be afraid to call for help. This time, call the manufacturer's technical support number. The tech support engineer will walk you through the steps necessary to get your new printer working happily with Windows and your Windows applications. And, if they get enough calls, they may even write the instructions well enough the next time so a mere human can read them.

However, if you don't have the time or patience to wait on hold for the manufacturer, or you really just want someone to do it for you, you should call your favorite nerd and bribe him or her to load up the new driver. In doubt about the best way to bribe a nerd? See Chapter 22, "Windows Problems and How to Solve Them."

More Fonts Please, Sir?

Windows makes it easy to get carried away with fonts. There are five different TrueType typefaces included with Windows and lots more available from a wide variety of sources.

Microsoft has two additional packages of TrueType fonts available, and there are zillions of other companies providing TrueType fonts of varying quality. If you do buy additional fonts (and who can resist the temptation?), the package will undoubtedly come with instructions for installing. Just keep in mind that fonts use space both on your hard disk and in your computer's memory.

A Long and Boring Note about Fonts and Font Technologies

In Windows 3.1, Microsoft introduced a whole new way to handle fonts, called TrueType. This was an enormous improvement over previous versions of Windows. It provides three major improvements to users:

☞ It gives users the ability to see on the screen what their documents will look like when printed (called "WYSIWYG," short for "What You See Is What You Get").

☞ It gives every printer the ability to print essentially similar-looking documents. This is called device independence.

☞ The fonts are fully scalable and therefore take up lots less hard-drive space.

The other major font technology for Windows is the Adobe Type Manager (usually called "ATM"). ATM provides the same three key elements of True-Type fonts.

There are other font technologies for Windows as well, but these two are the principal players in the game. Adobe has an edge in the quality and diversity of the fonts available, but TrueType is hard to beat for being simple and easy to use. Unless your primary goal is desktop publishing, stick to the TrueType fonts.

Mills's Third Axiom: No matter how big the print job, the printer will run out of paper when there is only one page left to print.

It Won't Print!

While Windows makes printing easier than plain-old DOS, you can still have some problems. Here is a short list of common problems and their solutions.

Nothing happens

Check to make sure that the printer is turned on. If it is turned on, make sure that it is "on-line." A printer can be switched on and still not ready to print. Many printers will have a button labeled "On-line" or "Select," with a corresponding light. When that light is on, it means the printer is ready to go.

The last page didn't print

This is more of a problem in DOS than in Windows, but still comes up, especially with laser printers. When this happens, press the on-line button (usually the upper-left button on a laser printer) so that the light goes out, then press the "Sheet Feed," "Form Feed," "Page Eject," or similarly named button (usually directly underneath the on-line button). Usually the light is on at this point. Then, when the page starts coming out, press the on-line button again.

The paper jammed

What to do if you get paper jammed in your printer depends on what type of printer you have. If you have a jammed dot-matrix printer, first turn off the power. Then try slowly backing up the paper, using the large knob on the side of the platen. If this doesn't work, try flipping up the little latches that hold the paper against the pin-feed pins, and gently pull the paper out. And if this still doesn't work, you may have to remove the platen completely. Get help for this, at least the first time. Taking the thing off isn't the problem but getting it back on may be.

If you have a laser printer, you don't have to turn the printer off to unjam it, but be careful. First, take the printer off line, and remove the paper tray. If you see a piece of paper sticking out, gently pull it back out of the printer and put the paper tray back. If you still get the paper jam signal, you will have to open up the printer and peer into its guts. Usually the source of the problem is pretty obvious at this point.

☞ *Never stick anything sharp into your printer. It can only make the problem worse.*

☞ *Don't try to back messed-up sticky labels out of your dot-matrix printer. Move the little lever on the left side of the printer that compensates for the thickness of the paper all the way to its thickest setting. Tear off the labels where they're feeding into the printer, and feed the jammed ones slowly forward through the printer until you've gotten all of them out.*

☞ *Watch out for hot parts. The print head on a dot-matrix printer and several parts on a laser printer can be hot enough to burn.*

☞ *Never force the paper, and try to avoid tearing it. This generally just makes the problem worse.*

Gibberish and How to Stop It

So, suddenly your printer starts printing a few characters on each page and then spitting it out. And when you press the on-line button, it won't stop.

Dot-matrix printers

If it's a dot-matrix printer, turn it off and go to the Print Manager. After you turn off the printer, you will probably get an error message from Print Manager. If you do, choose Cancel. Now, double-click on the Print Manager icon at the bottom of the screen. You should see a listing for your printer, with your print job that is messed up showing under it. Click on this print job, and then click on the Delete button on the button bar below the menu bar. Windows will ask you to confirm that you really want to do this, and when you click OK, the troublesome print job is history.

Now, return to your printer, manually feed the paper out till you can line it up with the start of a new page, and turn the printer back on and you are ready to try again.

In a dot-matrix printer, gibberish is usually the result of a previous printing from a DOS program that has changed some settings on the printer. When you turn the printer off and back on again, the settings are restored to the ones Windows knows about.

Laser printers (ink-jet too)

If you have a laser printer, it is a bad idea to turn it off in the middle of printing. This will usually leave a piece of paper stuck inside. So remove the paper tray. Then when the last sheet of paper has had a chance to get all the way out of the printer, turn off the printer, follow the steps above to cancel the print job in Print Manager, and start all over again from scratch.

One cause of gibberish on laser printers is common to those of us who switch back and forth between PostScript and PCL laser printers. If you tell Windows to print to a PostScript printer, and you forget to put in the PostScript cartridge, what you will get is page after page of PostScript language commands. Cancel the print job, turn off the printer, and insert the PostScript cartridge. Then turn the printer back on and restart the print job from scratch.

Chapter 17

JUST FOR WORKGROUPS—CAUSE THEY'RE SPECIAL

Cap's Rule: Networks are simple; it's the explanation that's complex.

WINDOWS FOR WORKGROUPS is what's called a peer-to-peer network. This means everyone's equal and there is no boss. Isn't that sweet? Mostly Windows for Workgroups looks just like regular Windows, but there are some differences, and this is the chapter where we cover the extra applications that come with Windows for Workgroups and how to share files and resources with other users.

We assume that your workgroup has been set up and installed already. Setting up any network is not for the faint of heart, and even the easiest ones, of which Windows for Workgroups is one, should be set up by those who enjoy these sorts of things. In other words, leave it to a nerd. Once your nerd gets everything working, you should be suitably thankful and appreciative, stroke it a few times, and then let it crawl back into its bat cave, er, cubicle.

Sharing Drives and Directories

The need to share files is a big reason for using Windows for Workgroups in the first place. With Windows for Workgroups, you get a new and enhanced File Manager with the ability to share your entire hard disk, or any single directory of it, with the others in your workgroup. Plus the new File Manager has a cute, if somewhat useless, tool bar at the top, right below the menu bar.

When you share a drive or directory with another user, you can control whether the other users can actually change the files on the drive or directory you are sharing or only look at them. And you can even prevent users from being able to see your files if they don't know the necessary password.

To share a directory on your hard drive, open up the File Manager and highlight the directory you wish to share. Then click on Disk on the menu bar, and click on Share As on the menu that drops down. The Share Directory dialog box, shown in Figure 17.1, will open. Type a name for the directory in the Share Name box, and add a snotty comment if you wish in the Comment box. Then, if you want to make this directory automatically available every time you start Windows, check the Re-share at Startup box. Finally, in the Access Type box, choose whether other users will be able to only look at your files (Read-Only), will be able to edit, move, or even delete them (Full), or will have to provide a password to have either of these abilities (Depends on Password).

Finally, if you want to require a password before your workmates can connect to your computer, type the password into the appropriate password box. This makes everybody with the password feel important. It

FIGURE 17.1:
Windows for
Workgroups lets you
share directories with
others in your
workgroup.

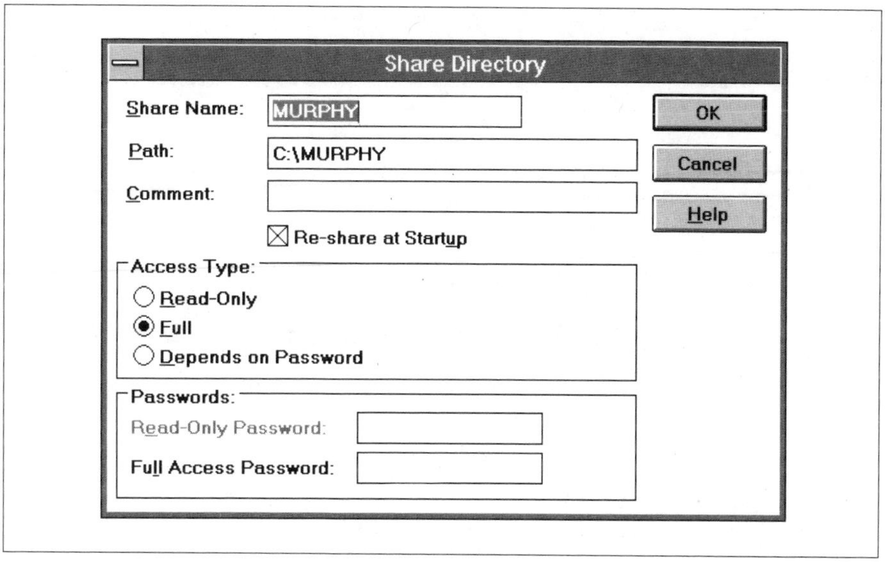

also makes them very annoyed when they forget the password. When you have everything as you want, click on the OK button, and the directory will be immediately available to the other users in your workgroup.

☞ If you share a directory, all the subdirectories below it will be available as well.

☞ To share an entire drive, simply share the root directory of that drive.

Connecting to a Shared Directory

Once one of your workgroup mates has shared a directory on his or her computer, you still need to connect to that directory in order to actually use it. You only have to do it once, though afterward you can have Windows for Workgroups do it automatically for you whenever you start Windows.

To connect to a shared directory on someone else's computer, first open the File Manager and click on Connect Network Drive on the Disk menu. This will open up the Connect Network Drive dialog box, shown in Figure 17.2.

Workgroups CH. 17

FIGURE 17.2:

Connecting to the drives on Charlie's computer

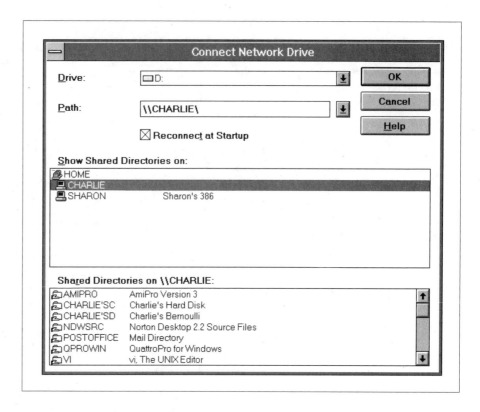

First, decide what drive letter the connection will look like on your machine. Windows for Workgroups automatically assumes that you want to use the next available drive letter, but you may well want to choose something a bit easier to remember. So, you might want to connect to the shared copy of Quattro Pro for Windows on your workmate's computer by making it your Q: drive, for example.

Next, click on the computer whose directory you want to share. A list of the available directories on that computer will appear in the Shared Directories box. Click on the directory you want to connect to, and the connection will be put into the Path box. If you want Windows to always reconnect you to this directory when you start up, make sure the Reconnect at Startup box is checked. If everything looks right, click on OK, and you will be immediately connected to the directory.

☞ You can't connect to your own computer using Windows for Workgroups. Silly, but I guess they figure you're already connected to it.

☞ Don't set up automatic connections to computers that aren't always left on and running Windows. Otherwise you will get annoying messages when you go to start Windows on your computer.

Sharing Printers

In most business situations, not everyone can have the exclusive use of a nice, speedy laser printer, except Bob, who plays racquetball with the boss. But perhaps you can coerce Bob into sharing his printer (a guy like Bob is bound to have skeletons in his closet).

The person who has the printer physically connected to his computer (Bob) simply needs to tell the Print Manager to share the printer, and the other users in the workgroup can then connect to it just as if it were connected to their computers.

To share the printer, Bob should open the Print Manager, and click on Printer on the menu bar and then click on Share Printer As. The Share Printer dialog box, like in Figure 17.3, will open. He selects his printer as the one to be shared, then types in a name in the Share As text box. This is the name other users see when they want to print to it, so the name should be as descriptive as possible (how about "Brownnose's Laser"). A comment in the Comment box can make the name even clearer.

By typing a password in the Password box, Bob can restrict access to the printer so that only those who know the password can use it. Finally, make sure the Re-share at Startup box is checked to make this hookup automatic every time he restarts Windows. Trust me, Bob—you do! Click on OK, and you won't have to worry about it again.

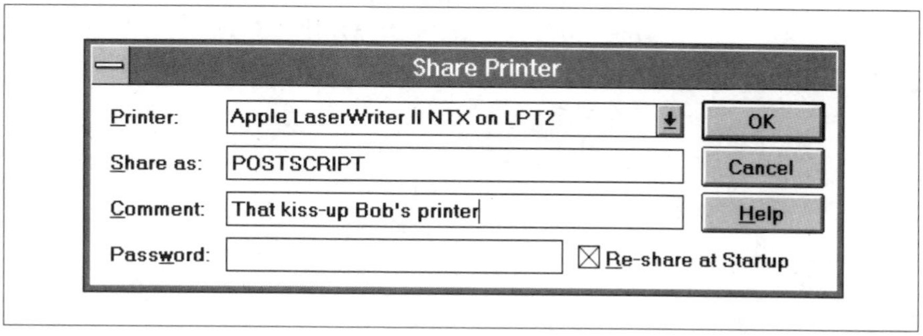

Workgroups CH. 17

FIGURE 17.3:
Set up the printer right and you won't have to do it again.

Share Printer		
Printer:	Apple LaserWriter II NTX on LPT2 ±	OK
Share as:	POSTSCRIPT	Cancel
Comment:	That kiss-up Bob's printer	Help
Password:		☒ Re-share at Startup

Connecting to Shared Printers

Once a printer is set up to be shared, you need to connect to it. Like sharing a drive, if you do this right the first time, you won't have to worry about it again.

Open the Print Manager and select Connect Network Printer from the Printer menu. Choose a device name to connect this printer to. If you don't have a printer physically connected to your computer, stick with the default of LPT1, but if you actually have a printer connected there, then choose one of the other LPT options. Next, click on the machine whose printer you want to connect to, in the Show Shared Printers On box, and a list of shared printers attached to that computer will appear in the Shared Printers On box. Click on the one you want to connect to.

Finally, make sure the Reconnect at Startup box is checked, and click OK. Phew. Aren't you glad that Windows will handle this from here on out?

☞ Try to connect printers to computers that are always on and always running Windows. This way they are always available to the rest of the network. Nothing is more frustrating than having your best (or worse, only) printer unavailable because Bob is on vacation and his computer is turned off.

Talking to Another User over the Network

Windows for Workgroups lets you "talk" to another computer on the network using the Chat program. Unfortunately, however, this is only an electronic conversation, so if you aren't much of a typist, it can be pretty painful.

To chat with another computer, click on the Chat icon in the Accessories group. Click on the little icon on the far-left side of the tool bar

and you will get the Select Computer dialog box.

Double-click on the computer you want to chat with, and Windows for Workgroups will "dial" the other person's computer. When that person notices that the little phone icon is ringing, and answers, you can type into your half of the chat box, and the words appear on your workmate's computer—handy for a quick question to someone several cubicles away, but not for lengthy discussions.

Sending Messages and Files to Others in Your Workgroup

You can use the limited version of Microsoft Mail that comes with Windows for Workgroups to send electronic mail to others in your workgroup. This mail can even include attached files that you want them to look at.

To send a letter to someone in your workgroup, all you need to do is click on the Compose button. Fill in the To: box, and send "carbon copies" to others in the workgroup by adding them to the Cc: box. Type in a subject and then the text of the message. When you have everything as you want it, click on the Send button, and the message will be sent to the mail addresses you specified.

☞ Use the Address button to pick the addresses from a list of addresses in your workgroup.

☞ If you type the names yourself, use the Check Names button to make sure that you got it right.

☞ To attach a file you want the other person to see, click on the Attach button and select the file to attach to the message.

☞ Get your favorite nerd to do the initial setup of Microsoft Mail. Some of the options can be a bit confusing. Once it is set up, you should be able to handle your mail on your own.

Using Microsoft Schedule+

Included with Windows for Workgroups is a limited version of the Microsoft Schedule+ program. This is a useful little program that keeps track of your meetings and ToDo list, as well as allowing you to schedule meetings with others in your workgroup. You can even use it to keep track of the schedule for conference rooms and other resources.

To run Schedule+ properly, you need to have set up your Microsoft Mail program and created the necessary post-office boxes and so forth. If this hasn't been done yet, get your computer resource person to handle the details. There are way too many options and possibilities in Microsoft Mail to be bothered with. The best possible situation is if someone in your workgroup has nerdish tendencies. If so, then let him or her be the postmaster and set everything up. If not, get your company's computer or network resource person to do the setup.

Once Mail is set up, you can start Schedule+ by just double-clicking on its icon:

Schedule+

Adding an appointment to your appointment book

Keeping track of your appointments using Schedule+ is easy. Just start up the Schedule+ program (we like to keep it open but iconized down at the bottom of the screen, ready for instant updating), and click on the Appts tab. Then, use your mouse to change the date to when you want to add the new appointment. When you have that day's schedule up, just click and drag your mouse across the time slot for the appointment, and then type in a description of the appointment.

If you want to add an alarm to remind yourself about the appointment, double-click on it once you have created it, and then check the Set Reminder For check box. An alarm is automatically set for 15 minutes before the appointment, but you can change the warning in the Beforehand box. Click OK, and an alarm is now set.

Adding a task to your task list

Schedule+ includes a task list as well as appointments. Just click on the Tasks tab to bring up your task list, and then enter in a new task by typing something into the New Task box. Click on the Add button to add the item to your task list.

To change the task you just added, simply double-click on it. This will let you set the priority and the due date, add reminders, and even make the task private so that others in your workgroup can't see the details of the task.

If you happen, just by accident, to click on your Games group while you're in Windows for Workgroups, you'll find something not mentioned anywhere in the documentation: the Microsoft Hearts Network. Click on the icon

Hearts

and you can play the hearts card game either alone or with others in your workgroup.

> ☞ *If you have a sound card, you can add sounds to the game by pressing F8.*

> ☞ *Select Contents from the Help menu to get all the rules and some advice on strategy.*

> ☞ *Use Alt-Tab to quickly hide your game from prying eyes.*

Workgroups CH. 17

4

So you thought you'd never have to deal
with DOS again, did you? Dream on. But if
you have a rude awakening, look here for
the basics of DOS, running DOS programs in
Windows, and DOS stuff you should never,
never do.

DOS:

It's Still Alive!!

Chapter 18

A DOS PRIMER

Anderson's Law: Established technology tends to persist in spite of new technology.

AS COZY AS things are in Windows, you may find that you need to poke around a bit in DOS. In this chapter you'll find some of the most basic maneuvers, as well as a section on running the DOS program MemMaker so you can squeeze out some extra conventional memory for all your programs to play in.

Lost at the DOS Prompt

At some point you're going to find yourself staring at a screen that's blank except for something that looks like:

```
C:\>
```

That's just DOS saying, "I'm sitting here patiently waiting for instructions from you. I'm at the C drive (your hard disk) in the root directory (that's \)."

The > doesn't mean anything in this case.

If you were percolating along merrily in Windows just before this happened, type

    EXIT

and press Enter, and you'll be swiftly escorted back into Windows.

However, if you're not in Windows and just want to potter around in DOS, read on.

Where Am I?

If you see a letter followed by a colon and a backslash (C:\) and maybe some other stuff too (like the > sign), you're in luck. DOS is set up to show you where you are. But if you have only a letter followed by the greater-than sign (C>), you'll need to type the letter "C" followed by the letter "D," and then press the Enter key to find out your location.

When you type in **CD** it will show on the screen as you type it, and when you press the Enter key, the cursor (that little flashing line) will move down a line and the screen will show something like

    C:\BOOKS

This means you are at drive C—the hard disk—and in the directory named BOOKS. If a directory (such as BOOKS) already shows at the prompt, typing in CD will only show that, yes, you are in the BOOKS directory.

You can always type this command, **CD,** to locate your current directory.

☞ If you type CD alone, it stands for "**C**urrent **D**irectory." If you include a directory name, you can remember it as standing for "**C**hange **D**irectory."

☞ Until you press the Enter key, nothing will happen. Press Backspace to erase your typing, letter by letter. You can continue to type in as many versions as you want because the computer pays no attention until you press that Enter key.

Changing Directories

The programs you install usually have their own directories. For example, a directory called QPW will have your Quattro Pro for Windows files. Word for Windows makes a directory called WINWORD. You can also organize stuff into directories based on function, such as a directory called GAMES for all your fun stuff.

Directories can have subdirectories of their own. So if you find yourself at a prompt like

```
C:\WINWORD\FISH
```

you are in the FISH directory (presumably full of fish stories), which is a subdirectory of your Word for Windows (WINWORD) directory. The WINWORD directory is in the root directory of drive C.

To change to another directory, use the CD command followed by the name of the directory.

```
CD \WINWORD\LETTERS
```

Then press Enter. This will take you to the LETTERS subdirectory under the WINWORD directory.

☞ A subdirectory is no lesser a being than a directory. The term subdirectory indicates that it is a directory under another directory, not that it is smaller or functions differently.

☞ You can always get to the root directory of a disk by typing

```
CD \
```

and pressing Enter. You can put a space between the "CD" and the "\" but it's not required.

Changing Drives

In DOS, the computer can only look at one disk (or drive) at a time. To direct its attention from one disk to another, just type in the new drive letter followed by a colon. For example, if you are at the A:\ prompt and want to look at drive C, merely type in

```
C:
```

DOS Primer
CH. 18

Make sure you include the colon and press Enter. To change back, type in

    A:

and press Enter.

☞ Sometimes, when you change drives, you will find yourself at, for example, \WINWORD\FISH, instead of the root directory like you expected. This is because the last time you left the drive, that's the directory you were in. DOS always "remembers" where you were the last time you visited that drive and plops you down there again. To get to the root, just type in

    CD \

☞ Don't change to a floppy drive unless a disk is in that drive.

☞ Your first floppy drive is drive A, and the second floppy drive is drive B. Your first hard drive is always drive C. Additional drives you may have will start with letter D and go on through the alphabet.

Scouting Your Location—The DIR Command

Once you know what directory you are in, you can poke around to see what else is in the area. Type in

    DIR

and press the Enter key.

All the files in your current directory will show up on your screen. If there's a lot of stuff, it will go scrolling by faster than you can read. To solve this problem, try one of the following:

    DIR /W

The "W" stands for "wide." This will give you the files in five columns across the screen, like in Figure 18.1. This is useful if you're looking for a particular name, but it leaves off all the other information about the files.

Or you can use

    DIR /P

which gives you a screen's worth of files at a time, as shown in Figure 18.2. Think of the "P" as standing for "page-at-a-time." Press Enter to get another screen's worth and so on until you've seen everything.

FIGURE 18.1:

What you get with
DIR /W

```
C:\AFTERDRK>dir /w

 Volume in drive C is BigDOS5Disk
 Volume Serial Number is 0000-14CA
 Directory of C:\AFTERDRK

[.]                  [..]                 [BITMAPS]            [ADMODULE.SDK]    3DBOUNCE.AD
AQUA.AD              CLOCKS.AD            DRAINO.AD            FADE.AD           GLOBE.AD
GRAFSTAT.AD          GRAV.AD              LASER.AD             LOGO.AD           MAGIC.AD
MESSAGE.AD           MONDRIAN.AD          MOUNTAIN.AD          NOCTURNE.AD       PUNCH.AD
PUZZLE.AD            RAIN.AD              RAINSTOR.AD          ROSE.AD           SATORI.AD
SGYRA.AD             SHAPES.AD            SLIDESHO.AD          SPHERES.AD        SPOTLITE.AD
STAINED.AD           STRING.AD            TOASTERS.AD          VERTIGO.AD        WARP.AD
WORMS.AD             WRAP.AD              ZOT.AD               AD_LIB.DLL        AD.EXE
ADINIT.EXE           README.TXT
            42 file(s)         815645 bytes
                             24764416 bytes free

C:\AFTERDRK>
```

FIGURE 18.2:

Looking at a
directory with the
page-at-a-time View

```
 Volume in drive C is BigDOS5Disk
 Volume Serial Number is 0000-14CA
 Directory of C:\WINWORD

.              <DIR>         10-24-92   11:22a
..             <DIR>         10-24-92   11:22a
CLIPART        <DIR>         01-03-93    1:34p
WINWORD   CBT <DIR>          01-03-93    1:30p
NORMAL    DOT       2885     04-11-93    4:17p
WORDMAC   CNV     153184     02-11-92    2:00a
XLBIFF    CNV     104960     02-11-92    2:00a
RFTDCA    CNV     174592     02-11-92    2:00a
WORDDOS   CNV     176640     02-11-92    2:00a
WRITWIN   CNV      66560     02-11-92    2:00a
WORDSTAR  CNV     109760     02-11-92    2:00a
LOTUS123  CNV     103424     02-11-92    2:00a
TXTWLYT   CNV     175984     02-11-92    2:00a
WPFT5     CNV     199856     02-11-92    2:00a
WORDWIN1  CNV     152576     02-11-92    2:00a
DBASE     CNV      47104     02-11-92    2:00a
CUSTOM    DIC        884     04-21-93    9:37a
SPELL     DLL     108576     02-11-92    2:00a
HYPH      DLL      78412     02-11-92    2:00a
Press any key to continue . . .
```

What You're Seeing When You Type DIR

When you see a list of files after typing DIR, the information is in five columns. First is the file's name, followed by the three-character extension. The extension is part of the file's name, though not all files have an extension.

Next is the file's size, in "bytes," or characters, followed by the date and time the file was created, or if it's been changed, the date and time of the most recent change.

If the directory you're in has subdirectories, you'll see those too. Unless you use /W, the directories will have <DIR> next to them in the listing so you can easily tell them from the files.

Reading a Command Line

When you look up a DOS command in the DOS manual or the DOS help system, you'll see all sorts of weird stuff after the name of the actual command. This is the command-line *syntax,* or format, and is actually there to *help* you. Hard to believe, isn't it?

The command-line syntax may have up to four parts:

- ☞ The command name itself
- ☞ The required part (called a required parameter)
- ☞ The optional part (called an optional parameter)
- ☞ Switches

The command name

An example of a command name is the command to find out the current version of DOS:

VER

Here, only the command is shown, since there are no required parts and no options or switches.

The required part

For a command such as the one to prepare a floppy disk for use by DOS,

    FORMAT *drive*

FORMAT is the command name itself, and the *drive* in italics is the required part.

The optional part

The command to find out the name of a disk (its "volume label") can also take a drive letter as a parameter, but here it is optional. So it is usually shown like this:

    VOL [*drive*]

where the square brackets indicate that the drive letter is optional. If you don't include it, DOS assumes you mean the current drive.

Switches

And finally, a command can have "switches," which are always optional but that act to modify how the rest of the command is carried out.

Put them all together, they spell "syntax"

Here's the DEL command, used to delete files:

    DEL [*drive:*][*path*]*filespec* /P

First in line is the command itself, DEL. The optional parameters are the drive and path. If you don't supply them, DOS assumes you want to perform the operation in the current directory. *Filespec* is the name of the file or files you want to delete. Adding the switch /P means that you'll be prompted to confirm every deletion.

Whew! That was pretty intense there, especially at the end.

DOS Primer
CH. 18

So if you want to delete all the files with the extension .TMP in your WINDOWS directory, and you want to be asked to confirm each one, you type in

```
DEL \WINDOWS\*.TMP /P
```

Remember that this way of showing the command syntax is pretty consistent in most books. It is also used by DOS versions 5 and above when giving command-line help. You get this help by including the /? switch after any command. So, if you see a command with all those brackets and slashes after it in a manual or other book, just remember that everything in brackets is optional and things with slashes (but not backslashes) are switches.

Copying Files

The COPY command is one command you might find useful if you want to move some stuff around and you don't want to start Windows.

Copying a file from where you are to somewhere else

To copy a file from the directory you're in to another directory, type

```
COPY BABS.TXT \LETTERS
```

This will copy the file BABS.TXT to the LETTERS directory on the same disk. Be careful here. If there isn't a directory called LETTERS, you will end up with a file called LETTERS in the root directory and you'll never know what happened to good old Babs. Probably not what you had in mind.

To copy the same file to another disk, type in

```
COPY BABS.TXT A:
```

This will put a copy of BABS.TXT on the floppy in your drive A.

☞ Don't forget to put a colon after the drive letter. If you don't, you will end up with a file called "A" on your hard disk.

If you want to copy this file to a directory on another drive, you have to specify the full path:

```
COPY BABS.TXT A:\OLDPALS
```

This will copy the BABS.TXT file to the OLDPALS directory on drive A.

Copying a file from somewhere else to where you are

To copy a file from some other directory to where you are can be done using the short form of the COPY command. Suppose the file MONET.DOC is on drive B, and you want to copy it to where you are on drive C. Type in

```
COPY B:MONET.DOC
```

If MONET.DOC happens to be in a directory called \PAINT-ERS\FRENCH, you would type in

```
COPY B:\PAINTERS\FRENCH\MONET.DOC
```

In both the examples above, a copy of the file MONET.DOC will end up in your current directory.

☞ This short form of COPY works only when the file you want to get is not in the same directory you are.

Copying multiple files

You can use the COPY command to duplicate several files at once. This requires the * wildcard. The * wildcard can stand for a group of characters in a file name. So, if you want to copy all the files in your current directory to the floppy in drive A, you type

```
COPY *.* A:
```

If you only want to copy the files with a .WK1 extension, type in

```
COPY *.WK1 A:
```

☞ Clues on using the * wildcard are in Chapter 13, "File Manager without Fear."

Remember, when you don't tell DOS where to find the file you want to copy, delete, rename, or whatever, it looks only in the current directory of the current drive. If the current drive is a floppy and doesn't have a directory structure, DOS will look through the entire floppy.

Making the Most of Memory Using DOS 6

If you have DOS 6, you have an extremely handy program called Mem-Maker. If you also have a computer with a 80386 or 80486 processor and extended memory, you can use MemMaker to free up some conventional memory and give your programs more room to play in.

To run MemMaker, go to the DOS prompt and type in

    MEMMAKER

Follow the prompts. Choose Express Setup. Answer No to any questions you don't know the answer to. If you need help at any point, press the F1 key for help.

After you answer the questions, MemMaker tells you to press Enter to restart your computer. Cooperate and press Enter. Then after some period of mysterious activity, you'll be asked to press Enter again. Go ahead.

When the computer has restarted (again), MemMaker displays a screen asking if your system appears to be working properly. If you haven't seen any error messages and everything seems to be OK, press Enter. If something too strange for words has happened, press the spacebar to select No and then Exit.

After you press Enter, MemMaker displays a memory before-and-after screen. You should at least act impressed.

Press Enter again to quit MemMaker.

Quit any programs that are running before starting MemMaker. Don't try to run it from inside Windows.

Chapter 19

DOS PROGRAMS AND HOW TO RUN THEM

Simmons's Computer Law: A good program to-day is better than a perfect program tomorrow.

IF ALL YOUR programs were written for Windows, you don't even need to look at this chapter. But the grim reality is that you probably have any number of programs that were written for DOS and you still have to use them.

In this chapter we tell you how to make those stubborn DOS programs behave nicely in the Windows environment—and if they don't behave nicely, how to kick 'em back into line.

Running DOS Programs under Windows

Some DOS programs are fairly easy to run inside Windows. Just go to the Program Manager, find the icon for the program you want, and double-click on it. It'll probably fill the entire screen while Windows fades away into the background (but ready and waiting to reappear).

Some stubborn programs are designed to run all by themselves and they refuse to share the computer with anything else. They don't know anything about this "Windows" stuff, nor do they want to.

To bring these programs into line, Windows uses something called a *program information file,* otherwise known as a *PIF.* Every DOS program gets its own PIF containing instructions necessary to shoehorn the program into Windows.

Many DOS programs come with their own PIFs, and Windows supplies most of the rest. When you click on a DOS program's icon, you are, in fact, starting that program's PIF.

☞ If you install a new DOS program that you want to run under Windows, see "Adding a New Program to a Group" on page 142. If Windows recognizes the program or the program supplies its own PIF, everything will be set up to run automatically.

☞ The PIF for a program is usually the program's file name with the extension .PIF. So the file that runs Quicken for DOS is called Q.PIF, and the file that runs WordPerfect 5.1 is called WP.PIF.

Using the PIF Editor

Windows includes a little program called the PIF Editor to let you accommodate those recalcitrant DOS programs. Most of what you can do with the PIF Editor is much better left for those with incurable nerdish tendencies. It is fairly easy to muck around with the PIF Editor and take a program that was working and make it *not* work. Since this isn't what we usually want to do, let's just leave those areas for those who *think* they know what they are doing. And try not to laugh too obviously when they start cursing.

For the rest of us, there are a couple of simple areas we can change in the PIF Editor that can actually help, and not get us into major trouble.

So fire up the PIF Editor by double-clicking on its icon in the Main group:

PIF Editor

This will bring up the PIF Editor, which looks like Figure 19.1. To change a PIF, however, you will need to first load it into the editor. So, click on Open on the File menu and find the PIF you want to change. Most will be either in your main Windows directory or in the home directory for the program you are trying to beat into submission.

Once you have the program's PIF loaded, you can change it. The *only* areas you should even consider changing, however, are the first four longish boxes, and maybe, if you feel really brave, the Memory Requirements settings. See "Who's Afraid of the Big Bad PIF?" below.

FIGURE 19.1:

Windows provides a PIF Editor to help tame your DOS programs.

PIF Editor - Q.PIF

File   Mode   Help

Program Filename: C:\QUICKEN5\Q.EXE

Window Title: Quicken

Optional Parameters:

Start-up Directory: C:\QUICKEN5

Video Memory: ● Text   ○ Low Graphics   ○ High Graphics

Memory Requirements: KB Required   320   KB Desired   640

EMS Memory: KB Required   0   KB Limit   1024

XMS Memory: KB Required   0   KB Limit   0

Display Usage: ● Full Screen   Execution: ☐ Background
                 ○ Windowed   ☐ Exclusive

☒ Close Window on Exit   Advanced...

Press F1 for Help on Video Memory.

DOS Programs CH. 19

The Program Filename box is where you tell Windows what the program's actual file name is. For Quattro Pro, for example, this will be Q.EXE; for WordPerfect, it will be WP.EXE. This will be right, so you won't need to fool with it.

The Window Title box is where you change the name that appears under the program's icon. Change this to whatever you want. Maybe you are mad at WordPerfect this week, so put Word Imperfect in here. Don't worry, you can't cause any harm here.

The Optional Parameters box is where you include any special command-line parameters that your program requires. Generally, you shouldn't be changing this unless the documentation for your program specifically tells you to, or you really know what it is you are trying to accomplish and how.

The Start-up Directory is where you set the initial directory your program will run in. This is one you might actually have to modify. If your program is loaded somewhere other than the normal, default directory, then you probably need to set this, especially if you are using a PIF that shipped with the program. Just be sure that what you type in here actually is correct, since if it doesn't exist, your program won't work. If in doubt, ask for help.

☞ Before you start trying to edit a PIF file, make a copy of it using the File Manager. Q.PIF becomes, say, QGOOD.PIF, or some such. Then, if you mess something up, it is easy to get back to where you started.

Who's Afraid of the Big Bad PIF?

If you're running a DOS program, and it seems to be behaving a bit erratically, it is just barely possible that it isn't getting as much memory from Windows as it really needs.

Windows tends to be a bit stingy with DOS programs, and usually that is fine. But some respond better with a bit extra. So, try this.

In the PIF Editor dialog box, there are two boxes next to Memory Requirements: KB Required and KB Desired. Type **-1** into both of them. This tells Windows to give the program as much regular DOS memory as it possibly can.

Sometimes this can help, but only do this if your program doesn't seem to be behaving as well as it should, since it will steal memory from everything else.

Running in a Window

When you start the DOS program, it'll probably appear full screen. If you're running in enhanced mode, you can pop the DOS program into a window. From within the DOS program, press Alt-Enter. The program will appear in a window, like in Figure 19.2. To go back to full screen, just press Alt-Enter again.

FIGURE 19.2:
Here's WordPerfect for DOS looking a bit uneasy inside a window.

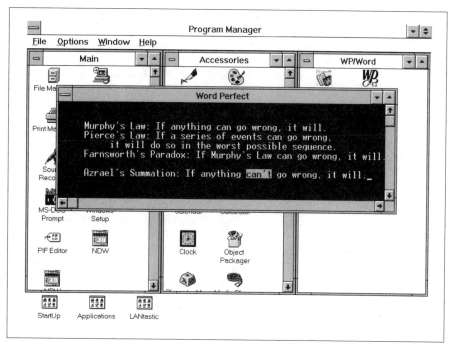

☞ If you have a 80386 processor or better and at least 2 megabytes of memory, Windows will automatically run in enhanced mode unless you tell it otherwise. For more boring details on enhanced vs. standard mode, see Chapter 6, "Starting Windows."

☞ You can move a DOS window or resize it or even turn it into an icon by clicking on the Minimize button. However, you can only close it using the DOS program's way. In other words, you can't close it by double-clicking on the Control box or by using Alt-F4.

☞ Graphics programs can run in a window, but so slowly as to be useless unless they're running in CGA mode. This eliminates any graphics program you're likely to have. Stick to full screen with them.

Getting That DOS Program to Print in the Background

You can persuade a DOS program to print while you work in another program. First, you need to open the PIF for the program. In the lower-right corner of the PIF Editor dialog box, check the box for Background and then click on OK.

Now you can iconize the DOS program after starting the printing process and go on to some other program while the printing churns away in the background.

Changing Fonts in a DOS Window

Sometimes you run a DOS program in a window and the text or what-ever is in the window is too small or too large to be useful. Click on the Control box and select Fonts from the menu that appears.

In the Font list box, click on a font size. As you click around, you'll get a preview of the selected font. The Window preview box gives you the window's size in relation to the whole desktop. Smaller fonts make smaller windows.

Select OK when you're done.

Leaving a DOS Program Temporarily

If the DOS program is in a window, just click on the Minimize button in the upper-right corner. When you want to go back to the DOS program, hold down the Alt key and press the Tab key until the name of the program appears. Release the keys and your program will pop back into its window.

If the DOS program is running full screen, hold down the Alt key and press the Tab key once. That should put you in Program Manager. If it doesn't, just keep tapping Tab until Program Manager shows up.

Quitting the DOS Program

Every DOS program has its own escape hatch and you have to exit that way. See Table 19.1 for the exit methods of some of the most popular DOS programs.

TABLE 19.1:

Escape Hatches from DOS Programs

To Leave This Program	Press These Keys
Lotus 1-2-3	/, Q, Y
Quattro Pro	Ctrl-X
Quicken	Esc, E
Word	Alt-F, X
WordPerfect	F7, N, Y
WordStar	Ctrl-K, X

DOS Programs That Don't Know When to Quit

If you're stuck with a DOS program that just sits there and refuses to do your bidding, don't reach for the reset button yet! Try these steps first.

The Terminator

Click on the Control box in the DOS program's window (if it's not already in a window, press Alt-Enter). Select Settings from the menu. Then click on the Terminate button. You'll get a box warning you severely, but what the heck, you're doomed anyway. Select OK.

Ctrl-Alt-Del

Try the three-fingered salute: Press the Ctrl, Alt, and Del keys all at once. You'll get a screen full of instructions. Press Enter and you should be back in Windows—sans the offending program.

Chapter 20

DON'T DO DIS DOS
(Commands You Shouldn't Use in Windows)

Dr. Langer's Law: Sooner or later the worst possible set of circumstances is bound to occur.

AS YOUR FINGERS perambulate around the keyboard, you may stumble across the DOS help system. (For those who are curious and have a few of their nine lives left over: Go to the DOS prompt and type **HELP.**) This chapter covers the DOS commands you should avoid like poison. Some are dangerous when used in Windows, others are dangerous anytime.

You don't have to pay any attention to this chapter if you never, ever venture outside the safe confines of Windows. But if you sometimes click on that MS-DOS icon and go to a DOS prompt, here are some commands that you should never, ever use as long as you're in Windows.

DOS Commands You Shouldn't Use in Windows

CHKDSK /F This command sends DOS scurrying to find odd-looking files and gets rid of them when they're found. Windows makes a lot of peculiar files and if you get rid of them, you're hosed.

DBLSPACE This is the DOS 6 disk compression program. This will do a lot for your hard disk but nothing for Windows. Exit all the way out to DOS. Close the window after yourself, please.

DEFRAG Another very helpful DOS 6 program. Useful for cleaning up your hard disk; extremely dangerous to your Windows.

EMM386 Turns expanded memory support on or off. If you run this while Windows is running, you'll have a memory lapse you'll never forget.

MEMMAKER If you have DOS 6, you should run MemMaker, but not in Windows. See page 228 for the skinny on running MemMaker.

MSCDEX Provides access to CD-ROM drives and shouldn't be run after Windows has started.

NLSFUNC A command related to settings for other countries. Use it in Windows and your computer may do a great imitation of a dead duck.

SMARTDRV This command belongs in your AUTOEXEC.BAT file. Have a guru set it up for you there, but don't run it in Windows.

DOS Commands You Shouldn't Use at All

The following commands are either useless to you or positively danger-ous. Feel free to look them up in the help system, but be sure you know what you're doing before you start fooling around with them—especially those with the Warning sign.

APPEND Allows DOS to look in directories other than the current one to find data files. Not nearly as useful as it sounds and downright dangerous in DOS as well as Windows.

ASSIGN Assigns a different drive letter to an existing drive. You don't want or need to do this (DOS 5 and earlier).

BREAK Controls how often DOS checks for Ctrl-C (or Ctrl-Break) while running programs. The default setting is OFF, which is what it should be.

CHCP **CH**anges the **C**ode **P**age that devices use to generate characters. Not something you could do easily, even if you wanted to.

COMMAND This is actually the file COMMAND.COM and is what runs the command interpreter of DOS. Don't delete it.

CTTY This command can disconnect your keyboard and monitor so that you have to use the reset button to get your computer back. It's not usable for anything you have to do.

DEBUG This sounds like something you might want to do. It isn't. It's a nerdish tool that not even nerds use any more.

DELTREE New in DOS 6, this command allows you to delete an entire directory and all its files and all its subdirectories and all *their* files—all at once. This is very powerful and very dangerous. Even the UNDELETE program won't save you if you use this command in error.

EXPAND If you mess up one or more of your necessary DOS files, a DOS expert can use this command to get them back from your original installation disks.

FASTOPEN This is supposed to speed up the process of opening frequently used files and directories. It doesn't work very well and causes mysterious problems.

FDISK You should never have to run this program. It prepares your hard disk for formatting when it is new. This was done when the disk was new and doing it again can cost you the contents of your hard disk. This one is strictly for experts.

GRAPHICS A specialized command that loads a memory-resident program to let you use the Shift-Print Screen keys to send a graphic screen to a Hewlett-Packard or IBM printer. If you need this, and you probably don't, have an experienced DOS user set it up for you.

JOIN An old-time DOS command that makes a whole drive look to be a subdirectory on another drive. This command was dropped in DOS 6 and was archaic even in DOS 5. Both useless and dangerous.

KEYB This command lets you install a foreign-language keyboard driver. If you need this, get a guru to set it up for you.

MODE A gut-level command that configures hardware attached to your computer. Most of this is done automatically by software these days. If you need to use it, you'll likely need help.

RECOVER This is a really nasty command that purports to recover data from a defective hard disk. Its reputation is so lousy that it's not even included with DOS 6. You do not want to use this command under any circumstances.

SET This command controls what are called environment variables. You don't care what they are. If you insist, type **SET** at the DOS prompt and press Enter. Didn't we tell you?

SETVER This has to do with the DOS version table. Don't tamper with this and you'll stay happy.

SUBST This is a command that tricks DOS into thinking that a directory is actually a drive. Tricky business that should be left to experts.

VERIFY This is an older fail-safe command designed to double-check that files are being written correctly to a disk. This slows down your computer dramatically and it doesn't work anyway. Normally it's OFF.

PART 5

Sooner or later your computer will turn on you and the only solution is hand-to-hand combat. This part shows you how to stay out of trouble (when you can) and how to bail yourself out when trouble finds you. There's a chapter on prevention, another on cures, and one more on those dreadful error messages that Windows sometimes barfs up.

I'm Mad as %@$#!

and I'm Not Gonna Take It Anymore!

Chapter 21

AN OUNCE OF PREVENTION

Hecker's Law: If you do your lessons every day, you never have to worry about a test.

COMPUTERS ARE DIABOLICAL machines created to help prove Murphy right. So if you want to avoid disaster, or recover from it once it's happened, you need this chapter. In it we will show you how to protect against

☞ An overly enthusiastic installation program (making an OOPS disk)

☞ Serious hard-disk problems (making an emergency disk)

☞ Damaged or destroyed files (Microsoft Backup for Windows)

☞ A virus attack (Microsoft AntiVirus for Windows)

☞ An accidentally deleted file (Microsoft Undelete for Windows)

Making an OOPS Disk

An OOPS disk is a floppy disk on which you keep your current configuration files. Its purpose in life is to make it easy to get back to where you started whenever you make a change that turns out not to have been as good an idea as you hoped.

It also protects you when an installation program decides it knows how to change your configuration for you, and it screws up. Of course, in a perfect world, none of this would be necessary, but this *is* a book about Murphy, after all.

Take a floppy disk that either has never been formatted or doesn't have anything on it you want to save, and insert it in the A: drive. This is one case where the B: drive isn't good enough. Open File Manager, and select Format Disk from the Disk menu. Check the Make System Disk box, and type in a nice, obvious label like "OOPS_DISK" in the Label box. Click on OK, and go ahead and tell File Manager that you know that all your data is going to be lost—that is one of the reasons you are formatting it, after all.

Once File Manager has formatted the disk, highlight the following configuration files:

```
C:\CONFIG.SYS
C:\AUTOEXEC.BAT
C:\WINDOWS\WIN.INI
C:\WINDOWS\SYSTEM.INI
```

Then drag the files to the A: drive icon at the top of the drive window and drop them. This will copy the files onto the floppy disk you just formatted. This operation will take two steps, by the way, since the files are in different directories. Now, if something goes wrong, you can simply copy the files back to your hard disk.

You should update this disk by copying the current configuration files onto it before you install any new software or hardware or make any changes to your configuration. Once you have made the change to your configuration, or installed the new software or hardware, wait several days to make sure that no problems have been caused by the changes, and then go ahead and copy the new files onto the floppy.

What Are CONFIG.SYS and AUTOEXEC.BAT, Anyway?

Most of us get up each morning and pour a couple of cups of coffee or other caffeinated beverage down our throats to get going. Your computer, however, doesn't function well on coffee, so it needs CONFIG.SYS and AUTO-EXEC.BAT to get it up and going. These two files tell the computer almost everything it needs to know about itself and the equipment that is attached to it. CONFIG.SYS loads drivers for all of your hardware, and AUTOEXEC.BAT handles your computer's equivalent to brushing its teeth and washing its face each time you start it up.

AUTOEXEC.BAT loads the programs that you need in order to connect to your network, tells DOS and Windows where to find files, and does other miscellaneous stuff. Your computer will run without either of these files, though not well, and if one of them gets changed in the wrong way, your computer won't run at all. So it pays to have a known good copy of both of them.

Making an Emergency Disk

An emergency disk is (surprise, surprise!) for emergencies. It has the tools on it you might need in case of serious problems. First, though, before you make the disk, run a virus scanner to make sure that your system is free of viruses. You can use Microsoft's Windows AntiVirus program or any other you have. For directions on running the Microsoft Windows AntiVirus program that comes with DOS 6, jump ahead to the section on DOS 6 freebies later in this chapter.

Once you have checked for viruses, use File Manager to format a high-density floppy disk in the A: drive. Make sure that the Make System Disk box is checked, and give the disk a suitable label, like "EMRGNCY_DSK."

Now, use Notepad to create a minimum CONFIG.SYS file and a minimum AUTOEXEC.BAT file on the floppy.

1. Open Notepad, and type in

```
FILES=30
BUFFERS=30
```

2. Then select Save from the File menu and type

```
A:\CONFIG.SYS
```

in the File Name box of the Save As dialog box.

3. Click OK to save the file.

4. Then select New from the File menu and type in

```
PATH=C:\DOS
PROMPT $P$G
```

5. Select Save from the File menu. This time, type

```
A:\AUTOEXEC.BAT
```

in the File Name box, and click OK. Then you can exit from Notepad.

You have just made an AUTOEXEC.BAT and a CONFIG.SYS file on the floppy drive in A: that have the bare minimum to get your computer going.

Now, copy the other files you may need to the floppy drive. In File Manager, change to your DOS directory, and in the file pane, highlight the following files:

```
MSAV.EXE
MSAV.HLP
MSAVHELP.OVL
MSAVIRUS.LST
MSBACK*.*
UNDELETE.EXE
UNDELETE.INI
UNFORMAT.COM
```

These are the minimum files that you may need to repair more serious damage. Now, take the emergency disk you have just created, and write-protect it. Put a nice, distinctive label on it, and store it someplace where you will be able to find it when you need it.

☞ For UNDELETE.INI to exist, you need to have configured Delete Sentry protection. See "Undelete for Windows" at the end of this chapter.

☞ How to write-protect a floppy is covered on page 171.

Gregg's Observation: Education is what you get from reading the small print. Experience is what you get from not reading it.

Freebies That Come with DOS 6

DOS 6 includes Windows versions of three very important utilities that can save your cookies. There are Windows versions of Microsoft Backup (really a limited version of Norton Backup), Microsoft AntiVirus (a limited version of Central Point AntiVirus), and Undelete (again, a limited version of the Central Point utility). All of these programs are excellent at protecting and recovering your data in times of stress. Here are some basic instructions for handling them. But if you have any doubts, don't be afraid to ask for help. Your favorite nerd will be glad to show you how they work, and if you use the AntiVirus and Backup programs regularly, you will earn its undying devotion.

Backups and Why You Really, Really Should Do Them

Unquestionably the single most important thing you can do to protect yourself from really serious disaster with your computer is to do regular backups. Every single book tells you this, and people have been ignoring it for years. Don't. If you do backups, you can recover from almost any disaster, and the worst that can happen is you lose the data that has changed since the last time you did a backup.

We know it is a pain to do a backup. But it's a lot more of a pain to try to reconstruct your data after a serious problem if you haven't done one.

Backing Up—It Only Hurts the First Time

With DOS 6, Microsoft has finally provided an easy-to-use, effective, and fairly speedy backup program. If you have an earlier version of DOS, we suggest you upgrade, but if you don't want to do that, the same backup technology is available from Symantec as Norton Backup. Central Point Backup and Fastback are two other popular and easy-to-use backup programs that work well with Windows. Each one of these has a somewhat different interface, but each of them will do an excellent and speedy backup.

The directions given here assume you're running the Windows version of DOS 6's backup program. The first time you run it, you have to go through a fairly lengthy process of teaching Microsoft Backup about your computer. It also checks to make sure that it can not only back up your files onto floppies but can also actually read them back.

Teaching Microsoft Backup about Your Computer

The absolute best way to handle your first time with Microsoft Backup for Windows is to get someone else to do it. Now is an excellent time to consider bribing your favorite nerd to help.

OK, you really want to do this yourself. No sweat. This isn't really difficult, just a bit intimidating. But if you're game, let's just do it.

First, start Microsoft Backup. You can do this by clicking on its icon in the Microsoft Tools group or by selecting Backup from the Tools menu in File Manager. Either way, once Microsoft Backup has had a chance to scan your hard disk to see what files are on it, a window will open up telling you that Microsoft Backup has not been configured and asking you if you want to configure it automatically now. Say yes, and you're on your merry way.

First, Backup will tell you to remove any floppy disks from your drives so that it can check to see if it can tell when there are floppies there. Remove any floppies, and click on OK.

Next, it will want to do a compatibility test to make sure that once it creates a backup it can read it. Choose which drive you want to test (the one you want to use for backups), and then click on OK. An informational window will open warning you not to try to use the floppy drives for anything else while the test is in progress. Humor it, and tell it that you understand.

Then a larger window will open with all sorts of boxes and stuff in it. This is the actual backup window, and if you look closely, you will see that it's asking you to insert a floppy disk into the drive. Again, humor it. You might as well, since that is the only way you can get this over with.

If the floppy you put in has some files on it, you will be warned and asked to either try a different one or allow Microsoft Backup to overwrite this one. Your choice, but once you have decided, it will start making a small backup onto the floppy. This backup will take two disks, so have a second one ready to go.

Watch the box where Microsoft Backup originally told you to insert a floppy and you will see it slowly fill with red as the backup continues. Once the first disk is full, you will be prompted to insert the second disk into the drive. Do so, and Microsoft Backup will finish its thing. One nice touch here—you don't have to tell Microsoft Backup that you have changed floppies. It's smart enough to figure that one out.

This is one of the few cases where you can ignore the drive light. It won't go out, no matter how long you wait.

Once the backup is complete, you will be prompted to insert the first of the two disks back into the drive so that Microsoft Backup can check that it can actually read the thing. Again, just keep humoring it so you can get this process over with.

Now Microsoft Backup compares the backed-up files against their originals on your hard disk. During the process you get to watch a window that looks remarkably like the backup window, but this time it's called the Compare Progress window. Insert the second floppy when you are prompted, and assuming everything went as expected, you will be told that all went well and that you can make backups with confidence that they will be readable. Which is the whole point, after all.

If for some reason, you get an error message telling you that something didn't work as it should have, call your nerd. This probably means that you have a hardware problem, but let your nerd deal with whatever the problem is. After all, that is why you have been cultivating it all this time.

Once all this *mishegoss* is done, you're ready to go on about your business and do a real backup. The nice thing is that because of all the testing, you can be pretty sure that if you ever need to recover something from your backups, you will be able to. Doesn't that give you a warm and fuzzy feeling?

Making a Backup

When you finally finish all that configuration stuff, just click on the Backup button on top, and you will be at the Backup window, which looks like Figure 21.1. This is also the window you will see when you first start Microsoft Backup after the first time. From here you select which files you will be backing up, where you are going to back them up to, and any options that you want to set.

FIGURE 21.1:

The Backup window is where you control what files you back up and how.

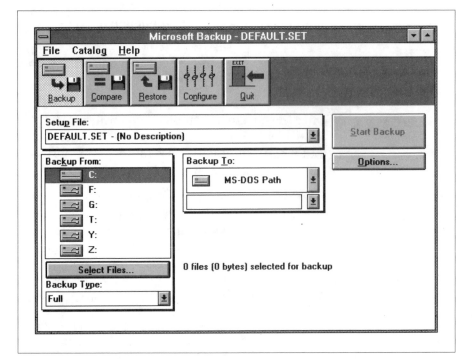

We strongly suggest that you get help from a friendly nerd or other computer re-source person to do the initial setup of your regular backups, but if that's not possible, you can do it yourself.

These are the important areas of the Backup window:

☞ **Setup File** lets you choose from a list of backups. When you first start, only the DEFAULT.SET file will be available.

☞ **Backup From** lets you choose which drives are included in your backup. Double-click on a drive letter to select or unselect all the files on that drive.

☞ **Select Files** lets you choose which files from the currently se-lected drive you want to back up. Click on Select Files. Use the right mouse button to select or unselect directories or individual files. (Double clicking and clicking with the right mouse button work the same for selecting in Microsoft Backup.)

☞ **Backup Type** lets you choose what type of backup to do: Full, In-cremental, or Differential. A full backup backs up everything, an incremental backup backs up all the files that have changed since the last incremental or full backup, and a differential backup backs up all the files that have changed since the last full backup.

☞ **Backup To** lets you choose which drive and type of floppy to save the files on.

☞ **Below the Backup** To area is an unlabeled area that shows backup statistics. In this area is a prediction of the amount of time and number of disks required for the current set of files. This prediction is usually on the high side of reality.

☞ **Options** lets you change the defaults. Don't change the defaults unless you really, truly know what you're doing.

☞ **Start Backup** does just that.

Once you have selected the files you want to back up, select Start Backup and put a floppy in the drive.

☞ Always number the floppies in a backup set as you use them. It's a lot harder later.

☞ Even though the Backup Statistics field usually predicts on the high side, always have at least this many disks available to do your backup. Nothing is more frustrating than having to scrounge around for disks when you find yourself short.

☞ Store backup disks away from stray magnetic fields, heat, and humidity.

Verifying Your Backup

Once you have made a backup, you really ought to verify that the floppies match what is on your hard disk—especially the first time you use a set of disks, in case there is a bad disk. To compare the files on the floppies to the hard disk, click on the Compare button. This will switch Microsoft Backup to the Compare window, shown in Figure 21.2.

These are the important parts of the Compare window:

☞ **Backup Set Catalog** lets you choose from a list of previous backups to compare.

FIGURE 21.2:
The Compare window lets you verify that your backup is good.

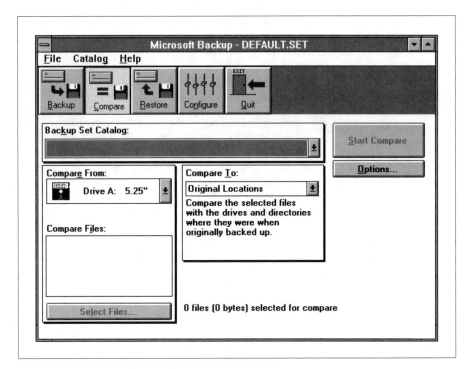

☞ **Compare From** lets you choose which floppy drive the backed-up files are on.

☞ **Compare To** lets you choose whether to compare the files to their original locations or to those on another drive or in a different directory. Normally this will be their original locations.

☞ **Compare Files** lets you choose which files to compare. Normally, you should select all the files by highlighting the drive and double-clicking or right-clicking.

☞ **Select Files** lets you choose individual files to compare.

☞ **Start Compare** does just that.

☞ **Options** lets you control beeps and whether to quit after the comparison is complete or wait for further commands.

Once you have selected the files to compare, click on the Start Compare button. Follow the prompts and if all goes well, you will have a verified backup that you can feel confident will allow you to recover your files successfully in the event of some disaster.

Using Your Backup—Restoring Files

The real reason you create a backup is in the rare, but sooner or later inevitable, event that you need to restore a file or, worse, a whole hard disk. If you have had a major disaster and need to restore your entire hard disk, get help.

When you call your favorite nerd in a panic because you need to restore your hard disk, the absolute first question asked will be, "Of course, you have a backup, don't you?" This will be said with arched eyebrow and a slightly sarcastic tone. Then you can blandly look him or her straight in the eye and say, "Of course. I always do backups." This will the most shocking news this person has ever heard. But it will earn you an amazing amount of moral credit.

The steps to restore files from a backup are exactly the same as to compare them, and the window looks the same, except for saying "Restore" instead of "Compare." Just select the files you need to restore, and then click on the Start Restore button.

☞ Use Microsoft Backup to transfer files between computers. Just back them up onto floppy, and then restore them on the other computer. Select Retrieve from the Catalog menu to retrieve the backup catalog off the last floppy of the backup set.

Tauber's Axiom: Trust everybody, but always run a virus scanner.

Viruses—What They Are and How to Avoid Them

Viruses are programs that are written with the deliberate intent of causing you and your computer grief. They range from the merely annoying to those that will destroy all the data on your hard disk.

If you only buy shrink-wrapped software from commercial outlets, never share disks with *anyone* else, never let anyone else use your computer, don't download programs from bulletin boards, and always wash your hands after using the bathroom, the chances of your getting a virus are very small. But if you work in an environment where computers are shared among several people, your chances of catching one of these bugs eventually is pretty high.

Where Viruses Come From

Viruses are written by computer vandals. Slimy little mole-like creatures whose blighted lives are devoted to making others as miserable as they are. They then take the product of their twisted psyches and put it on a bulletin board someplace, usually hidden inside a harmless-looking piece of shareware.

So a common source of computer viruses is a poorly supervised bulletin board. Since this is the province of nerds, you're unlikely to get one this way. But, if one of your friends or coworkers hands you a disk and tells you what a great new game he got, you might want to think twice about accepting the disk. In the first place, if the disk is commercial software, using it would be software piracy. Even more to the point, though, you have no idea where that disk has been. It could well harbor a virus, waiting to destroy your hard disk.

Murphy's Constant: Files will be damaged in direct proportion to their value.

Using Microsoft AntiVirus

DOS 6 includes an excellent AntiVirus program, which is a limited version of Central Point AntiVirus. If you ever share disks with a friend or a coworker (and who among us doesn't), you absolutely should run Microsoft AntiVirus or some other antivirus program, once a week or so. And use it to check, or *scan*, each and every floppy disk you put in your computer. It only takes a moment to scan a floppy, but it can save you days of grief.

To check for a virus, start up Microsoft AntiVirus by double-clicking on its icon in the Main group:

AntiVirus

Once you have it up and running, you will see a screen that looks like Figure 21.3. Select the drive you want to check by clicking on it in the Drives window, and then click on the Detect button. Microsoft AntiVirus will check the files on the disk to make sure that none of them contains a virus that it knows about.

Wait a minute. What if a new virus comes along that AntiVirus doesn't know about? There's a coupon on the last page of your DOS 6 manual that lets you order a couple of updates for Microsoft AntiVirus. Send it in and for a mere $9.95 each you will get two updates, and more than enough junk mail to keep your postal carrier unhappy for years. Plus directions on how to order additional, regular updates to Microsoft AntiVirus. This is far and away the easiest way to keep your protection current, and we recommend it highly.

FIGURE 21.3:

Pick the drive you want to disinfect.

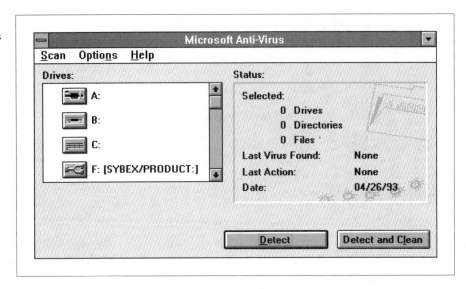

Undelete for Windows

In spite of your best intentions, sooner or later you will delete a file you wish you hadn't. Not to worry. If you act immediately, there is every likelihood that you can recover the file completely. Just don't wait. Your chances of undeleting a file immediately after deleting it are nearly 100 percent, but they go down rapidly as time goes on. DOS will tend to figure that since there's no longer a file stored in that spot on your hard disk, it can safely use the space for something else. Once that happens, your file is lost.

As soon as you realize that the file you just deleted was not the one you meant to delete, click on the Microsoft Undelete icon in your Microsoft Tools group, or select Run from the File menu and type in

    MWUNDEL

and click on OK. This will start the Microsoft Undelete for Windows program. Use the Drive/Dir button to select the drive and directory where the file was located, and you will see a list of deleted files along with some information about them. Click on the one you want to undelete, and then click on the Undelete button.

While you're in Undelete, click on the Options menu item and select
Configure Delete Protection. Choose Delete Sentry and then click on
OK. Just keep clicking on OK until it is happy, and you will have signifi-
cantly improved the chances of being able to recover a deleted file.
And you won't even have to remember the first letter of the file.

Chapter 22

WINDOWS PROBLEMS AND HOW TO SOLVE THEM

Dienes's Law: No problem ever solves itself.

WINDOWS TRIES HARD to be friendly, but like an oversized Alsatian, it can be just too overpowering and drool-laden. Most of the problems you have with Windows are fairly easily solved, however, unlike those with the Alsatian.

This chapter supplies the answers to Windows problems in the general categories Strange Messages, Dumb Mistakes, and Weird Behavior (sounds like a day at the office, doesn't it?).

At the end is a section of advice on drivers and other stuff that didn't fit anywhere else.

Strange Messages

One day you're bopping along, minding your own business, and Windows suddenly pops up a message that makes no sense. Look here for translations and ways to respond.

Windows says it can't find my program

The icon you clicked on represents a program that Windows can't find any more. Perhaps the program was deleted from your hard disk or moved.

☞ Highlight the program icon, then select Properties from Program Manager's File menu. The dialog box that opens shows where Windows *thinks* the program is.

☞ Open File Manager and use the Search command to look for the program file. If you find it, either move it to the directory Windows wants it to be in or change the Command Line in the Properties dialog box to reflect where the program is.

☞ See Chapter 12 for more on the Properties box and Chapter 13 for information on using the Search function in File Manager.

File Manager shows the wrong stuff on my floppy disk

If File Manager gets confused about what's on your floppy, press F5. This will make File Manager look at the floppy again.

Windows says there's no disk in the drive

If Windows says there's no disk in the floppy drive:

☞ If it's a $5\frac{1}{4}$ drive, make sure the door is latched.

☞ Make sure the disk isn't in upside down or backward.

☞ Try a disk you know is good. If you still can't read it, your floppy drive may be misbehaving. Call your repair guru.

File Manager tells me "Access Denied"

You're trying to copy a file to a floppy and File Manager tells you "Access Denied." Wow, just like in a spy movie! But the facts are probably much more mundane:

☞ The floppy is full. So you'll either have to put in a new disk or get rid of some of the files on the current disk.

☞ The disk is write-protected. Take the disk out and replace it. Or you can remove the write-protect tab (on a $5\frac{1}{4}$-inch floppy) or close the write-protect window (on a $3\frac{1}{2}$-inch floppy). See "What's Write Protect?" on page 171.

Windows says the file is already in use

You'll get this message if the file you're trying to open is already open somewhere else. Check to make sure the file isn't busy in some other application. If you're on a network, someone else may be hogging the file. You can wait for that person to close the file, or you can cruise your workmates' cubicles until you find the guilty party.

Windows won't let me leave

You're trying to exit Windows, but you get a message saying

```
Application still active
Quit the application before quitting Windows
```

Cures   CH. 22

This just means that you still have a DOS program open. Look at the bottom of your screen and you'll probably see a program icon there. If not, use Alt-Tab to find the program that's still open. Exit the program and then you can exit Windows.

Dumb Mistakes

Murphy's Realization: If you're already in a hole, there's no point in continuing to dig.

We all make mistakes of the oh-no-what-have-I-done-now variety. Look here to find ways out of the hole.

I deleted a program icon

No need to panic if you accidentally delete a program icon. After all, the icon is just the representative of the program, not the program itself. But you will have to reinform Windows of the program's existence. See "Adding a New Program to a Group" on page 142. OK, it's not a new program to *you*. But as far as Windows is concerned, it is.

I forgot my screen saver password

If you forget the password for your screen saver, you're not going to be able to get back to Windows. All you can do is poke the reset button and restart your computer. You'll lose any work that isn't saved.

This is such a drag that we advise you to first stomp around, and rant and rave for a while. You'll feel better and you may even remember the password. If you don't, do the following:

1. Push the reset button.

2. When the computer is done rebooting, start Windows by typing **WIN** at the DOS prompt.

3. Double-click on the Control Panel icon in the Main group. Then double-click on the Desktop icon.

4. In the dialog box that opens, click on the Setup button. You'll get still another dialog box, where you should clear the check box that says Password Protected. Click on OK until you're out.

Don't set a password here again. As you can see, anyone willing to re-boot your computer and screw up your files can easily get access to your stuff.

I can't find my window

It is possible, though not easy, to scoot a window around on the desk-top until it virtually disappears. To locate a stray window, try these steps.

1. Press Alt-Tab until the name of the prodigal program pops up. Re-lease the Alt-Tab keys. Still not visible? Go on.

2. Press Ctrl-Esc to bring up the Task List. Click on Cascade. Every window that's open will be rounded up and corralled into the cen-ter of the screen.

I know the file is in this directory

You've selected Open from the File menu. The Open dialog box is star-ing back at you and there's no sign of your file!

Look at the bottom of the dialog box for a box marked List Files of Type. Click on the arrow to see a list of file types. Select something with the same extension as the file you're looking for, or to see every file in the directory, select All Files (*.*). The files that are of the file type you selected will now be in the File Name list.

☞ For more on the use of the * wildcard, see "Using the * Wildcard" on page 163.

Cures
CH. 22

I saved a file yesterday, and now it's gone

If you're sure you saved a file and you can't find it, it probably ended up in a directory other than the one you intended. See "Finding Lost Files" on page 162 for help in finding stray files.

Weird Behavior

Every so often Windows goes on a bender and ends up doing things you'll regret. When the going gets weird, the weird look in this section.

My mouse has gone on strike

If your mouse refuses to work at all, it isn't asking for more money, just improved working conditions. So, what's your problem?

☞ If you start Windows and there is no mouse pointer at all, press Alt-F4 to exit Windows, and turn off your computer. Check the back of the computer box to make sure that the mouse's tail is securely plugged in and that the cable hasn't been chewed through by your cat. Then turn the power back on, and try again.

☞ If you still don't have any mouse pointer at all, and you used to, chances are your mouse isn't on strike, it just quit. So you'll have to hire a replacement.

☞ If you still don't have a mouse pointer, and you never have, chances are you have the mouse plugged into the wrong port. Try changing where the tail plugs into the back to another connection point that looks the same. Windows doesn't like to have a mouse plugged into the COM3 or COM4 port, even though most DOS programs don't care. If you can't find a likely-looking connection point that helps, get help.

☞ If the mouse pointer or an hourglass is on the screen and is stuck in the middle and won't move around, chances are Windows is confused about what kind of mouse you have. Exit Windows and type

```
CD \WINDOWS
SETUP
```

This will change to your Windows subdirectory if you aren't already there, and then will run the Windows Setup program. Check what kind of mouse Windows thinks you have installed, and change it to match what you really have.

Most of the major mouse brands can safely be used as "Microsoft or IBM PS/2," but if that doesn't seem to be cutting it, try for a specific one for your brand of mouse. Check your mouse manuals to see if you need to install any special drivers for your mouse, and how to do it if you do.

My mouse jumps around like it has ants in its pants

If your mouse used to work fine, but now seems to be jerky and jumps around the screen a lot, chances are its little mouse ball needs to be cleaned. First, take a cloth with a *little* glass cleaner on it and wipe the mouse pad and the bottom of the mouse.

Now, turn the mouse upside down, and take the little ring around the outside of the mouse ball and turn it counterclockwise a quarter turn or so. It should pop off. Carefully remove the mouse ball and wipe it with the moistened cloth. Gently remove any stray cat hairs, dust, etc. Blowing into the hole will help with this. Now, put the mouse ball back in and put the ring back on.

If your mouse jumps erratically all over the screen, and it hasn't ever worked right, or hasn't since a new piece of hardware was installed, chances are you have an *interrupt* conflict. The interrupt can frequently be changed for either the mouse or the new piece of hardware, but you will need help with this. Time to review the current balance sheet with your nerd, and figure how large a bribe is in order.

The clock has the wrong date or time

Your clock doesn't know anything about daylight savings time (or anything else for that matter). So if the clock shows the wrong time or date, you can fix it.

Double-click on the Control Panel icon in the Main group. In the Control Panel window, double-click on the Date/Time icon. You get a box that looks like this:

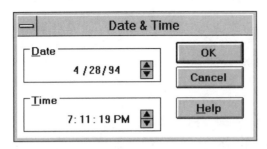

Click on the part of the date or time you want to change, then use the spin buttons to adjust the number up or down. When you've got things the way you want them, click on OK.

All I get is the splash screen

OK, everything has been working fine, and suddenly when you go to start up Windows, you see the initial splash screen, then nothing. You try pressing the Escape key several times, which makes you feel slightly better but doesn't do anything to help. So, you try clicking the mouse a few times and still nothing happens. Great, now what?

Well, the first thing to understand is that Windows has gone out to lunch and invited your computer to go with it. This may seem obvious but is worth saying anyway. There are a few things you can try, and some of them even have a faint hope of success, but if all else fails, you may well have to completely reinstall Windows. Yuck.

So, let's do the obvious stuff first. Reboot your computer. You can try pressing Ctrl-Alt-Delete, but usually that isn't enough when this happens. Just turn the power off, and wait ten seconds or so while you do something else constructive, like consider computercide. Or something more constructive, like try to find your original Windows disks, just in case. Then, turn the power back on, and when all that start-up stuff is done, type

    CD \WINDOWS

to take yourself to your Windows directory.

Now the first question to ask yourself is, what new software or hardware did I just install? If the answer is anything other than "nothing," you have a real good guess at what the culprit is. Hopefully, you took our advice and created an OOPS disk before you started. You did, right? Good.

While you are in the Windows directory, type the following:

```
COPY WIN.INI WIN.NFG
COPY SYSTEM.INI SYSTEM.NFG
```

This makes copies of the nonworking versions of your Windows initialization files. Now you can copy the ones off your OOPS disk. Place the disk in your A: drive and type

```
COPY A:*.INI
```

which will copy the two .INI files over the top of the ones that didn't work. Then, try starting Windows again. If all goes well, you should start up OK this time. If you want, you can use Notepad to look at the two .NFG files to see what is different.

If this doesn't work, there is one more thing you can try before throwing up your hands and calling in your favorite nerd. With the OOPS disk still in drive A, type

```
COPY A:\CONFIG.SYS C:\
COPY A:\AUTOEXEC.BAT C:\
```

to copy your computer's start-up files back in case that was what got munged. Then reboot your computer by pressing Ctrl-Alt-Delete. When your computer gets done doing its start-up thing, try one last time to start Windows. If you still get nowhere, call for help.

My program is running way too slowly

If your program begins to run more slowly than usual, try the following:

☞ Maybe you have too many windows open at once. Close some of the other programs.

☞ Leave Windows and then restart it. Sometimes that works.

☞ Maybe you're running out of hard-disk space. Leave Windows completely and type **CHKDSK /F** at the DOS prompt. Look for the number described as "bytes available on disk." If that number is very small, go back to Windows and try deleting excess files. See Chapter 13 for information on deleting files in File Manager.

☞ If you have DOS 6, leave Windows and run the DEFRAG program on your C: drive. Just type **DEFRAG** at the DOS prompt. Consult your DOS manual if you get confused.

☞ If none of this helps, call on some friend with computer smarts. See "How to Bribe a Nerd" later in this chapter for advice.

It is very important that you leave Windows entirely before you run either CHKDSK or DEFRAG. If you don't, you may wreak havoc on your hard disk.

Program Manager is different every time I start

It's very annoying to get everything set up just the way you like it, only to have it disappear when you restart Windows. To make Windows open up on Tuesday morning just the way you closed it on Monday night, select Save Settings on Exit from the Options menu in Program Manager.

On the other hand, maybe you like Windows always to open up in a particular way, but after you've messed about in Windows for a while, you have icons strewn all about the landscape, program groups in disarray, etc. To make Windows open up on Tuesday morning just the way it did on Monday morning, set things up just they way you want them. Then while holding down the Shift key, double-click on the Program Manager Control box (in the upper-left corner).

Then Program Manager will always open up looking just the way it did when you double-clicked. (For this to work, make sure the Save Settings on Exit option is *not* selected.)

The floppy drive makes weird noises when I start File Manager

File Manager has this annoying (or endearing, depending on your perspective) habit of remembering how it was set up each time you leave.

The noise you hear is File Manager searching for a floppy that used to be in the drive. Sad, isn't it?

To make File Manager more forgetful, open the Options menu and click on Save Settings on Exit to remove the check mark.

I pressed Alt-Tab and nothing happened

If you hold down the Alt key and press the Tab key, you can cycle through all your open programs. This feature is aptly named the Cool Switch. If it gets turned off, it doesn't work.

To turn the Cool Switch back on, double-click on the Control Panel icon in the Main group. Double-click on the Desktop icon. In the dialog box that opens, look for the Fast Alt+Tab Switching box. Click on the box to put an X in it. Then click on the OK button.

Advice from Dear Murphy

Sooner or later you'll be driven to install a new driver. Here's how to do it. Also in this section are miscellaneous bits of good counsel.

Installing a new driver for Windows

If you get a new mouse, keyboard, video card, sound card, CD-ROM, or other new toy, you probably need to install a new driver for it. If you got a new printer and need to add it to your available printers, go back to Chapter 16 and review how to add a printer.

If you added a new keyboard, mouse, or video card, or have changed to now be on a network, double-click on the Windows Setup icon in the Main group of Program Manager:

Windows
Setup

This will let you change your settings for these things. When you are done, restart Windows. Choose Change System Settings from the

Options menu, and make the changes you need to make. When you are finished, let Windows restart itself.

If you need to add a driver for a new toy, however, such as a new sound card, you use the Control Panel. Double-click on the Control Panel icon in the Main group, and then double-click again on the Drivers icon in the Control Panel.

Click on the Add button, and you will see a list of possible drivers to add, including Unlisted or Updated Driver. Use this one to load a driver off the floppy disk that came with your new toy if the driver isn't included in the list you see. If you do see your new toy listed, click on it.

How do I tell how many colors my video driver supports?

Windows itself is pretty much limited to some 20 colors, but lots of programs that run in Windows will use many more. And there is lots of really neat wallpaper out there in 256 colors. So, to see if the driver you are using supports more than the basic 16 colors, double-click on the Windows Setup icon in the Main program group.

Choose Change System Settings from the Options menu. Under Display, you will see the driver that Windows is using. If it is VGA or EGA, you have the basic 16 colors, period. If it is 8514/A or TIGA, you have 256 colors or more. And if it isn't one of these, it probably says specifically in the name, like "Super VGA 800x600, 16 colors."

Most of the Super VGA cards or special Windows accelerator cards support at least 256 colors, and many now support as many as 16.7 million colors. But stick to 256 colors unless you have a specific need for more. The extra colors will tend to slow down Windows a bunch.

Finding and getting rid of those pesky temp files

Windows has this annoying habit of leaving miscellaneous temporary files behind itself. Now, if you always start and stop Windows like you are supposed to, no problem. Windows will usually do a good job of cleaning up after itself in that situation.

But things happen sometimes, and one doesn't always do things the right way. Windows can create some temporary files that it doesn't clean up when you are forced to exit in a more brutal way than desired. So, how to clean them up?

The first thing to understand is that you should *not* do this from within Windows. This is one of those things you absolutely must go back to DOS to do. And we mean *all* the way back, not just out to a DOS window. When you get to DOS, type the following to help find the temporary files:

```
CD \
DIR ~*.TMP /S
```

This will give you a listing of all the files that start with ~ and have the extension .TMP. The neat thing it will do, though, is tell you which directory they are in. Starting with version 5 of DOS, you can get a directory listing that includes subdirectories as well, so take advantage of this to find your temp files. Now, when you find them, change to the directory where they are (usually something like \TEMP, but anything is possible). If they are in the \TEMP directory, the command to change to it would be

```
CD \TEMP
```

Then, once you get to the directory where Windows left them, type

```
DEL ~*.TMP
```

to delete the files. You won't generally build up too many of these, so you aren't likely to run out of space on your hard disk because of them, but it's always nice to keep a tidy hard disk.

Using SYSEDIT to make Windows start automatically

If you want Windows to start automatically whenever you fire up your computer, you will need to use an editor to add its command to your AUTOEXEC.BAT file. Windows provides a special editor called SYSEDIT that will do the job nicely.

Use File Manager to locate the file SYSEDIT.EXE. This file will be in your Windows SYSTEM directory. Double-click on the file, and you will start up the System Configuration Editor program, which automatically loads the four files that control how your system and Windows behave. You'll get a screen that looks like Figure 22.1.

FIGURE 22.1:

Getting at those files that control Windows

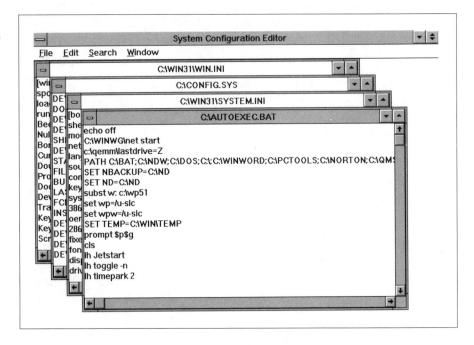

This program works just like Notepad, but opens four files instead of one. The top window will be the AUTOEXEC.BAT file. Go to the last line of the file, and add the command **WIN** below it. This should be on the last line, with nothing else on that line. Then double-click on the Control box to close SYSEDIT.

If you are *sure* that you haven't made any mistakes, when you are prompted to save the current changes in AUTOEXEC.BAT, click on the Yes button. If you have any doubts at all, click on the No button to exit SYSEDIT without any change being made.

☞ If your computer already starts Windows automatically, and you don't want it to, just remove the line that starts it.

☞ Never, never, never make a change to any of the files in SYSEDIT without copying the current, working versions to your OOPS disk first.

☞ The changes you make with SYSEDIT will not actually occur until you reboot your computer. But exit Windows properly first.

A Nerdish Note about Your System Configuration Files

The SYSEDIT program opens four files: CONFIG.SYS, AUTOEXEC.BAT, WIN.INI, and SYSTEM.INI. What are these four files and why are they important?

CONFIG.SYS is the first file your computer loads when it boots up. This file controls the loading of various and sundry drivers to allow your computer to work with the hardware you have attached to it. This includes things like memory managers and hard-disk drivers. As its final act, it automatically loads AUTOEXEC.BAT.

AUTOEXEC.BAT is the second file that your system uses to figure itself out. Here are a mixture of DOS commands, like PATH, with program names like WIN. Each line of the file is a separate command that is **auto**matically **exec**uted by your computer when it starts up, saving you from having to type each one of them in every time.

SYSTEM.INI is the file that Windows uses to know how to talk to the hardware attached to your computer. You almost never want to mess with this one, since it is very easy to totally screw it up so that Windows won't start at all. This file is the Windows equivalent of the CONFIG.SYS file for DOS. (But you still need both.)

WIN.INI is the file that Windows and its little programs use to keep track of how they are supposed to look. When you add or delete fonts, or change the color of your desktop, all that goes here so that you don't have to do it again the next time you start Windows. This is very much like the Windows version of the AUTOEXEC.BAT file.

Each of these files provides untold hours of amusement for nerds, who will twiddle and tweak them for hours on end. You, on the other hand, should keep your interaction with them to the minimum. And never change any of them without copying the old, good one to your OOPS disk.

Cures
CH. 22

How to Bribe a Nerd

Throughout this book, we suggest that when you run up against something that is really beyond what you want to have to deal with, you get a favorite nerd to help you. That is good advice, but how do you find one? And having found a nerd, how do you keep it?

Finding a nerd is pretty easy, really. We all know people who not only appear to know more than is really healthy about computers but actually seem to like them. They will spend countless hours fiddling and tweaking their own computers, and will drop into a totally incomprehensible dialect at the mere mention of certain key phrases, like "RAM" and "Video Accelerator." These are the unmistakable signs of nerddom.

So, having found one, how does one develop a relationship with this weird being? First, it is important to remember that nerds are, in limited ways, almost like people, and they respond to a wide variety of stimuli, but all are bribable to help you in your time of trouble or need. You will need to find exactly the right combination that works on your particular nerd, but we present here some basic guidelines.

Ms. Martin's
Fail-Safe Rules of Nerd Bribery

1. Nerds thrive on caffeinated beverages. So have a fresh cup of coffee or a favorite soda waiting when your nerd comes to call. Not only will the bribe be appreciated for itself but the thoughtfulness will be noted.

2. Junk food is excellent. Nothing pleases like a nice, high-calorie, low-nutrition treat. And remember that serious problems call for serious treats. When you are really desperate, go beyond the simple Twinkie to serious chocolate sin.

3. Do backups. Absolutely nothing will make your nerd more willing to help you than the knowledge that you have a recent backup.

4. Reciprocate. Nerds are somewhat limited and usually have areas that they don't do well at. Like life. So, offer your expertise in an area the nerd may be weak in.

5. Try to be specific about the nature of the problem. Write down the exact wording of the error message you got. Or the exact sequence of events that preceded the crash. Nerds respect precision.

6. Be honest. If the problem is caused by something you did, fess up. It makes the nerd's job much easier if it doesn't have to guess about what you did.

7. Praise, especially public praise, works wonders. Nerds will positively preen if you start telling your friends about the miraculous rescue of your data.

8. Don't be afraid to overbribe. You will build up a balance sheet in your favor, and when you are really desperate, your nerd will pull out all the stops. Grown men tremble at the sight of a nerd in full attack mode.

Cures CH. 22

Chapter 23

WINDOWS ERROR MESSAGES YOU LOVE TO HATE

Marker's Rule: There are no secrets, only obfuscations.

WINDOWS MAY BE a thing of beauty, but it's a long way from being a joy forever. Sometimes the error messages in Windows are cryptic and unhelpful in the extreme. Other times, they're just plain terrifying. In this chapter, you'll find the ones you're most likely to come across and the true facts on how to deal with them.

Application Execution Error: Cannot Find File; Check to Ensure Path and Filename are Correct

Cause This means your program is not where Windows expects to find it. The program has either been moved or been deleted from your hard disk.

Fix Make sure the program is on the hard disk and in the directory where Windows is looking.

Application Execution Error: Unexpected DOS Error #11

Cause Who knows? It's not a DOS error, even though you get it when running a DOS program.

Fix Click on OK to make the error message go away. Try restarting the DOS program. If that doesn't work, exit Windows and start again. If you get this error repeatedly, get a guru to help.

Application has violated system integrity

Cause Jeez, this does sound serious. But it's the same as a General Protection Fault except created by a DOS program instead of a Windows program. It means the DOS program did something that Windows didn't expect.

Fix Shut down everything you can, exit Windows, and restart your computer. If clicking on OK doesn't work, try pressing Ctrl-Alt-Delete. If that doesn't get you out, hit the reset button.

Disk is full

Cause Not much of a mystery here. The disk doesn't have room to store the file you want to save.

Fix   Replace the floppy with one that does have room. Or remove some files from the disk to make room.

Extremely low on memory...

Cause   Windows is having trouble finding enough memory to run your programs.

Fix   Quit any programs you're not using and try again. If this doesn't work, exit Windows and restart it. If Windows doesn't want to let you exit, open a small program like Notepad. Exit the program and *then* try to exit Windows again. Use Ctrl-Alt-Delete only as a last resort.

General Protection Fault

Cause   This is the catchall Windows error. It means something has gone wrong. It could be any one of a zillion things. The message you get may not even say "General Protection Fault." It'll probably say "An error has occurred in your application" and then give you a choice to "Ignore" or "Close" the application.

Fix   The safest thing to do is close the application that's caused the error plus *every other* open application and exit Windows. If, in the process of closing applications, you must save files, save them with new file names because the data in memory after a GP fault may be corrupted. After you've exited Windows, restart your computer using Ctrl-Alt-Delete and then restart Windows.

Insufficient Disk Space

Cause   Windows has run out of room on a floppy or on your hard disk.

Fix   If you're working on a floppy, put in another one or clear some room on the current one. If you're not copying files to a floppy, close down your applications and exit Windows. Delete any excess crud on your hard disk, like files with the extensions .BAK and .TMP or any old programs you don't use any more. Then restart Windows.

Errors CH. 23

Insufficient memory to run this application

Cause Windows is telling you it can't bear to go on like this. Memory is running low or something called "system resources" is running low.

Fix You don't really have a choice. Quit what you can and try again. If it's still droopy, exit Windows and restart it.

Not a valid filename

Cause You've tried to give a file a name that's forbidden by the DOS Police (they patrol in Windows, too).

Fix Check the sections on legal and illegal file names in Chapter 13.

Not ready error reading drive A:

Cause Windows can't find a disk in drive A, probably because there isn't one there.

Fix Make sure there's a disk in the drive and that it isn't upside down or backward and that the drive door is latched.

Parity error

Cause This means that an attempt to read data from memory has failed. It's caused by faulty memory, an overheated PC, electrical problems, or faulty software.

Fix Get help. You can turn off the computer and restart it. It may even appear to work, but don't be fooled. Sooner or later (and probably sooner) it's going to take another dive.

Share Violation: File Already in Use

Cause A program is trying to use a file that's being used somewhere else. You may be trying to move or delete a file in File Manager when the file is open somewhere else on the desktop.

Fix Look around for the offending file and close it. It's also possible, if you're on a network, that another user has the file open on his machine. In that case, look around for the offending user and persuade him to give it up.

System error: Cannot read/write from Drive C:

Cause Windows can't read or write to your hard disk.

Fix Not usually good news. Have a computer guru look at the thing, but odds are that your hard disk is going south...never to return.

System Violation Error

Cause Another error caused by one of those pesky DOS programs.

Fix All you can do is click on OK to make the error message go away. Your DOS program will close down, taking any unsaved work with it. You should exit Windows at this point and restart it.

Unrecoverable Application Error

Cause This is what a General Protection Fault was called in Windows 3.0. It also could be caused by any of a number of foul-ups.

Fix All you can do is try to escape with as much of your work intact as possible. Try to close down your applications and exit Windows gracefully. If you're not allowed out by the front door, try the Ctrl-Alt-Delete back door. If all else fails, press the reset button.

Errors CH. 23

6

In this part, we cover all the ways that Windows can part you from your money. One chapter is on ways to make Windows run faster and smarter. Another chapter is on stuff you'll love but that has no redeeming social value.

Decorating Windows

Chapter 24

WAYS TO MAKE YOUR POCKETBOOK THINNER AND WINDOWS HAPPIER

Borawski's Law: The one you want is never the one on sale.

THE FACT IS that just to run Windows, much less any actual programs, takes more memory, processor power, and hard-disk space than virtually any DOS program written before it. In this chapter we present some of the ways you can spend your money to make Windows work even better, with some specific recommendations for the best and most cost-effective ways to do that.

A Cautionary Disclaimer and Shameless Offer

The recommendations we make are based on our own personal experience with hardware and software products we have used. They are not intended to be the definitive answer but to point you in the right direction. There are numerous magazines out there that run mega-comparisons of products. We read them and we find lots of useful ideas in them, as we're sure you will. But what we recommend here we have lived with long enough to know we like.

So if some manufacturers feel slighted, we apologize, and make the following offer: Send us your best, and let us live with it for a while, and we'll be happy to let the world know what we think. There, we promised it would be shameless!

Memory—The First Place to Spend Your Money

Absolutely the first place to spend your money to improve Windows is on memory. If you only have 2MB of memory, upgrade to at least 4MB, and preferably to 8MB or even 16MB. You will see a difference in the speed of several hundred percent. Really, no kidding.

If you have 4MB, you should at the very minimum double it, and if you can swing it, go all the way to 16MB. And if you have 8MB already, spend your money on a faster video card instead. Not because 16MB wouldn't be faster—it would be—but because on most computers it's difficult to get from 8MB to 16MB without having to throw out the 8MB you already have.

What will all this cost you? If you have 4MB, and you want to go to 8MB, figure somewhere around $150–$200 to upgrade, including getting the store to do the upgrade for you. To go from 2MB to 4MB, the cost is the same, since you can't take advantage of the 2MB you already have.

And to go to 16MB from anything else will cost you somewhere in the $600–$700 range. Probably not worth the money, unless you either run a lot of programs all at once or use really big ones like AutoCAD, CorelDRAW, or Paradox for Windows.

If you are lucky and have a newer machine, it may be possible to go to 12MB or 16MB without throwing out the memory you already have. This upgrade will be considerably cheaper (say $300–$350) and may be worthwhile if you've already done the things we suggest in the rest of this chapter.

Should you get more than 16MB? No. Windows won't use it, and it can even get confused by it. If you want to run Windows NT, then yes, get absolutely as much as you can afford. But until the next version of regular Windows is released for the rest of us, stop at 16MB and spend the rest of your money somewhere else.

TECHNONOTE

Why You Can't Get 7MB or 11MB of RAM for Your Computer

Most motherboards made in the last several years have eight slots for memory SIMMs. Because of the way in which your computer accesses its memory, these slots *must* be filled in batches of four, so the choices for how much memory you can install on your computer are seriously limited. SIMMs come in 256K, 1MB, 4MB, and (soon) 16MB sizes, though most computers built before the last year or two will not support the 16MB SIMMs. Many motherboards will not support mixing sizes.

So, if you have only eight slots, you can have 1, 2, 4, 8, 16, or 32 megabytes of memory in your computer. Or, if your computer supports the 16MB SIMMs, you can have 64MB or 128MB. (We don't even want to think about any program that requires 64MB of memory.)

If you install eight 1MB SIMMs, you have filled all your slots and you have topped out. You can't upgrade your memory without pulling those eight little SIMMs and using them as bookmarks or something. But since there are now some newer machines that let you add SIMMs one at a time, check the manual for your machine before making assumptions about what you can or can't do with memory.

Making Windows Look Better and Run Faster at the Same Time

Once you have your computer up to 8MB of memory or more, the next place to look at spending money is on the video system. Some people start here because it's sexier, but spend your money on memory first if you want to get the maximum bang for the buck.

Your video system has two parts to it. The video card does all the work and makes the biggest difference in the speed of what you see. The video monitor (technospeak for the TV thing) just displays what the video card tells it to, but the differences in how well it displays it and how easy it is to use what is displayed are almost as big as the differences in cost.

Video cards

When you go to spend money on video cards, your choices break down into how fast you want to go and how much money you have to spend. A basic VGA card costs under $100 and will do nothing to help Windows run faster. This is what most computers bought more than a year or two ago will have. They are prime targets for a video upgrade.

One of the accelerated Super VGA cards, such as those based on the S3 chip, will make Windows run significantly faster and cost somewhere in the $150–$300 range. They are a good choice for those on a limited budget, and the fastest of them are quite good indeed.

At the high end of the video card spectrum are the cards based on TIGA, 8514/A, mach32, and other high-end technologies. They will make Windows fly but also make the money fly out of your wallet. Expect to pay somewhere in the $350–$1000 range for these cards. The ones we have used and like are the Graphics Ultra series from ATI Technologies.

So, what should you get? The answer, really, depends on how much money you have to spend and what other places you have to spend it on. You should certainly move up to at least one of the "optimized" cards in the $150–$300 range. These provide really noticeable improvements over a basic VGA card and are well worth the money. If you have the money to spend and have already installed enough memory, pop for one of the accelerated graphics cards.

Monitors

Your video monitor is one of the most neglected parts of the average PC today, and yet it's the one place you are most aware of while you work on your computer. The problem is that getting a good video monitor is expensive. Most of the better video cards will support truly astounding resolutions of 1024×768 and even 1280×1024 or more. But it's simply impossible to work with these resolutions on an older 14" monitor, which seemed like pretty hot stuff at the time it was bought a couple of years ago.

Today's graphics require a minimum of a 15" monitor, and 17" is becoming more and more necessary.

The problem is that these monitors cost big bucks. The generic 14" monitor that shipped with most computers a couple of years ago cost somewhere around $300–$500. But a good, 15"–16" name-brand monitor will set you back anywhere from $700 to upwards of $1000. Not cheap. And the 17"–20" monitors start at $1000 and climb right through the ceiling.

If you intend to use Windows for more than playing Solitaire, figure on at least a 15" monitor. Good ones come from a lot of companies, but one of the better bargains we have seen is the one from Mag Innovision. The NEC 4FG is very nice in an environment without a lot of glare, but will run a bit more. And the new Nanao F series monitors are very nice indeed, but a bit pricey.

A 17" monitor is a great upgrade to your video system if you can afford it. It allows you to run at a higher resolution, yet still be able to see what is going on. Our favorite here is the Nanao, but the NEC 5FG and ViewSonic 17 are also excellent choices.

Bigger and Better Hard Disks—Necessary, but Boring

Windows and Windows programs seem to take up more and more space on your ever-shrinking hard disk, so what's a person to do? Spend money, of course.

In the last couple of years, the speed and especially the size of hard disks have improved dramatically while the price has come down. Anyone buying a new computer today shouldn't even think of buying less than a 120MB hard drive, and realistically a 200MB hard drive makes more sense. So what should you do with your old computer? Add a second hard drive, or just replace the one that is there with a newer and much bigger one.

Don't worry much about what kind. If you are adding a second one to an existing computer, you may need to make sure that it will work with your current one, but if you are simply replacing the one you have, get the most bang you can for the money you have. Figure to spend somewhere around $1.50–$2.00 per megabyte of storage space.

What about removable drives? Again, probably not. Unless you have a need for serious data security that requires you to be able to lock up your hard drive at night in the company vault, these are probably a bit more bother and certainly a bit more money than they are really worth. They do have advantages where infinitely expandable storage space is required, but they are not trivial to install. We have a Bernoulli, and like it, but spent the better part of a weekend getting it to work right.

Software to Make Windows Work Better

So far, all we have talked about are hardware solutions. There are also some excellent software solutions to make Windows work better, faster, and easier.

Norton Desktop for Windows

The Norton Desktop for Windows is the best known of the replacements for Program Manager, and its strength is that it's a complete replacement for both the Program Manager and the File Manager, integrating the two of them into a comprehensive, easy-to-use shell that has some real advantages over plain Windows alone. Included with Norton Desktop are a whole suite of useful little utilities as well, including calculators, an icon editor, a Windows batch-file language that allows you to automate tasks in a pretty sophisticated way, excellent backup and antivirus programs, and even a rather cute screen-saver program.

DOS 6

Hunh? DOS 6 as a Windows enhancement? Yes. If you haven't made the upgrade to DOS 6 already, Windows is a good reason to do it. Included with DOS 6 are excellent antivirus and backup programs, which have Windows versions included, and a Windows interface to the Undelete program as well. Plus, of course, DoubleSpace. No matter how big your hard disk, it seems like sooner or later it isn't big enough. DoubleSpace lets you increase the apparent size of your hard disk by about 60 percent, with no appreciable loss of speed. While not as good as Stacker, it does have the advantage of being included free.

Stacker

The best known of the disk compression utilities, this is also the best. Version 3 added a cute Windows interface and a vastly improved DOS interface as well. This will make your hard disk seem very nearly twice as big as it really is, with no loss in speed on a reasonably fast computer. If you have DOS 6, get the upgrade to version 3.1. This version provides the same seamless integration into DOS as DoubleSpace, but with a higher compression ratio.

Disk caches

Windows spends a lot of time storing or retrieving stuff from your hard disk, so anything that speeds up this process is a definite boon. A disk cache is designed to do just that, by using part of your computer's main RAM to store the most recently accessed disk information readily at hand. A good disk cache can make a major difference in how fast Windows runs if you have the memory to spare. Our personal favorite is Norton Cache, which is included as part of the Norton Utilities, but we have also had excellent success with SuperPC-Kwik.

Better Windows CH. 24

Windows ships with a disk cache, SMARTDrive. Like lots of stuff that gets thrown in for free, it's nice enough if that is all you have, but we wouldn't spend money on it.

Other Shells and Utilities

While we use and love Norton Desktop for Windows, there are lots of other programs out there trying to convince you that they are the ultimate replacement for the Program Manager, the File Manager, or both. Some are a definite improvement, some are not. We include here a personal list of some of the possibilities. There are lots more. All of these provide substantial enhancements over plain Windows, but none have made us dump Norton Desktop yet.

PC Tools

Central Point Software has a new Windows version of PC Tools that some people really like a lot. Personally, we found it a bit hard to get to know, though it certainly seems powerful enough for the most confirmed nerd, and configurable enough to keep even a hopeless twiddler busy for a while.

Dashboard

Hewlett-Packard has two Windows utilities. Dashboard is a cute little program launcher and organizer that one could easily grow to love. It's small, quick and easy to use, and doesn't take up 10MB of your hard disk. In fact, the entire thing installs in about 1MB of hard-disk space. Definitely worthy of consideration.

New Wave

New Wave, the other Hewlett-Packard Windows shell, is a whole lot more than just a shell. It adds a whole additional layer of potential goodies to your desktop, but it is large, complicated, and not really supported by a lot of software. Generally, this one you should leave for the serious nerds to play with.

XTree for Windows

XTree for Windows, version 1.5, is a replacement for the File Manager that we should like a lot. We have used the DOS version of the program for years and really like it, but somehow we just can't seem to work up the same sort of enthusiasm for the Windows version. Probably because the Norton Desktop handles virtually everything that this does, plus a whole lot more, and is seamlessly integrated into our working world.

WinMaster

WinMaster version 1.5 from PC-Kwik is a replacement for the Program Manager with some real potential. It provides a useful improvement on the Program Manager for launching and organizing your programs, plus some excellent file and disk utilities. Included are a disk cache that is among the best in the industry and several other file and disk utilities designed to speed up your hard disk. What it doesn't have that Norton Desktop has is an integrated File Manager replacement.

Too Nervous for Bungee Jumping? Try PC Upgrading

It is possible to do all this upgrading yourself. You don't have to be a nerd (or play one on television). Just reach for *The PC Upgrade Guide for Everybody* by Dan Gookin (SYBEX, 1993). It will calm your nerves and tell you everything you need to know.

Better Windows
CH. 24

Chapter 25

WAYS TO SPEND MONEY *AND* HAVE FUN

(As If You Needed Help)

Digger's Law: Money can't buy happiness...but then happiness can't buy computer equipment.

IN THE LAST CHAPTER, we talked about ways to make Windows work better. This chapter has advice on how to make Windows *play* better. However, you might consider getting advice from your accountant on how to write off your new Sound Blaster card as a business expense since it improves your business presentations. Just remember to sound sincere when the IRS audits you.

Buy a Sound Card

Sound cards have become the basic minimum for new play toys for your Windows computer. They let you record sounds in special .WAV files and play them back, either through headphones or speakers attached to the back of the sound card. These can have a serious side, since they easily let you add sound effects to your business presentation, or a more playful side, letting you assign truly disgusting noises to common, everyday actions that Windows performs.

When combined with a CD-ROM drive and external speakers, these cards turn your ordinary PC into a multimedia-capable wonder machine. You can do some truly amazing things, but none of it comes easy. Probably the simplest way to turn your computer into such a wonder machine is to buy a complete package that includes all the goodies at once and make the store where you buy it install everything and get it to work together. These complete packages have the definite advantage of using components that are known to work together, and the manufacturer has already found out all the quirks to making it all work. However, it means spending your money in one fairly large chunk all at once.

If you want to just add a sound card now and worry about adding other goodies later, you can keep your costs down to a quite reasonable level. A simple sound card can be had for under $100, while the better 16-bit ones run up in the $200–$250 range. Try to go with one of the better, 16-bit cards if you can swing it, since they will integrate better with other goodies, like CD-ROM, when you go to add them later.

One we like a lot is the Sound Blaster 16 ASP from Creative Labs. This has all the connections you will need, lots of neat software, and you can use it with a CD-ROM drive if you decide to get one later.

Get a Modem and a Fax

A modem or combination modem/fax board *almost* belongs in the previous chapter. While lots of people seem to go through life without connecting their computers to the outside world at all, and they appear to show no signs of deprivation, for others this would be unthinkable.

If your goal is to be able to connect to the outside world to collect and send electronic mail (e-mail) or to be able to connect (log on) to CompuServe, GEnie, Prodigy, or a local BBS to download neat new files and pictures, all you really need or want is a modem. Don't get anything slower than 9600 baud.

You don't really need to know what those numbers mean, by the way. Just understand that the bigger the number the faster your computer can talk to another computer, assuming the other computer has at least as fast a modem. Good, inexpensive modems can be had from a wide assortment of vendors. We like the ones from Practical Peripherals—they're good *and* cheap.

If you want to be able to send and receive faxes, however, you will need a special modem called a fax modem. The problem here is that the technology hasn't quite caught up to the need. You can buy any number of fax modems that let you send the document that you created in your computer to another fax machine, and there is plenty of software that will handle this fine. But you can't easily send a document or other piece of paper that didn't start life on your computer. You could get a scanner to scan it into your computer, then send it, but this adds one more layer of complication and grief.

And you can receive faxes from other fax machines fairly well, but your hard disk will rapidly get too small, and the document you get is not a text file that you can use in your word processor but an *image* file that must then be translated by some sort of optical character recognition software into a document. Does this sound horrible or what?

If you need to be able to send documents you create on your computer by way of fax, go ahead and get a fax modem and some software to support it.

Specialized Video Cards

Windows has opened up a whole new world of graphics and video possibilities for the ordinary user. There are cards that let you connect your computer to a cable TV box and have reruns of "MASH" running in a window on your PC. There are other cards that let you connect to a VCR, video camera, or other similar source and capture images for inclusion into your next presentation or document or whatever. You can combine these images with sound to create truly amazing effects if you have the artistic skills and are willing to take the time to learn how it all works together. While this technology is still in its infancy, there are already some exciting possibilities. And the price of admission is dropping daily, to the point where real people can play with this stuff.

CD-ROM

A couple of years ago, the price of the CD-ROM drive was $1000 or more, and there was almost no software available for it anyway.

Boy, has that ever changed! Prices have dropped to a few hundred bucks, and the amount of software that is being created is exploding.

Some of the best games for PCs now come on CD-ROM, letting them add astounding graphics and sound, and the more serious uses are also steadily increasing. There are encyclopedias with full-color graphics, animation, and sound, or you can have the complete works of Shakespeare on a single CD.

Large programs, such as CorelDRAW and Borland C++, are now available on CDs and in many cases have additional features not included with the floppy-disk versions.

Should you have one? Sure, if you can afford to. The technology and software are still in their early days, but since the manufacturers have settled on a standard, you can be fairly sure that the hardware you buy today will be usable tomorrow.

One problem you can have is getting everything to work together. Make the store where you buy the hardware hook everything up and get it all to work. This can be especially important if you buy a sound card now, a video card a little later, and then a CD-ROM drive at a different time. Since you haven't bought them all as a package, it can be a bit tricky to get them to work together. Make sure that the store where you buy the package is going to get it all working before you plunk down your VISA card and sign on the dotted line.

Buy After Dark

Screen savers used to be absolutely necessary to keep your screen from developing burned-in characters when you left them on too long. Today, screen savers are no more necessary than a pet rock, yet screen savers are more popular and more ornate than ever.

The very best is Berkeley Systems' After Dark. Not only does it have wonderful tropical fish and stained-glass shows, you can combine different effects.

After Dark is worth buying for its flying-toasters screen saver alone. But, in fact, you can spend many nonproductive hours fiddling with thirty-plus modules.

Glossary

50 TERMS THAT WILL AMAZE YOUR FRIENDS

(and Confound Your Enemies)

active window The window that keyboard or mouse movements act on. Many windows can be open, but only one is active at a time.

ANSI Pronounced "ANT-see." Stands for **A**merican **N**ational **S**tandards **I**nstitute. This is a numerical code for characters used by Windows and Windows programs. The first 128 characters coincide with the ASCII character set.

application A collection of files that may include several programs. Lotus 1-2-3 is an application that consists of any number of files constituting a single package. Applications are also grouped by type, such as word processing application, database application, and so forth.

ASCII Stands for **A**merican **S**tandard **C**ode for **I**nformation **I**nterchange (pronounced "AS-key"). Developed back in the sixties as a standard numerical code for characters used on all computers. Today, ASCII usually means a normal text file as opposed to one in code unreadable by humans.

associate   To connect all files with a particular extension to a program. When you double-click on a file name with that extension in the File Manager, the associated program is opened.

attribute   A bit of code in a file that gives specific information about the file's status. The four file attributes are read-only, hidden, archive, and system. A file can have none or any number of the attributes. You can modify these but you shouldn't. (Remember to pronounce with the accent on the first syllable, not the second.)

AUTOEXEC.BAT   A batch file consisting of DOS commands and program names. Each line of the file is a separate command that is **auto**matically **exec**uted by your computer when it starts up, saving you from having to type each one of them every time.

background   All of the screen area behind the active window. Can also mean a process that is going on other than in the active window.

baud   The speed at which data is transmitted over a communications line or cable. This is not the same as bps (bits per second), but it matters not.

bit   Short for **b**inary dig**it**. Represents a single switch inside a computer set to 0 or 1. There are millions of them in every computer. Eight bits make up a byte, the basic unit of data storage.

bitmap   A picture or image file that is made up of pixels. Pictures made in Paintbrush are automatically saved as bitmaps (with a .BMP extension).

boot   A simple name for the complicated process your computer goes through when starting up. Restarting by pressing Ctrl-Alt-Delete is a "warm boot." Starting up from a power-off is a "cold boot."

bootable disk   When your system starts up, it looks for a disk first in drive A. If none is there, it goes to drive C. When a disk is found, the computer examines the disk to see if it contains the *system* files. When a disk with system files is found, the computer uses that disk's information to get the system running. If a disk with system files is in drive A, that disk will be used to tell the computer about itself. Computers can normally be booted only from drive A or drive C.

bps Short for **b**its **p**er **s**econd. A unit of measurement for the communication speed of modems and fax modems.

buffer An area of memory set up to speed the transfer of data, allowing blocks of information to be moved at once. Better than nothing, but inferior to a cache (see below).

byte A basic measurement of capacity. A byte is eight bits. For all intents and purposes, a byte equals a single character.

cache A sophisticated hardware or software product that does what buffers should do, only faster and smarter. Speeds everything up in a most amazing way.

CMOS Stands for **C**omplementary **M**etal-**O**xide **S**emiconductor. It's the area in your computer that stores the most basic configuration information about what hardware is in your machine.

CONFIG.SYS A file read by your computer very early in the start-up process. This file controls the loading of various and sundry drivers to allow your computer to work with the hardware you have attached to it. This includes things like memory managers, your mouse, etc. As its final act, it loads AUTOEXEC.BAT.

configuration A set of values in a program or for a device, such as a printer. The values will be things such as how menu options work or whether a printer uses legal-size paper.

DDE Stands for **D**ynamic **D**ata **E**xchange. An older standard for updating information in two programs at the same time. It is being replaced by OLE, for the most part.

default The setting that a device or program will have without any intervention from you. Usually you can change the default settings, but you shouldn't unless you have a good reason.

dialog box A window that opens to ask you impertinent questions or request input. Windows programs are knee-deep in dialog boxes.

DLL Short for **D**ynamic **L**ink **L**ibrary. A file with information needed by one or more programs. Don't delete these because your programs will be dysfunctional without them.

driver A program made up of instructions to operate things that are added to your computer, such as printers, a mouse, expanded memory, and so forth.

expanded memory A kind of memory that is used to get around the limitations of DOS, which will only use a maximum of 640K of memory.

extended memory Memory whose address is greater than 1MB. Not used by most DOS programs, but Windows loves this kind of memory.

INI files Pronounced "IN-ee". Stands for **INI**tialization. These are the files that contain the instructions about how you have set up an individual program. For example, the WIN.INI file remembers all the stuff about the colors and wallpaper you've chosen and other settings for Windows. Don't mess about with the .INI files unless you really, truly know what you're doing. (And even then, make copies of the original files just in case.)

initialize To prepare for use. With disks, this means to format the disk so it can be read. Programmers use this term to mean to get everything in the program to a known beginning state.

kilobyte One thousand bytes (actually 1024). Abbreviated as K or KB.

landscape A printer setting in which the characters are printed sideways along the length of the page. The opposite setting is "portrait."

macro Essentially a little program that you write yourself to automate a frequent task. Most word processor and spreadsheet applications have ways for you to write macros. The Recorder is Windows' feeble attempt at a macro writer.

megabyte One million bytes (or 1,048,576 bytes). Abbreviated as M or MB.

memory resident A program that starts when your computer starts but then retreats into the background and waits for you to activate it. Also called a TSR (for **T**erminate and **S**tay **R**esident). All memory-resident programs use up chunks of your conventional memory, so there's a real limit to how many can be running at a time.

modem A contraction for **mo**dulator-**dem**odulator. A device that hooks up to phone lines so your computer can communicate with other computers.

multitasking Using more than one application at a time. Most of the time in Windows, you're task switching—moving back and forth between applications—not actually using more than one at the same time.

OLE Pronounced "O-lay." Short for **O**bject **L**inking and **E**mbedding. An automatic way for Windows programs to share data.

on-line To be connected and in a state of readiness. A printer is said to be on-line when it's ready to print. On-line is also used to mean being connected to another computer via modem.

optimize Computer jargon for "improve the performance of."

parallel A port on your computer usually used to connect to a printer. Can also be used to connect other devices, such as an external drive or a network card, to your computer.

peripheral A device attached to the outside of your computer. This includes the monitor, keyboard, mouse, and printer.

PIF Short for **p**rogram **i**nformation **f**ile, it's pronounced "Piff," as in piffle. It's a file containing instructions to help Windows manage those rowdy DOS programs. The file tells Windows just what the DOS program expects to find (in memory, for example) and helps things operate smoothly.

port A connector on your computer for plugging in external devices. At a minimum, computers will have one serial port and one parallel (printer) port.

portrait A setting to make the printer line up characters horizontally in the usual way. The opposite setting is "landscape."

PostScript A page description language. Used on many printers to provide high-quality text and graphics output, but can also be used to control video displays.

protocol A set of rules that determines the flow of data and how it's used. The modems at either end of a communication line have to be using the same protocol to talk to each other.

serial A particular type of port. Mostly used by modems but also occasionally by a mouse, a scanner, or a weird printer. Communicates one bit at a time.

swap file This is the same as virtual memory. It's space on the hard disk that Windows uses to increase the amount of memory available to Windows programs.

system resources A portion of memory that is set aside for Windows to keep track of all its pieces. If that portion of memory gets too full, Windows will refuse to start any new stuff.

WYSIWYG Stands for **W**hat **Y**ou **S**ee **I**s **W**hat **Y**ou **G**et. Pronounced (we kid you not) "Wiz-ee-wig." Used mainly in word processing programs, it means that what you see on the screen is a pretty good facsimile of the printed page.

Mega-Index

Are you ornery enough to take on The Murphy's Mega-Index?

There's a **MURPHY'S LAW OF INDEXES** too. It says that even if you list something in an index ten different ways, someone will always come along ornery enough to look for it an *eleventh* way!

If you look for some information in our index, and you do not find it listed the *first way you look it up,* let us know. We'll add your eleventh way of looking it up to future indexes AND you will earn yourself a place in indexer's Heaven!

Throughout the index, we have used certain typographical conventions to help you find information. **Boldface** page numbers indicate primary explanations. *Italic* page numbers indicate illustrations.

Italic page numbers indicate illustrations.

Boldfaced numbers indicate primary explanations.

Del key
  Ctrl-Alt-Del (rebooting), 22, 76, 236, 304
  deleting with, 122
  deleting files with, 160
  deleting groups with, 141
  Shift-Del (Cut), 124
  in Write program, 175
Delete Font File from Disk check box,
    Fonts dialog box, 101–102
deleting
  with Backspace key, 122
  confirmation for, 149, 160, *160*
  vs. cutting, 122–123
  with Del key, 122
  directories, 160
  files, 160
   in DOS, 225–226
  fonts, 101–102
  groups, 141
  icons, 66, 137, 264
  system fonts, 102
  temporary files, 24, 272–273
  Undelete for Windows program,
    258–259
DELTREE command, DOS, 239
desktop, **18**. *See also* screens; windows
  assigning sounds to events, 108
  Clock program on, 189
  color settings, **96–98**
  copying to Clipboard, 123
  cursor blink rate setting, 96
  date settings, 106
  icon settings, 95
  keyboard settings, 111
  mouse settings, 104–105
  patterns
    changing, 91–92
    editing, 92
    vs. wallpaper, 91
  screen savers, 57, **92–93**
  sizing grid, 95
  time settings, 106
  wallpaper, **18**
    16-color vs. 256-color, 94, 95
    memory for, 95
    vs. patterns, 91
    selecting, **93–94**
    sources of, **94–95**
desktop case, **26**. *See also* computers
Desktop dialog box, Control Panel,
    90–96, *91*
  Border Width setting, 95, 113
  "Cool Switch" option, 92

Cursor Blink Rate option, *91*, 96
Edit Pattern dialog box, 92
Fast "Alt+Tab" Switching option, *91*, 92
icon for, 90, *90*
Icons options, *91*, 95
Pattern box, 91–92, *91*
Screen Saver options, *91*, 92–93
Sizing Grid options, *91*, 95
Wallpaper options, *91*, 93–95
dialing telephone numbers, 187–188
dialog boxes, *85*, **85–88**, 305. *See also*
    windows
  Alt key in, 73
  check boxes, **88**
   in Norton Desktop for Windows, 88
  Control box, *85*, **85–86**
  drop-down lists, *85*, 87, **87**
   opening, 73
   scroll bars in, 87
   selecting multiple items in, 87
   text boxes in, 87
  I-beam pointer in, 86
  scroll bars, *85*, 87, **88**
  spacebar in, 73
  spin buttons, *85*, 87, **87–88**
  Tab key in, 73
  text boxes, *85*, **86**, 87
  vs. windows, 17
digital clock, Clock program, 189
dimmed commands, 81
DIR command, DOS, **222–224**, *223*
directories, **15**, **151–154**. *See also* File
    Manager
  APPEND command and, 239
  changing
   in DOS, **221**, 222
   in Program Manager, 69
  copying files to different, 159
  creating, **152–153**
  deleting, **160**
  DELTREE command and, 239
  determining current in DOS, 220
  expanding and collapsing, **154**
  FASTOPEN command and, 239
  icons for, *153*, **153**
  listing contents of in DOS, **222–224**,
    223
  moving to next higher, 154, *154*
  naming, **152–153**
  path names for, **152**
  renaming, **161**
  root directory. **152**, 209
   changing to in DOS, 221, 222

Boldfaced numbers indicate primary explanations.

in drop-down lists, 87
in group windows, 137
in windows, *78*, **81**, *81*
Scroll Lock key, 39
SCSI drives. *See* hard-disk drives
Search dialog box, File Manager, 162,
    163, 262
Search menu, Cardfile program
    Find command, 187
    Go To command, 187
Select Computer dialog box, Windows
    for Workgroups, 212–213
Select Files dialog box, File Manager, 158,
    170
selecting
    data, 120, *121*
    files, 158
    items in drop-down lists, 87
    wallpaper, 93–94
serial ports, **307**. *See also* ports
Set command, Calendar program, 185
SET command, DOS, 239
Settings command, Control menu, 75, 236
Settings menu, Clock program, 189
Setup command buttons, 82, *82*
Setup program
    Custom setup, 54
    Express setup, 54
    running, **53–54**
SETVER command, DOS, 239
Shape tools, Paintbrush, 180, *180*
Share Directory dialog box, Windows for
    Workgroups, 208–209, *209*
Share Printer dialog box, Windows for
    Workgroups, 211, *211*
"Share violation: File already in use"
    message, 263, 282–283
shared directories
    connecting to, **209–211**
    creating, **208–209**
shared drives
    connecting to, **209–211**
    creating, **208–209**
shared printers
    connecting to, **212**
    creating, **211**
shelling out, **16**
shelling to DOS, **16**
shells, **294–295**. *See also* File Manager;
    Program Manager
    Norton Desktop for Windows, **292–293**
        check boxes in, 88
    vs. Program Manager, 146

Shift key, 39
    + clicking, 158
    + Del (Cut), 124
    + Ins (Paste), 124
    + Tile button (horizontal tiling), 117
    Ctrl-Alt-Shift (cheating in Solitaire),
        191
    selecting data with, 120
SIMMs, 289. *See also* memory
SIPs. *See* memory
Size option, Control menu, 86, 112
sizing
    desktop grid, 95
    DOS windows, 234
    windows, 78, 86, **112–113**
Sizing Grid options, Desktop dialog box,
    91, 95
SL microprocessors, **28**
slash (/). *See also* backslash (\)
    in DOS command syntax, 225
SMARTDrive program, DOS, 238, 294
software, **18–19**
    for backups, 250
    bug fixes in upgrades, 9
    memory requirements of, **42–43**
    microprocessor types and, 28
    versions of explained, 8–9
    Windows requirements for, 7–8
Solitaire program, **191**
Sound Blaster, **27**, 298
sound cards, 108
    installing drivers for, **271–272**
    Media Player program and, 190
    purchasing, **298**
    Sound Recorder program and, 192
Sound dialog box, Control Panel, **108**
Sound Recorder program, **192**
sounds
    adding to Hearts Network game, 215
    assigning to events, 108
    Media Player program, **190**
    SPEAK.EXE program, 108
    speaker drivers and, 130
    SPEAKER.DRV program, 130
spacebar
    Alt-spacebar (Control menu), 73
    in dialog boxes, 73
SPEAK.EXE program, 108
speaker drivers, 130
SPEAKER.DRV program, 130
special characters, 188
speed, of microprocessors, **29–30**
spin buttons, *85*, 87, **87–88**

334

SYBEX

FREE BROCHURE!

Complete this form today, and we'll send you a full-color brochure of Sybex bestsellers.

Please supply the name of the Sybex book purchased.

_____

How would you rate it?

____ Excellent   ____ Very Good   ____ Average   ____ Poor

Why did you select this particular book?

____ Recommended to me by a friend
____ Recommended to me by store personnel
____ Saw an advertisement in _____
____ Author's reputation
____ Saw in Sybex catalog
____ Required textbook
____ Sybex reputation
____ Read book review in _____
____ In-store display
____ Other _____

Where did you buy it?

____ Bookstore
____ Computer Store or Software Store
____ Catalog (name: _____)
____ Direct from Sybex
____ Other: _____

Did you buy this book with your personal funds?

____ Yes   ____ No

About how many computer books do you buy each year?

____ 1-3   ____ 3-5   ____ 5-7   ____ 7-9   ____ 10+

About how many Sybex books do you own?

____ 1-3   ____ 3-5   ____ 5-7   ____ 7-9   ____ 10+

Please indicate your level of experience with the software covered in this book:

____ Beginner   ____ Intermediate   ____ Advanced

Which types of software packages do you use regularly?

____ Accounting	____ Databases	____ Networks
____ Amiga	____ Desktop Publishing	____ Operating Systems
____ Apple/Mac	____ File Utilities	____ Spreadsheets
____ CAD	____ Money Management	____ Word Processing
____ Communications	____ Languages	____ Other _____

(please specify)

Which of the following best describes your job title?

_____ Administrative/Secretarial _____ President/CEO

_____ Director _____ Manager/Supervisor

_____ Engineer/Technician _____ Other _____
                                                    (please specify)

Comments on the weaknesses/strengths of this book: _____

_____

_____

_____

_____

Name _____

Street _____

City/State/Zip _____

Phone _____

PLEASE FOLD, SEAL, AND MAIL TO SYBEX

SYBEX, INC.

Department M

2021 CHALLENGER DR.

ALAMEDA, CALIFORNIA USA

94501

SYBEX

SEAL

...More Murphy's Laws

Nothing is as easy as it looks.

(But Windows comes close. See Chapter 1 for how and why—pages 3–10.)

Perfect documents will develop errors on their way to the printer.

(Mastering printers is covered in Chapter 16—see pages 193–206.)

It's a mistake to allow any mechanical object to know you're in a hurry.

(Get the best of ornery hardware with Chapter 3—see pages 25–39.)

For every vision, there is an equal and opposite revision.

(Do your own revisions with Chapter 10—see pages 111–118.)

You can never do just one thing.

(Chapter 11 tells you how that can be a plus—see pages 119–130.)

When you don't know what you're doing, do it neatly.

(Tidy up your Windows with Chapter 8—see pages 89–102.)

Established technology tends to persist in spite of new technology.

(DOS is the best example. See Chapter 18 for all you need to know—pages 219–228.)